DATE DUE

2 5 '81			
FEB			
FEB 2 5 1981			
MAY 10 1986			
SEP 10 1986			

DEMCO 38-297

CRITICAL ESSAYS IN MODERN LITERATURE

TITLES IN THE SERIES

The Fiction and Criticism of Katherine Anne Porter (Revised) by Harry J. Mooney, Jr.
Entrances to Dylan Thomas' Poetry by Ralph Maud
Joyce Cary: The Comedy of Freedom by Charles G. Hoffmann
The Short Stories of Ambrose Bierce by Stuart C. Woodruff
The Fiction of J. D. Salinger (Revised) by Frederick L. Gwynn and Joseph L. Blotner
James Agee: Promise and Fulfillment by Kenneth Seib
Chronicles of Conscience: A Study of George Orwell and Arthur Koestler by Jenni Calder
Richard Wright: An Introduction to the Man and His Works by Russell Carl Brignano
Dylan Thomas' Early Prose: A Study in Creative Mythology by Annis Pratt
The Situation of the Novel by Bernard Bergonzi
D. H. Lawrence: Body of Darkness by R. E. Pritchard
The Hole in the Fabric: Science, Contemporary Literature, and Henry James by Strother B. Purdy

The Hole in the Fabric

> ὅσοι μὲν οὖν τὰς ἀθέους ἀσκοῦσι
> φιλοσοφίας . . . ταύτας εἰς γέλωτα
> πολὺν ἄξουσι τὰς ἱστορίας
> ἀλαζονείαις ἀνθρωπίναις αὐτὰς
> ἀνατιθέντες, ὡς οὐδενὶ θεῶν μέλον
> ἀνθρώπων οὐδενός.
> Dionysius Halic. *Rom. Ant.* II 68.2

> To be sure, the professors of the atheistic
> philosophies . . . will also laugh these reports
> to scorn and attribute them to human
> imposture, on the ground that none of the
> gods concern themselves in anything
> relating to mankind.

STROTHER B. PURDY

The Hole in the Fabric   Science,

Contemporary

Literature,

and Henry James

UNIVERSITY OF PITTSBURGH PRESS

Published by the University of Pittsburgh Press, Pittsburgh, Pa. 15260
Copyright © 1977, University of Pittsburgh Press
All rights reserved
Feffer & Simons, Inc., London
Manufactured in the United States of America

Library of Congress Cataloging in Publication Data

Purdy, Strother B   birth date
The hole in the fabric.

(Critical essays in modern literature.)
Includes bibliographical references and index.
1. James, Henry, 1843–1916—Criticism and interpretation. 2. James, Henry, 1843–1916—Influence. 3. Fiction—20th century—History and criticism. I. Title.
PS2124.P78   813'.4   76-6667
ISBN 0-8229-3330-4

I wish to thank the Librarian of Cambridge University for granting me visitor's privileges, and my chairman, Joseph Schwartz, with my other colleagues in the Department of English at Marquette University, for granting me time for research, and the benefits of their comments on parts of this study. My thanks also to Mr. J.T. Fraser for permission to quote the Wu-men Hui'k'ai poem from *The Voices of Time* (New York, 1966). With apologies to Mr. Nabokov for the displeasure caused him by the book's interpretation of *Ada*, I have reduced my direct quotation from that novel to the amount generally accepted as "fair use."

Matrī et filiae et praecipuē uxorī eximiae hunc librum dēdico

Dr. Einstein tells us that when velocities are attained which have but just now come within the range of our close investigation, extraordinary things happen—things quite irreconcilable with our present concepts of time and space and mass and dimension. We are tempted to laugh at him, to tell him that the phenomena he suggests are absurd because they contradict these concepts. Nothing could be more rash. When we consider the results which follow from the physical velocities comparable with that of light, we must confess that here are conditions which have never before been carefully investigated. We must be quite as well prepared to have these conditions reveal some epoch-making fact as was Galileo when he turned the first telescope upon the skies. And if this fact requires that we discard present ideas of time and space and mass and dimension, we must be prepared to do so quite as thoroughly as our medieval fathers had to discard their notions of celestial "perfection," which demanded that there be but seven major heavenly bodies and that everything center about the earth as a common universal hub.

Scientific American, *December 1919*

Contents

1. Introduction • 3
2. The Henry James Murder Mystery • 18
3. Murder as a Literary Art • 28
4. Terror in Henry James • 47
5. Science Fiction • 56
6. Time and the Visible World • 67
   Relative Time • 67
   Henry James's *Sense of the Past*
   and Some Analogues • 80
   Ada • 93
7. The Erotic • 132
   The Awkward Age and *Lolita* • 132
   Sex and *The Turn of the Screw* • 149
   The Feminine Psyche • 159
8. Nothingness • 182
9. Postscript • 198

Notes • 205
Index • 223

The Hole in the Fabric

CHAPTER ONE
Introduction

New sciences have opened space and time with dimensions unsuspected by our fathers. • Teilhard de Chardin

Perhaps the hardest thing in all literature . . . is to write anything original. • Lewis Carroll

Contemporary writers have begun to explore the hole in the fabric that Henry James found. Others, in other ways, found it too, of course—Niels Bohr and Albert Einstein, J. Robert Oppenheimer and Edward Teller, the physicists celebrated by Friedrich Dürrenmatt, who destroyed what we now look back on as if it were the safe certainty of eighteenth-century Deism or medieval Catholicism, the Euclidean universe of up-down, left-right, and explorable surfaces. From the point of view of certainty of knowledge, as well as from that of certainty of cultural and physical security, it is today as if the dark nebula *Loch im Himmel*, the "hole in the sky" discovered by William Herschel in 1781, had proved to be real, and as dangerous as it would have been to Ptolemy. We always exaggerate the security of former epochs in order to take more satisfaction in lamenting the insecurity of our own. Whatever we say about our own is therefore to be taken with a grain of salt. It can very much be doubted, for instance, whether we are indeed dealing with levels of interpersonal violence, rebelliousness in youth, hypocrisy of those in power, racial prejudice, or military irresponsibility that are higher than any experienced before in comparable human societies.[1] On the other hand, we have definitely lived for the last several years, since the international deployment of Teller's hydrogen bomb (perfected in 1954), with a threat of almost immediate extinction that gives to politics and warfare a dimension that they could not have previously had. The individual victim of politics and warfare does not, of course, expect to be killed any deader, or even die more painfully, than he would have in the siege of Tyre or the Thirty Years' War; nor does he expect that his culture and

4 • *The Hole in the Fabric*

civilization will be any more completely destroyed than were those of the Etruscans, the Mohendjodarans, or the Narragansetts. It is the scale and the possible finality of this modern technological war that lend it its horror. The strong probability that this planet is going to be swallowed up by its expanding sun in 5×10^9 years is not especially terrifying—it is too far away and too impersonal, like Death in the abstract. The mere possibility that fellow men can arrange a small but sufficiently apt imitation of that final destruction—say, one hundred Auschwitzes—within the next thirty minutes is very terrifying, to anyone who thinks about it.

At the same time it is perhaps finally impossible to avoid saying that Christian metaphysics has been impaired in its capacity to conceptualize the world. That it continues to sustain as many individual human beings in various forms of sustainment as do Hinduism, Buddhism, Islam, and a variety of less intellectualized faiths is irrelevant, as is the fact that contemporary political and social conditions have caused great changes in the thinking and policies of Christian churches. An anthropomorphized Creator, effecting such a perfectly concealed personal interest in the four billion anthropomorphs of the planet, is a concept that no longer attracts the impassioned counterarguments of a Voltaire; it simply has ceased to figure in art, literature, music, politics, government, war, geometry, philosophy, or the culture it once formed and dominated in an important way. This leaves once more, or, it could be, as never before, a gap in the conceptual apparatus with which a culture protects itself against the unknown while guarding its gains. To have accomplished within the same generation both what may come to be seen as the completion of the loss of faith in a universe guided by divine wisdom, and the perfection of ultimate weapons of destruction, is the sadly ironic predicament of mid-twentieth-century Western man.

The body of knowledge that made possible the combined creation and destruction just mentioned is that of nineteenth- and twentieth-century science, starting with geology and progressing to nuclear physics. It has gone from strength to strength, starting in the seventeenth century, building up an ever more impressive record of advancement in knowledge, provable and physically graspable in the things, the machines, it has enabled technology to build. Yet at the same time its grasp of the nature of physical reality has weakened, and in that the final irony is added. For advances in knowledge have brought advances in the knowledge of how little is known, and the "how little is known" has an increasingly corrosive effect upon the "what is known." It is known for instance, that germs cause disease, but it is no longer known with the same exclusive certainty that it was thirty years ago. That is, other things than germs also cause disease, but we do not know exactly what they are. Medicine had a classic dependability well into the modern period that was sustained by the rigorous exclusion of theories of disease and treatment that did not conform to the clear and eminently demonstrable discoveries of the nineteenth century.[2]

Mathematical knowledge may be said to have doubled between 1850 and 1900, doubled again from 1900 to 1950, and again from 1950 to 1970, but it still has become increasingly apparent, as Einstein pointed out, that precision in mathematics has little relation to reality.[3] Until the late nineteenth century, mathematicians were generally confident that their subject dealt with physical reality, and that the problems it generated were capable of solution, given time and application, in a manner parallel to that of progress in other disciplines. David Hilbert, in his famous address to the Second International Congress of Mathematicians in Paris in 1900, in which he set the new century an agenda of twenty-three as yet unsolved mathematical problems, spoke in ringing tones of how "this conviction of the solvability of every mathematical problem is a powerful incentive to the worker. We hear within us the perpetual call: There is the problem. Seek its solution. You can find it by pure reason, for in mathematics there is no *ignorabimus*."[4] Few would care to make such an assertion today; with the limitative theorems of Kurt Gödel (1930) and Alonzo Church (1936) it became clear that the unsolvability of certain problems, the unanswerability of certain questions, basic to the nature of mathematics, had to be formally recognized. In these areas, mathematics seems now more like a game of human invention than an uncovering of the numerical aspects of reality. The best that can be hoped for the game is that it teaches us about reality, and, as Howard DeLong puts it, there is in that hope the suggestion of an "incommensurability between reality and our ability to understand it completely."[5]

Physics has had to face the same poverty within riches, being forced to recognize that theories of rational order and clarity, while perfectly suited to serve as the basis for a high level of technological control of the world, must coexist with, and for the purposes of advanced theory be replaced by, theories of disorder and obscurity. The standard meter may be kept at 0° centigrade in a light vacuum in the International Bureau of Weights and Measures at Sèvres and continue faithfully to serve as the cornerstone of a vast and powerful technology; but the conception upon which it was founded, the separate existence of a standard in measurement, unaffected and unaffectable by human thought or passion, has evaporated. Because it is now known that no measurement made by human beings or their tools is unaffected by the fact that human beings or their tools made it.[6] The subatomic structure of matter departs more radically from the classical models as the particle accelerators grow larger, and the results of such discoveries force reappraisal of the whole accepted structure of reality. The "dimension" of time, for instance, can hardly be retained as an independent linear progression against which the processes of physical reality are thrown and by which they are measured, if it can be reversed in relation to some interactions but not in relation to others. A notable public exposure, since the 1920s, has been given to the better-known formulations of the scientific departures from a static (and secure) Newtonian model[7] of the universe as a balanced and self-perpetuating mechanism, such as Clausius and Kelvin's second law of thermodynamics, widely and somewhat spectacularly touted as "heat-death," and Werner Heisenberg's indeterminacy principle, along with the primary intellectual event of this century, Einstein's theory of relativity, popularly summed up as "Everything's relative," and at least partly responsible for a spread of relativistic thinking in areas as widely separated as literary criticism, linguistics, and the writing of history.

Finally, since approximately 1960 the world has faced the deep of space in which it is poised with an entirely new consciousness—in 1957 (with Sputnik) the heavens opened, joined the earth, and circumscribed it in a way that was profoundly shocking and disorienting. There was no longer "our sky," "the skies of Andalusia," "the sky over Japan," and so forth, but one medium, in which you could revisit your starting point in an hour and a half by proceeding straight ahead—at a speed orders of magnitude beyond any that human beings had ever experienced. Nor was there an "up" into space from the earth distinguished from a "down" with the 360-degree unity enforced by orbital machinery; "up" and "down" had to be replaced by "around."[8] In 1960 it became the declared goal of a nation on Earth to reach, to send several of its citizens to, another celestial body, and in 1969 this was accomplished. We now face travel into space as a fact, whether or not we choose to go on with it. That we should choose not to go on with it would be, of course, as if no one in Europe had sought out America again after Columbus returned from his voyage of discovery—that is, highly unlikely. Our astronomy has now been disordered, in the sense that while the landscape of space has not changed any, its intellectual and emotional effect upon us has. While we were, seemingly permanently, earthbound, our speculations about other peoples and other voyages in space necessarily had the daydream quality of projections of our own "Voyages to the Moon." From the moon looking out, Earth and the sun take a place more similar in scale to the billions of other equivalent stars, and more on a scale with the billions of other planets those similar stars probably have. By entering space, in other words, we have inescapably entered, or faced, the overpowering mathematics of space. This includes the overpowering possibility of other cultures than ours, in a wide spectrum from inconceivably less developed than we, in our painful progress away from insectile lusts for destruction as we refine our weapons, to inconceivably more developed, developed through billions of further years of time. Our Project Ozma, named with such a pleasing sense of literary proprieties, sends hopeful messages from us to these other worlds, leaving more or less open the question of what we are to do with an answer—including the first and most practical matter of whether or not lay humanity should be told of it!

These matters, to my mind and to the minds of some others the central matters of our time, are not so to others. Indeed, if we take them up one by one, how can we even assert them as matters of general consciousness? In 1960 it was popular to reflect upon the hydrogen bomb, and popular reflection led, as it so often does, to a popular misconception: that hydrogen bombs are like TNT bombs only more powerful. Encouraged in this delusion by government officials, many of them sufficiently ignorant themselves to escape the charge of hypocrisy, Americans by the thousands took up the construction of World War II-style bomb shelters. How many people remember the shelter craze? More to the point, how many today think about nuclear warfare? It has not gone away in the meantime; it has rather undergone considerable further development. In the matter of payload and accuracy, for instance: A Russian SS-9 "Scarp" ICBM, one of the 288 currently deployed, measuring 10 by 120 feet before shedding two of its three stages, carrying a 15,000-pound payload at 12,000 miles per hour, could arrive most anywhere "from Central Asia," but spatially straight down, finishing a ballistic trajectory above the earth's atmosphere, taking some three minutes for reentry, and landing within 35 feet of the selected aiming point. Or in the matter of surprise: The MIRV "spacebus," whose thermonuclear passengers get down on trajectories for unpredictably selected targets, has made the concept of defense even more laughable. Its orbital launching system brings the warning time to a city about to be incinerated from the previous thirty-odd minutes to something like ten to fifteen minutes, provided no mistakes are made in detection.[9] Hardly time to include the public in the warning, which leaves them in a position resembling that of creatures receiving a divine judgment—indeed, but for the fact that it lies in the hands of men rather than gods, what would be the point of "thinking about nuclear warfare"? And while the intellectual force of Christianity is long gone, its logic unused in contemporary conceptualization,[10] the average Western man is content to go on without any thought on the loss at all, making vaguely comforting ritual gestures in the direction of the church.

In the same way, the average man is content with his time, his space, and his stable world, its surface only slightly ruffled when an electrical failure stops the clock, a midnight TV broadcast shows men eating something from a tube a quarter of a million miles out in the blackness of space, or an odd line on the importance of the SALT talks appears in his newspaper. If we can question how many men have intellectually digested Copernicus' 1540 relegation of the earth to inferior astronomical status (a satellite of the sun), how many fewer may have digested Harlow Shapley's 1918 demotion of the sun to an ordinary star fifty thousand light years from the center of the galaxy, or Walter Baade's 1952 demotion of the galaxy (once our "universe") to one among many, quite undistinguished in size?[11] Most of us, geocentric, anthropocentric, and humanistic, like Thomas Mann's Serenus Zeitblom, look upon such astronomical figuring as a *Teufelsjux*—a good medieval judgment. We cannot be said to have accepted Jacques Monod's challenge to awake to a state of universal "lonely strangeness."[12]

But such consciousness of the world is not our subject. That subject is centrally the literary consciousness, that of the writers of imaginative fiction. That is, not "how the facts of contemporary science affect (popular) thinking," but "how the facts of contemporary science have affected contemporary literature." In literature, the most striking and noticeable thing is, on first glance and in general terms, how strongly the situation parallels that of the public, average consciousness I have been describing. The makers of what is generally called the modern spirit or the modern age in literature are Thomas Mann, James Joyce, Marcel Proust, Franz Kafka, T. S. Eliot, Ezra Pound, Virginia Woolf—almost without exception, we might say, uninterested in science, if not uninterested in technology as well.[13] Were they aware of the dramatic way in which the conceptual world was being changed in their time by advances in knowledge and in technology? They could only have been so aware in the abstract, of course, for while they could testify to the march of industrialization across the countryside or to the giant slaughter of World War I, they had finished writing, or were dead, before World War II and the dawn of the Atomic Age—Proust in 1922, Kafka in 1924, Joyce along with Woolf, in 1941. Thomas Mann and T. S. Eliot lived well into the new era, to 1955 and 1965 respectively, but the major work of both men was done thirty or forty years earlier, and neither was capable of a response, or interested in making one, to events from 1945 onward. Other modern pioneers lived and live on—Ezra Pound, André Malraux, Jean Paul Sartre, John Dos Passos, all of whom did important work in the twenties and thirties; fictionally speaking, they still belong to that period more than to any since. Clearly, the *modern* novel, like the modern poem, does not touch the issues I have described; for that we must turn to the contemporary. Sartre's *Nausea (La Nausée,* 1938), Malraux's *Man's Fate (La Condition Humaine,* 1933), Dos Passos' *USA* (1930–1936), like Joyce's *Ulysses* (1922) or Kafka's *Trial (Der Prozeß,* 1924), *retain* a great deal of relevance to our present conditions, but it is rapidly becoming the kind that Molière and Aeschylus have, the generalized and sempiternal kind. As Thomas Mann remarked in his introduction to *The Magic Mountain (Einfuhrung in den Zauberberg,* 1939), the conditions of life that his hero, Hans Castorp, enjoyed in that novel, one of the cornerstones of twentieth-century fiction, disappeared in the outbreak of the 1914 war with which he closes its events. The same thing is true of the other modern greats—most of all William Faulkner and Dos Passos, perhaps, least of all Joyce and Kafka, but inescapable for all—their world is not ours.

In the matter of *technique* in fiction there is, of course, a definite and markable continuity. The writers of today could not write as they do without having read Joyce and Mann; the revolutionary novel of Joyce was not so revolutionary that it could have existed without the previous existence of the novel of James; that of James depended upon that of Anthony Trollope and Charles Dickens, on the one hand, and upon that of Gustave Flaubert on the other. Flaubert could not have existed without Honoré de Balzac, Dickens without Henry Fielding, and so throughout time, or throughout the life of any fictional form. Nevertheless, the difference between modernism and contemporaneity can be specified as well in the matter of technique. Richard Ellmann and Charles Feidelson, in *The Modern Tradition: Backgrounds of Modern Literature* note, for instance, that while Flaubert told the Goncourt brothers that neither plot nor character interested him, and that he intended *Madame Bovary* only to convey a gray color, "it had, nevertheless, a pronounced and steady plot, and a profound study of character." It did not, in other words, actually incorporate the revolutionary break with the previous novel that Flaubert may have intended. Ellmann and Feidelson go on in their survey to point out that André Gide intended with *The Counterfeiters* and its novelist-hero (seventy years after Madame Bovary) to "strip the novel of virtually all its customary elements."[14] They do not go on to point out that *The Counterfeiters* has the usual elements of plot and character, or that Gide never wrote a novel stripped of its customary elements. Modernism developed more than one theory of a new novel; but, with the lonely exceptions of James Joyce and Gertrude Stein, it did little to put one into practice. It is the postmodern generation, or the contemporary, that can use such terms as *nouveau roman* in a more than superficial sense.

If the great twentieth-century writers who made the modern novel are to be set aside as not relevant to this study, lacking the reference to special contemporary conditions dependent upon work in science since 1925, how then can Henry James be properly a part of such a study, of science and contemporary literature? How can it be said that he found the "hole in the fabric"? James has, of course, his well-attested place in literary history, just before the moderns, bridging the gap between them and the Victorian novel, and is given his full measure of praise for having established in perfected form the psychological novel, as well as the novel of *style indirect* in English. He was born in 1843, lived most of his life in a world much closer, technologically, to Chaucer's than to ours, and died in 1916, full of uncomprehending horror at the "abyss" the relatively mild antics of the First World War had opened up under all that he knew. He was very much a man of the nineteenth century. His works are sufficiently read that we can say they are part of the unconscious experience with theme, character, plot, and the literary use of the language with which living writers approach their subjects. And we can say that this Jamesian presence, as a part of the fifteen-hundred-year literary history of the language, exists independently of the chance that the living writer in question does *not* intend to write sentences that will sound like those in *The Golden Bowl*, using extended syntactical structures as a device for probing human consciousness, and independently of the chance that the writer does *not* intend to describe the Anglo-American social relation, or the relation between American and European culture, metaphorically or otherwise. The choices made by James throughout the spectrum of literary structures impinge upon those of any writer following, as being preexistent, and as being known. They impinge upon Kurt Vonnegut, John Barth, Vladimir Nabokov, Samuel Beckett, John Fowles and Arthur Clarke, who write in English, in this wide sense; they impinge upon Alain Robbe-Grillet, Eugène Ionesco, Günter Grass, and Jorge Luis Borges in a limited sense, of literary conception with far fewer linguistic overtones (the linguistic cannot be eliminated, though; it is clear that Proust's French sentence structure has affected the sentence structure of several subsequent writers in English), and as literary conception less familiar, less a part of an education in fiction.

But how does James impinge upon these contemporary writers in a way that Dickens and Balzac, or Kafka and Proust, do not?[15] It is that he *marked out* several areas within the novel that have now become central to it. These areas were not necessarily those which interested *him* most, nor did he conceive of them in the same terms we do; but while the "modern" generation that immediately followed him left them alone, the contemporary generation has taken them up and is pushing their exploration further. These are, first, the tale of supernatural horror, often with murder or mysterious death, that poses the problem of an "other world" without metaphysical location (*The Turn of the Screw*, *Cat's Cradle*, *The Erasers*, *The Killer*). Second, the novel of disoriented time, in which human consciousness moves, or is moved, outside linear time, with the possibility of existence on parallel time tracks (what is now sometimes called the "time fork") and the possibility of being trapped inside time out of order (*The Sense of the Past*, *Slaughterhouse-Five*, *La Maison de Rendez-Vous*, *Ada*). Third, the psychological novel of erotic theme in which the essence of the sexual relation between men and women is located outside and beyond the physicality (*The Awkward Age*, *Roderick Hudson*, *Ada*, *Lolita*). For a writer whose inherited convention was one of repression of the facts of sex along with an idealization that claimed a meeting of souls above and beyond the sordid physical level, that might seem a small matter for remark. There is a difference here, though, no less important for being a subtle one, in that James did not locate evil in a specific metaphysical entity and did concentrate on the relations of men and women. His contemporaries were generally satisfied with the moral equation that a union between a man of good will and a woman of good will would be a happy one, and that if such a union turned out to be unhappy instead there was simply an undiscovered lack of good will, a moral obloquy, in one or both partners. In that, the subtly psychological George Eliot was at one with the allegorical Charles Dickens and Nathaniel Hawthorne. Their aphysical simplicity is today often replaced by a positivistic celebration of physicality in the novel, heralded, but as yet not fully developed, by the work of Alfred Kinsey, of William Masters and Virginia Johnson, and of other sexologists. Now we find that unhappy unions are the result of sexual inadequacy, which is in turn correctable by counseling. This has replaced the emphasis on associational (Freudian) depth analysis, which was founded upon the same idea: Human unhappiness (which is about as close as it came to identifying evil) is founded upon sexual misperformance, and sexual misperformance upon childhood trauma. The current rise of the erotic novel takes first Freud, now Masters and Johnson, as its guide, placing the physical relationship in the foreground and deriving the other relationships, be they good or ill, from it.

Such logical positivism has served literature no better, or less well, than it has served science: The very real advance D. H. Lawrence made in the erotic novel is tied to such absurdities as the idea that impotence is naturally allied to the application of inhuman efficiency in the management of industry, and that in search of the fully satisfactory mutual orgasm the individual rightly dispenses with social and moral ties. Even such a travesty of intellectual organization was lacking when the sexual veil was fully lifted, in such erotic works as Frank Harris's *My Life and Loves* or Henry Miller's *Tropic of Capricorn*, to expose a moral and intellectual void. The writers who have now combined sexual freedom with literary sophistication have turned back, or have been forced to turn back, to the fact that men and women make their own heaven or hell out of their lives with each other up to, including, and beyond the generative component of their relationship. In understanding this, James emphasized what is now being realized as the central area of reassessment, the feminine point of view, and prepared the way for the downfall of the male-oriented psychological and positivistic models. He himself suffered none of the cultural shock we are now experiencing over this collapse of Freud, Dewey, and Skinner; and the new erotic novel, or the new novel with an erotic component, will be better than his. As it seeks its fully successful form, we can note how much closer John Fowles's *Magus* is to *The Golden Bowl* than to *Lady Chatterley's Lover*, Nabokov's *Lolita* to *The Awkward Age* than to *Justine*.

Fourth, and finally, is that matter of nothingness, which has become the leading subject in several main areas of contemporary literature. In fact, the contemporary literature that is of most technical and thematic interest occurs in two forms: pure assertion of nothing (Beckett, Grass, Ionesco); and the assertion of nothing tempered by the assertion of something else, or *other*, that takes its origin from science fiction, with or without falling back upon man's own resources as an alternative to despair (the existentialist position)—William Burroughs, Borges, Vonnegut, Nabokov. But how can nothing be anything, it might be objected, to examine either under the heading of literary influence, or as a literary theme? This difficult point is less open to a philosophical or logical definition than it is to identification by literary embodiment: The two greatest presentations of the problem of nothing in our century are Beckett's *Waiting for Godot* and Henry James's *The Beast in the Jungle*, despite all the intervening efforts of Dreisers, Manns, Bellows, even—and here we must pause over a literary spirit truly above any chronological taxonomy—Kafkas, to give it literary form. Beckett and James have the final sinister mastery of this ever more pressing problem of our age, the problem that Vonnegut has represented as the problem of what to do with useless people—what do useless people do with themselves, but seek death? The confidence of philosophy in handling it has recently had a series of weakening shocks; in the comparison of what James and Beckett share in their perception of it we can find no superior philosophical escape from it, but we can more clearly see what literary genius is capable of, suspended, as it were, like Milton's dovelike spirit, but not Milton, over an abyss.

In all the four cases or conceptual foci I have named, there is a direct bearing or influence emanating from modern scientific research; and the contemporary writers I consider in relation to them are for the most part, and in differing degrees, aware of that research and of at least some of its consequences for man in relation to the world. The supernatural mystery, as a literary form, cannot but be affected by changes in the scientific view of the mystery of the supernatural, or, defined another way, the mystery of the natural that lies beyond the limited capacities of our sense impressions of micro- and macrostructure. Most directly and simply, the possibility of intelligent life, superior to our own in intelligence and in mastery of nature, located elsewhere in the universe, impinges more and more upon literature as a whole, escaping from its previous confinement within the boundaries of "science fiction," that nowhere-land of (in most cases) neither true fiction nor true science. The matter of time in the novel cannot help being influenced, despite the very real difference between our time, space-time, and the "time" of physical interactions, by physicists' speculations, some of which have been proved by experiment, concerning the slowing of time in inverse proportion to velocity (Einstein's clock paradox); the reversibility of time in most physical processes, but perhaps not in all (the C[harge] P[arity] T[ime] puzzle); and the lack of application of any one time to separate bodies in space not in gravitational contact (the possibility that we are either in another planet's past or in its future). The matter of the place of the erotic in literature has as well undergone a drastic social reevaluation, undoubtedly connected to scientific work, first in the invention of the twentieth-century science of psychoanalysis, second in the statistical and physiological studies done by Kinsey and his followers. In the final area, that of philosophically apparent nothingness, we can point to the application of the technology science has given this century, a vaporization of matter and man's hopes along with it.

The effect of this book is not meant to be an attempt to modernize

Henry James, in the style of a fond Elizabethan scholar proving that Shakespeare predicted aerial bombardment, or an exasperated classicist proving that there is no moral problem not covered by Homer. It is a book partly about Henry James as a portentous event for the contemporary novel, rather than an accession to the usual view that Henry James is a portentous event in the historical development of the novel. For all his exaltation by graduate faculties, he is not given credit for having had much to do with subject matter outside the society he lived in and reported upon, a social world destroyed by World War I. Indeed, while we give formal acknowledgment to the idea that our great writers—Milton, Shakespeare, Homer, Cervantes, Tolstoy—are always "alive" to us (as long as we read them), that their genius spans the generations and keeps them in a state of deep communication with us and relevance to our concerns, we are in fact, in our own minds and in the minds of our students, undergoing a historical phase of such change, physical change in our world brought about by the relentless and destructive advance of science and technology into areas we thought most secure and unalterable, that we are having very great difficulty in managing any communication at all with the past, specifically in this context the literary past, without excluding from our minds the present and the imagined future. That kind of exclusion is, in fact, an everyday part of the scene in the university literature courses that deal with dead writers.

I think such exclusion is a mistake, and I hope this book will have a corrective effect upon it in one small area, the fiction of Henry James—and in our view of "contemporaneity" itself. We all *know* the present has no identity apart from the past on which it stands, but we do not really believe it. So I wish to show that the fictional themes concerning our leading contemporary writers have been adumbrated before them, not in such generality as to be self-evident (what age has not dealt with the problem of relations between the sexes, or the identification of a metaphysical force in life?), but in rather specific, complex, and subtle details. And that they are profoundly affected by contemporary science, but not in any simple or direct way (the attempt to assert some such has been the rock upon which most surveys of science in literature have foundered). Rather I wish to show contemporary literature suspended between a revolutionary science and a literary tradition faced with the problem of expressing what has never been known before, and which is only indirectly known, inside a literary medium it has inherited from the dead. The writer I have selected upon which to base the literary component of this demonstration is Henry James, because he is the one I have found to be involved not only in one, but in four, of the major contemporary concerns. What *all* those concerns are, or which other past writers have shown the way to the present in terms of one or more of them, I make no effort to define.[16] Henry James is relevant to contemporary literature and relevant to the human condition; that is no less and no more than we claim for any writer, past or present, whose work we find worth reading and encourage others to read. Within that general relevance I find specific relevances that I think have escaped the attention of many who study literature; in an effort to increase their pleasure and interest in the work of James and in the work of Beckett, Nabokov, Barth, Vonnegut, Grass, Robbe-Grillet, Clarke, Borges, and other living writers, I present the evidence and assertions of the following pages. I hope too that the reader will find a coherent and challenging account of the interpenetration of science and contemporary literature, free of both the wild claims of equivalence between the metaphors of science and literature and of the opposite fatuity, which sees physics and poetry as locked in deadly combat.

CHAPTER TWO
The Henry James Murder Mystery

Sky Pilot . . . you'll never reach the sky • *The Animals*

What ties together the Jamesian concepts echoed by contemporary writers, and makes their relation to contemporary literature so potent, is the matter of *absence* in James, primarily *absence* of what the novel always assumed as present before, the existence of understandable, predictable, *agency* in human affairs. As a primary metaphor for that essential aspect of this metaphysical complex, I propose the murder mystery in which the identity of the murderer is, and remains, unknown. This is *The Turn of the Screw*. But before taking up Jamesian specifics, I should like to locate the contemporary situation with a look at a novel that I take to be typical, though even less a murder mystery in the conventional sense of the term—Kurt Vonnegut's *Cat's Cradle* (1963).

A few years ago, this book could have been dismissed as belonging to the narrow and not-central-to-literature genre of science fiction; but for reasons I hope shall become clear as I proceed, that classification (or dismissal by classification) is no longer possible. The only thing that may prevent the science-fiction novel from becoming the dominant novel form, at least in the West, within another generation, is a change in terminology, an abandonment of the pejorative label "science fiction" (human affairs grotesquely intermixed with imaginary nuts and bolts) for something like "the (new) modern novel" (human affairs shown in the necessary relation they necessarily bear to real nuts and bolts). At least one novel, Nabokov's *Ada*, has already passed this line of demarcation.

In Vonnegut's story a man named Jonah, of indeterminate middle age, starts collecting information about a famous deceased scientist, Dr. Felix Hoenikker, popularly known as "the father of the atom bomb." With the collected data he wants to write a book, *The Day the World Ended*, centered upon the events of August 6, 1945, when the first atomic bomb was exploded over Hiroshima. Jonah's researches bring him into personal contact with the

Hoenikker children—the midget Newt, the psychotic Angela, and the "Boy Scout" Frank, now a general and second in command of the Central American island republic of San Lorenzo. He soon discovers that the three have in their possession their father's last, and potentially most destructive, invention, "ice-nine," a form of ice that freezes water between 32° and 114°F on contact. By a series of hilariously blood-chilling and believably inevitable events, one of their samples comes into contact with the ocean, and the world really does end, making Jonah's book project otiose. Thanks to the "stupidity and viciousness of all mankind" the final triumph of mind over matter is attained, or once more attained.[17] As the book's first sentence ("Call me Jonah.") darkly hints, this is the voyage of the *Pequod*—but on a planetary scale.

Such a bleak and hopeless prospect for mankind is not unusual in modern fiction, or postatomic fiction. What is of special interest is that Vonnegut's hero starts out a Christian but ends up a convert to a new religion widely practiced in San Lorenzo, Bokononism. Bokononism is the private revelation of a totally skeptical mocker with humanitarian principles, Bokonon, who lives in self-created exile on the island in order to give his religion the attraction of outlawry. He has arranged with his partner, the island's dictator, to have Christianity the official religion and Bokononist practices punishable by death. The opening passage of the Bokononist Bible, *The Books of Bokonon*, includes the statement, "Nothing in this book is true," which is a rehearsal of the antinomy of the liar.[18] This first principle of Bokononism, placed on the reverse of the title page of *Cat's Cradle*, states something always true about fiction, or something meant to be further unsettling, that, in effect, the statement that Bokononism is untrue is untrue *is untrue*.

Now Bokonon was called upon by his disciples to explain the terror of ice-nine, and he told them "that God was surely trying to kill them, possibly because he was through with them, and that they should have the good manners to die."[19] This we know to be untrue, because we know Bokonon knows nothing of God and his plans—that is, if we take Bokonon at his word. Two other occurrences should be mentioned: First, in the last days, after ice-nine has frozen the world, Frank Hoenikker takes to studying ants and finds that they have already developed a way to get water, and thus to survive, for a time at least:

> They did it by forming with their bodies tight balls around grains of *ice-nine*. They would generate enough heat at the center to kill half their number and produce one bead of dew. The dew was drinkable. The corpses were edible. (p. 186)

Frank is puzzled and upset, repeatedly challenging Jonah to tell him who taught the ants this little trick. The second occurrence is the last in the book: Jonah is driving along the main road of San Lorenzo, wrestling with an idea that possesses him but that he cannot make sense of—that he should climb to the top of the island's highest mountain and plant some symbol there, some expression of the end of the world. The car passes a figure seated at the roadside. It is Bokonon. Jonah stops, goes back, and asks the master what he is thinking. Bokonon replies that he is writing the final sentence to *The Books of Bokonon*. It is that if he were a younger man he would climb to the top of the island's mountain, take up some of the ice-nine, and by tasting it, "I would make a statue of myself, lying on my back, grinning horribly, and thumbing my nose at You Know Who" (p. 191).

This is the equation of the fiction I wish to discuss, in and out of the work of Henry James: There is *not* nothing, but it is nothingness that threatens man. There *is* something else, beyond man but inextricably bound up with him. Here in *Cat's Cradle* it takes the form of truth hidden within the antinomy of the lie; the trick the ants have implausibly learned; the waiting of Bokonon by the road to give Jonah the answer to the question he will come to ask; the impossibility of ruling out Bokonon's having expressed the will of God to his disciples. The world is not empty, but afflicted with a terrible absence of agents and motives. If it were simply empty, the fiction too could be simply empty, as so much of the post–World War I fiction was, denying Christianity while replacing it with physical processes like evolution or sexual instinct. Vonnegut, like James, may share with many twentieth-century writers an unwillingness to project Christian metaphysics, but he is not so simple-minded as to the matter of metaphysical, or supernatural, *presence*.

The Henry James Murder Mystery

In the work of Henry James there is no metaphysical system—efforts to find either Christianity or his brother William's principles in it have proved unconvincing[20]—but there is a metaphysics in the sense I employ here: not simply an ethical code tacitly based upon a belief in a power beyond man (in James, as in most Western writers, atheist or otherwise, we can take this to be a survival from Christian or Christian-derived training), but an assertion of an *Other*, or *others*, possibly another dimension, accessible by passing through a painted door or a mirror reflection, but another dimension that does not show itself beyond giving hints of its presence. It is therefore a mystery, as well as something missing.

If the mystery is a murder mystery, the dramatization can be simple: There is a murder, but there is no murderer. Or there is what we can intuit to be a murder, but a murder which if seen from certain points of view is not a murder at all. *No murderer* is what Edgar Allan Poe flirted with in *The Murders in the Rue Morgue*, the flirtation being quickly given up for a shift to a real, and only unusual, murderer (an orangutan). *No murder* is what Robbe-Grillet flirts with, in works like the mirror-reflective *Last Year at Marienbad (L'Année dernière à Marienbad)* and *La Maison de Rendez-Vous*. Henry James's greatest murder story, *The Turn of the Screw*, is possibly both *no murder* and *no murderer*, and it also has the metaphysical dimension that both Poe's and Robbe-Grillet's examples lack.

Its murder is that of little Miles; its question is, "If he *were* murdered, who murdered him?" The only person in the room with him, or with his dead body, is the governess, yet it is very difficult to pin the crime on her. Her responsibility for the disastrous situation in which she finds herself has been underscored heavily by modern critics generally of a Freudian persuasion; their charges against the governess, and the countercharges brought by more traditionally minded interpreters of the story, have formed one of the most intense clashes of twentieth-century American literary criticism.[21] If we are to hold her responsible we must note that she got away unapprehended, for the teller of the tale, Douglas, knew her several years later when she was the governess of his sister. We must also note that she used most devilishly clever means to bring about what must have been a heart attack on the boy's part: a little hint there, a surprise question about school here, a restraint calculated only to indicate suspicion, a glance, an expression—such barely definable marks of terror she must have surrounded him with, to the extent that his frail organism finally gave in.

Not many of the Freudian critics go this far, to suggest that the governess is a murderer, but it is only the logical extension of their approach to the story. We now consider it quite reasonable to say that you "did" what you unconsciously wished to happen, and acted indirectly to allow to happen, although our courts of law still, in most cases (that is, nonpolitical cases), strictly divide the thought from the act. The problem with the Freudian reading is not that it makes the governess into a monster of self-deceit and repressed hostility; it is the problem of Freudianism itself. In its applied and literary forms it is too simple. After explaining the hidden instinctual basis for many kinds of acts, it leaves the stage metaphysically bare. It is a physical, or material(istic) system; while James's story is a metaphysical story about the supernatural, and we destroy its connection to contemporary literature, as well as its point, if we insist upon dissolving, or leaching out, the metaphysical element.

It is just as possible to claim that there is no murder in *The Turn of the Screw*, which is the only thing to do if you absolve the governess of responsibility for Miles's death and yet wish to keep the supernatural out of the story, or out of the interpretation of the story. The governess is alone with the body; he must then have died of natural causes, or of unnatural but physical causes. Which? His guilt over his disgrace at school; his distress over his sister's abrupt decline into a kind of *dementia praecox*; his despair at the news that his uncle, his last remaining relative and surrogate father, has no love for him; his frenzy over a guilty secret. All perfectly possible, only no more supported by anything else in the story than a claim, that I might invent now while writing this sentence, that he was poisoned by the maid, who last served him food.

The third possibility is the interpretation that James's contemporaries put on the story, only without considering its consequences, the consequences that contemporary literature is exploring. That is, Miles was killed by an outside force, an undefined and undefinable force exerted across a boundary naturally and physically impervious to the exertion of such force. He is killed by Peter

Quint, a man several years dead. All James will say is that Miles's heart, "dispossessed" (by Quint), stopped. What might be called the ghost of Quint appears at the window, but only to the governess; Miles cannot see it (the governess is the only one in the house who "sees," in the sense of *admits* seeing, any of the presences of the living dead). The governess is, in fact, one of James's vessels of heightened consciousness, to whom values, acts, life itself, assume an intensity, a visibility, a *palpability* not granted to lesser and duller souls; but she can do no more than fumble toward a description of the enemy she is facing in her role as protectress of the children. That description is: "It was like fighting with a demon for a human soul."[22] Elsewhere she allows herself terms little more specific than those she uses in conversation with the children, and she has from the beginning of her fears taken a vow—of great usefulness to the horror effects in the story—that she would never lead the children in the direction her thoughts were taking by naming to them the agents—Jessel, the dead governess, and Quint, the dead valet—that she felt certain were operating against them, and constantly in their thoughts. It is thus that her conversation with Miles, even moments before his death, is perfectly adapted to the indefinability of the evil that surrounds them. After their last meal together, Miles says, "Well—so we're alone!" (p. 129), referring both to the fact that the maid has left the room after clearing away and, presumably, to the fact that Mrs. Grose is now on her way to London with the raving Flora. With the governess's reply the exchange continues:

"Oh, more or less." I fancy my smile was pale. "Not absolutely. We shouldn't like that!" . . .
"No, I suppose we shouldn't. Of course we have the others."
"We have the others—we have indeed the others," I concurred.
"Yet even though we have them," he returned . . . "they don't much count, do they?"
I made the best of it, but I felt wan. "It depends on what you call 'much'!"
"Yes"—with all accommodation—"everything depends!" (p. 129)

The dreadful tease here for us is that throughout both Miles and the governess could be referring to the servants of the house. The governess quite certainly, with her pale smile and her wan feeling, is talking about Jessel and Quint, and for Miles as well the term "others" is unusual, along with any reference of companionship, for servants of the nature of those left in the house. That leaves the reference suspended. Even if both Miles and the governess mean directly "Quint" and "Jessel," the task of identification is only begun—what exactly are Quint and Jessel?

The governess thinks that by questioning Miles, by getting him to speak the truth—about school and about his theft of her letter to his uncle—she can end the "communication" he has with the dead servant. She thinks, wrongly as it turns out, that "he knew when he [Miles] was in presence, but knew not of what, and knew still less that I also was [in presence] and that I did know [that I was in presence]"(p.134). I mean she thinks wrongly in that she thinks she is shutting off the communication between Miles and Quint when she can see the face of Quint at the window and can also see that Miles cannot see it. She is sure that he could before—that he saw Quint looking down from the window when he was out on the lawn, for instance. This is apparently true, but it only means that thanks to her momentary influence Miles cannot communicate with Quint. It does not mean that Quint cannot communicate with Miles, or "reach" Miles. In another few moments he does so, and takes Miles's life away.

But that leaves Quint no better defined than he was before. It is perfectly possible to bear down on the "demon" used by the governess and say he is clearly a soul in hell, come to claim for his companion there one who shared his crimes in life. It is not too hard to fit that into Christian metaphysics, with a little bending and pulling. It bears heavily, though, on two pieces of criminal evidence: that Mrs. Grose was aware of sexual misbehavior between Quint and Jessel when they were both alive, and that Miles's headmaster will not have him back at school at any price. If Mrs. Grose had been aware of an illicit relationship, or criminal acts, between or shared by Miles and Quint, she would have spoken; since she did not, she was not.[23] The reason for Miles's being sent down from school was, he tells the governess in the last scene, because of things he *said*, not things he did. What are such potent things to say? We must depend upon our governess to tell us, *faute de mieux*; hers is the recording consciousness: "Say that, by the dark prodigy I knew, the imagination of all evil *had* been opened up to him: all the justice within me ached for the proof that it ever could have flowered into an act" (p. 106).

The search for the act, the something definable and graspable, is perhaps her fatal error, that which prevents her from saving the boy. It leads her to stay at Bly with him, alone, to face the evil down, instead of fleeing with him to London. On the other hand, what good would that have done? If Quint is "the imagination of all evil" he clearly goes wherever the mind that has been opened up to him goes. Indeed, the governess's certainty that Miles and his sister Flora are "steeped in their vision of the dead restored" (p. 81) brings up the interesting possibility that the governess has become privy to the children's vision, or the children's thoughts, and that the appearances of the dead she experiences—Quint on the roof, Jessel and Quint on the stairs, Jessel in the schoolroom—are not something independent, but a view of what the children and only the children see, a view, in other words, into their heads and into their minds, rather than into the supernatural.

So *The Turn of the Screw* is a ghost story if you want, but a ghost story extremely difficult to fit into established metaphysics or, put more simply, into any scheme of Western religious belief.[24] That is stated on the assumption that the scheme of belief used by a culture can handle all occurrences of the supernatural within that culture. Quint's force as a Christian "demon" depends upon the commission of mortal sin on Miles's part, and James has carefully constructed the story so that attribution of such sin to Miles cannot be made. It is an interesting sidelight on this point that in Jack Clayton's film version of the story, *The Innocents*, the governess is asked by Mrs. Grose, when things have reached a state of emergency, whether she ought not to contact the vicar of their church. The governess rejects the suggestion, as indeed she must if James's story is to be followed, which leaves us with the question of why the suggestion was put into the film when it is not in the story. Part of the answer seems clearly that we, as Christians watching a ghost story, expect such a suggestion to be made. We know that if demons come as ghosts, with hellish designs, they may be put to flight by an appeal to God and his angels, by the rite of exorcism that the church has prepared for such emergencies. James included no such scene, we must grant, because he did not want to. He turned his vision of evil here, as elsewhere in his fiction, away from the Christian framework. Since his evil here is supernatural in form, he turned as well his embodiment of the supernatural away from the Christian, and away from the religious, framework. The conventional Clayton also has the governess turn to her Bible for sustenance in her dark hours of despair; James has no such scene. For such reasons I prefer to call his story a murder mystery.

From the conventional point of view, what is most striking about *The Turn of the Screw* is what is *not* in it. There is not, in short, any of the comfort Western man has, or has come to depend upon, in the face of horror. There is no appeal to religion; there is no appeal to outside help; there is no outside. Bly, with its dark, haunted lake, is all. The uncle in London wants nothing to do with the children, wants never to hear from the governess. Their exchange of letters is something of Beckettian malevolence in blunted communication: He sends on to her the headmaster's letter, unopened; hers to him, when all else has failed and she is desperate enough to break his condition of employment that she never write to him, is intercepted and burned by Miles. There is no definition of the evil, either in the matter of what has been done, or in the matter of what is threatened.[25] There is simply something existing parallel to the lives of the characters, or to life, that is inimical to life and capable of destroying it. It is *not* life; it is *anti*life; it is definable best as it appears most strikingly, as *absence*. A contradiction in terms if you like, for how can a negative quantity exert a positive force of harm? A "taking away" sums it up. An appearance of cessation of all life when the dead servants appear is what comes out strikingly in the governess's descriptions of the events. Here is the scene during which she first sees Quint, on the roof:

It was as if, while I took in—what I did take in—all the rest of the scene had been stricken with death. I can hear again, as I write, the intense hush in which the sounds of evening dropped. The rooks stopped cawing in the golden sky, and the friendly hour lost, for the minute, all its voice. (pp. 36–37)

And here is the way the governess intuits the nearing of Quint or Jessel, invisibly, when she is alone with the children:

After these secret scenes I chattered more than ever, going on volubly enough till one of our prodigious, palpable hushes occurred—I can call them nothing else—the strange, dizzy lift or swim (I try for terms!) into a stillness, *a pause of all life*, that had nothing to do with the more or less noise that at the moment we might be engaged in making and that I could hear through any deepened exhilaration or quickened recitation or louder strum of the piano. Then it was that *the others*, the outsiders, were there. (p. 88, italics added)

Quint and Jessel are just a little touch of what, in Vonnegut's terms, we call *ice-nine*, a visitation of stillness to the world. As Vonnegut's Jonah sees his world after the visitation, "the air was dry and hot and deathly still. . . . There were no smells. There was no movement" (p. 179). Both Quint and ice-nine are human inventions, hypothetical, even "impossible" approximations to antimatter, the physical correlative to a universe of utter indifference to man. The Dickensian sentimental humanism shared by James and Vonnegut, though buried at stratigraphically variant sites in their literary psyches, leads one to adopt a force, once human, that *desires* something human, and the other to adopt a force that is the product of charmingly human weakness—the urge to tinker. Both love man too much to leave him any comfort in these fictions, any feeling of a universe upholstered with him in mind. Of that cozy feeling, more in the next chapter.

CHAPTER THREE
Murder as a Literary Art

My motive in calling *The Turn of the Screw* a murder mystery is to bring out the unsettling aspects of its mystery of agents and motives; yet in the average murder mystery there is no such mystery of agents and motives, none that is not fully cleared up by the last page, at any rate.[26] The fact is that this very popular and very modern literary form is undergoing large contemporary changes, changes that bear examination in the light of the theme of this book, and changes that bring it closer to the form of *The Turn of the Screw*, even though to the world of 1898, into which *The Turn of the Screw* was born, it could hardly be called a murder mystery, for it had clearly too much mystery (left much greater at the end than at the beginning) and too little murder. There was enough death in it, of course—but Miss Jessel committed suicide; Miles and Flora's parents simply died in India, whether by *thuggee* or by typhoid fever; Quint was found dead outdoors at Bly. Was he murdered? No, the time had simply come for him to pass out of life, so that he might take the life of little Miles. Was Miles murdered? That question cannot be answered to the satisfaction of anyone applying the classic standards of the murder mystery.

For the murder mystery was a nineteenth-century invention, an outgrowth of the rational or Radcliffe school of the Gothic novel (rather than the Walpole-Lewis or fabulous school), and from the beginning has derived its effect from its certainty, its assumption of a metaphysical order that is *there* and need not be questioned or, for that reason, included. The possibility of its being challenged may be flirted with to give a sense of unusual and extradimensional danger, as when Conan Doyle pits Sherlock Holmes against Hindus who take no cognizance of Christian values, or Mormons who consider bloodshed a divine commandment; but the outcome is a foregone conclusion—these are exotic *frissons* and no more. Or, as in the work of Charles Williams (*Many Dimensions, War in Heaven*), violent death may be thrown against the screen of the Christian mystery itself. This is, in the end, even more comforting, bringing out into the open and showing in triumph those supernatural agents which sustain us above the void of not-knowing. When the criminal is found and led off to punishment, there is generally no ominous foreboding that this is a recurrent drama, that new victims and new murderers will follow one another through an infinity of future time or until some factor in the human equation has changed; there is only the feeling that rationality and justice have triumphed, day has once more driven back night. There is little concern for next evening.[27]

For that reason, the tacit assumption that here is a horror we are going to work out, defeat, and punish, the murder mystery as we have come to know it in the West need not state any metaphysics. Its author may harbor personal convictions of Bahai, Rosicrucianism, Shintoism, or Presbyterianism, but as long as he writes within the conventions of the form he is Deist, and his characters inhabit a mechanical universe where immutable laws, discoverable by reason, pursue an impartial course.

There are naturally variations; so rich and popular a form never cleaves to a totally dependable outline. The Alexandrian Tawfīq el Hakīm's excellent *Maze of Justice* (1947) depicts a murder along the upper Nile that is not solved by the hero, and never will be solved. That is, we are led (perhaps too easily, following our preconceptions of the East) to see Egypt as the land of shifting shapes and indeterminate contours, the land pumped up so romantically by Lawrence Durrell in his *Alexandria Quartet* and caused, in vicarious frustration and despair, to assume the fatalism we imagine endemic in the region. *Vicarious* is the saving word: We look on as spectators; this is not our world, but the world of hopeless creatures, or creatures having ways of sustaining hope into which we need not inquire.

Another kind of variation can be seen in Agatha Christie's *They Came to Baghdad* (1951), which allows into the normal equation of the murder mystery the international nefariousness of the Cold War and national plans for slaughter on a large scale. On the safe assumption that since 1945 it is practically the rule in literature to view killing in war as pointless horror, we should find the neat structure of the murder mystery overthrown here, washed out in the glare of such large-scale perfidy; the neat single or double or triple but *individual murder* overwhelmed by the numerical superiority of mass murder—even the mention or threat of mass murder.[28] But that does not happen in *They Came to Baghdad*, probably because the foreground events are of the same old comfy sort, with identifiable and punishable villains, while the names of political leaders and of locations in China and Russia are omitted or made imprecise.

Thus, the murder mystery can survive, if it skirts lightly two main dissolving effects: that of death on a large scale, and that of death inside a metaphysical context strange to the reader. What it cannot survive is death in no context, or a context of utter strangeness, from which there is no evident means of rescue by the familiar. Such strangeness is metaphysically threatening. It is probable that readers of murder mysteries prefer them to be written without supernatural agency, not only because such agency usurps the role of reason in them, but because it calls into question their own beliefs about the supernatural. The Freudian rewriting of *The Turn of the Screw* is one that brings comfort and solace to the modern reader—to be told that "it was all dreamed up by a sexually frustrated governess" (read St. Theresa of Avila) is to be (re)assured that we do not have to worry about it.

Since most writers who have worked in the murder-mystery form since its inception have not thought to challenge it, examples of such metaphysical "threats" are rare. Feodor Dostoevski took up the form, partly from Poe, who is generally credited with having invented the murder mystery with detective-hero, and made it the backbone or structural framework of his three greatest works: *Crime and Punishment, The Possessed,* and *The Brothers Karamazov*.[29] The last has only one or two rivals for being the greatest investigation of the human condition in Western prose fiction, but neither it nor the other two contains the absence that so marks *The Turn of the Screw*, for the horrors with which Dostoevski sears us are only preliminaries to his vision of the final triumph of Christ over the Grand Inquisitor. Specific readers may find the being of Smerdyakov, or the questions posed by Dmitri Karamazov, unanswerable, but the novel itself, that Dostoevski wrote to include them, does not find them so. Dostoevski certainly "challenged" the form; he blew it sky high, or wide, so that it included all the final questions about the relation of man to God. The solution of his murders still comes, though, and it is comforting. The difference between that solution and that comfort and those we have come to expect in the murder-mystery form is simply the difference between working a chess problem and undergoing the death of a loved one.

Needless to say, there aren't many Dostoevskis! The work of Charles Williams, mentioned earlier, is similar in applying final mysteries of Christianity to the question of murder, but it is not to be compared in any other respect. A search for the equation of *The Turn of The Screw* within the matter of sudden death leads inevitably into contemporary literature.

ALAIN ROBBE-GRILLET

One contemporary murder mystery, written with skill and power, that truly undermines the form without casting it into conventional metaphysics is Alain Robbe-Grillet's *Last Year at Marienbad* (1961), in which the heroine, "A," is shot by the mysterious "M," her companion and possibly her husband, because of her involvement with the hero and narrator, "X," who himself is killed by a fall in the gardens adjoining the palatial hotel where the story takes place. Yet neither of these events, one a murder, can be taken as having definitely occurred, mainly because Robbe-Grillet deprives the reader of locating cues in time. The reader does not know whether the lives of A and X terminated as shown, and the scenes in which they appear afterwards are actually previous in time to their deaths; or whether the later scenes are truly later, and the deaths only imagined by X, or by both X and A. The outer frame of the narrative itself may be death, for X, A, and M seem trapped in the hotel rather than just spending a holiday there; the events of the "last year" of the title are much the same as those of the present year, and the garden through which they wander has all the earmarks of a labyrinth. Robbe-Grillet has deliberately undermined the tight linearity and chronological dependability of the murder-mystery plot, so that while all the elements are there, they are not "composed." That is left for the reader to do, so that he may see, in terms of the *nouveau roman*, that reality is not given to producing scripts, not hospitable to the mind-set of any human culture, and not even chronologically linear (I shall discuss that point further in chapter 6).

In *La Maison de Rendez-Vous* (1965), Robbe-Grillet gives the death of Edouard Manneret the same kind of dimensionless treatment. There is a play within the novel called "The Murder of Edouard Manneret"; it is performed at the *maison* of the title, a house of prostitution in Hong Kong. Yet when one of the narrators, Johnson, is stopped by a police patrol, he is told that Manneret has just committed suicide. Johnson then takes the ferry across to Kowloon and goes to Manneret's house. Manneret comes to the door to meet him. A few pages further on, the first-person narrator is told by Lady Ava, the manager of the *maison*, that Manneret was murdered by someone who knew the house and rifled his safe. The impersonal (authorial) narrator next gives this description of the crime: "As usual, Manneret had left the door of his apartment open. Before he has had time to turn around, the dog has leaped on him from behind and broken his neck with a single crunch of its jaws."[30] After this the girl with the dog leaves immediately. In his hotel room, Johnson sees a headline in the newspaper announcing Manneret's "accidental" death. Lady Ava and the first-person narrator now rehearse the details of the murder: A crooked Chinese policeman had come to blackmail Manneret and then murdered him with a folding stiletto, arranging the body afterwards over fragments of a broken wine glass so that Manneret might be presumed to have fallen upon them in a drugged state and so died. After this, the Eurasian girl Kim, whom we have seen with the dog, "remembers that she has killed [Manneret]" (p. 128). The events of Kim's visit to Manneret with the dog now begin to unreel again, with the author's note: "If Manneret has already just been murdered, this scene takes place earlier, of course" (p. 130). At the end of the novel Johnson returns to Manneret's apartment and shoots him as he sits rocking in his chair. To separate the whole further from an experience in which the reader can locate himself, Robbe-Grillet has Lady Ava confess, in one of the last sections of the book, that "she has never gone to China; the fancy brothel, in Hong Kong, is merely a story people have told her" (p. 134). If the reader wants a murder mystery from this murder mystery, he must compose it himself. That is, after all, what the characters themselves, Lady Ava, Johnson, Kim, Manneret (who is writing at his desk), are doing.

The effect of this dislocation practiced upon the murder mystery by Robbe-Grillet is as serious and destructive, in principle, of the values of traditional literature as that of any work so far mentioned. But the effect is blunted by Robbe-Grillet's playfulness (his presentation of many plots rather than a true absence in plot) and by his objectivity. There are no moral issues in *Marienbad* or *Maison de Rendez-Vous*, and no hint either that there might be any. Nor is there any appeal to the supernatural. The reader is baffled, but not really moved out of the position of power he is used to enjoying in the pursuit of a mystery. Robbe-Grillet seems linked more closely to the utter blankness of objectivity in writers like Gertrude Stein, or in the concretists, than to the moral seriousness of James or of Vonnegut. His work is also notably erotic, in the manner of sadistic suggestiveness, and more allied to the metaphysical absence of the contemporary erotic writers than to the absence I have posited in James and in the metaphysically more explorative of the moderns.

EUGÈNE IONESCO

The contemporary writer who "takes on" the full metaphysical implications of murder, only to reject them or to reject any implications yet imagined, is Eugène Ionesco. *The Killer (Tueur sans gages,* 1959), describes the career of a multiple murderer who has terrorized the inhabitants of a great modern housing development. He never fails to get his intended victim and ruthlessly kills old and young, rich and poor, seemingly at random. His method is bizarre: He shows his victims a picture of a colonel, stretching it out over the water of a pool until they fall and drown. The police and the authorities, like the victims, show a strange passivity in the face of his continued depradations; they do not even pursue him. The hero of the play, Bérenger, decides with impetuous idealism that he will pursue and capture the killer, but he is sadly ineffectual in a series of attempts that grow more and more confusing to him and result finally in his own death. He finds his own friend's briefcase to be filled with incriminating evidence—photos of the same colonel, a map, and a diary listing both murders accomplished and murders planned ahead—but when he rushes out with it to the police he finds that it has been left behind and that various people he meets in the street carry apparently identical briefcases. He is involved in a dream absurdity that makes rational action impossible.

Rational interpretation may be felt to be impossible as well; to many people Ionesco's work is a hangover from the Dadaism that celebrated meaninglessness. But *The Killer*, viewed in the context of its author's own philosophy and in terms of what can be seen as a comprehensible set of internal symbols, is a coherent attack on conventional value systems, both political and metaphysical, current in the West. Like *Marienbad*, it is therefore an attack on the conventional murder mystery too, but in place of *Marienbad*'s lack of specific location amid value systems it has a specific denigration of religion (Edouard, Bérenger's tired and ill friend, who carries the clue to the mystery about with him but whose attitude is only passive acceptance), state planning (the Radiant City haunted by the killer and for that reason soon to be abandoned), and bureaucratism (the members of the Civil Service are safe from the killer's attack until they retire or resign, trading a death-in-life for protection against the real thing, real life and real death), and political allegiance (the figure of Mother Peep represents a "mystification" common to all the new political faiths that have usurped the role of religion). Thus, Bérenger is left in the bare existential situation —alone, and with no other reality than that he *is*, and will die. Ionesco once wrote: "The eternal truth which we forget throughout history, the truth which we fail to consider . . . is both simple and trite: I will die, you will die, he is dying."[31] Bérenger does not die very well, babbling a pathetic tirade of mingled threat and plea, bravado and cringing parody of Christian humility, as the killer slowly advances on him. Ionesco, in effect, does not hold out much hope, either in his plays or in his existential outlook, that there is any nice or heroic way to die.

TWENTIETH-CENTURY VIOLENCE

The murder mystery has thus taken part, like all other forms of fiction, in the "loosening of the center" noted by Yeats and Eliot in the postwar period, the loss of connection between its structure and that of a conventional metaphysics. The form has a natural dependence upon the way death is viewed in the culture for which it is written; it is perhaps true that it could not be written at all until there arrived a combination of social factors, including urban life and Victorian sexuality, enabling at once a keen, intellectualized interest in death and a conventionalized insensitivity to its horror. Robbe-Grillet's open manipulation of the sexuality may be as damaging to the form as Ionesco's manipulation of its horror, but more common and shared is the fact that the murder mystery in contemporary forms no longer "makes sense," and that writers like Robbe-Grillet and Ionesco are interested in showing us how provincial, bourgeois, and *petit rentier* our views of "sense" are, including our confidence in its existence. In such an effort they are far from the Jamesian example, *The Turn of the Screw*, that I used to initiate this discussion. Their *absence* is a simpler thing than James's, for it is mainly a denial of what other people, or people in general, believe. It is a negation, filled, especially in Ionesco, with the same scorn that inspires Sartre's epochal *Nausea*, a novelistic equivalent, we might say, of "They (ordinary people and their beliefs) make me puke." James, for all his own private and sometimes ill-concealed scorn for parts of his own culture, was fictionally beyond that point, and at the point of simple exploration of what there is, and might be, that affects the consciousness of human beings. The murder mystery, I am tempted to conclude, has yet to reach the point at which James placed it with his little potboiler of 1898.

There are elements of particular application to the contemporary era that I have not taken up in the murder mystery, however, and to some extent these bear upon the questions of metaphysical absence and the "other." "Senseless" or "meaningless" outbreaks of savage personal violence seem to many people—to many Westerners—the most puzzling and disturbing "problem of our time." That adolescents should murder and rape, schoolchildren set fire to their teachers or commit aggravated assault combined with property damage, is as threatening to them and their sense of security as any of the other developments I mentioned earlier. It also seems analogous to them to modern political movements, like National Socialism in Germany, that make free use of violence, actual and threatened, with the same barefaced impudence that marks the attitude of the urban juveniles. Presumably those who feel this alarm merge their fascinated horror with the general contemporary appeal of violence for entertainment purposes to account for the popularity of books and films featuring ultraviolence: Anthony Burgess's *Clockwork Orange* (1962, in 1972 made into another "mind-blowing" film by Stanley Kubrick); the genre of Italian Westerns, developed in the 1960s as a logical extension of the violence in the original Hollywood Westerns, which now appears both relatively mild (not more than a dozen killings per film, and no depiction of gore) and relatively motivated in contrast; the films of Sam Peckinpah, which first restored the supremacy of the American Western in this respect and then went on to new heights with *Straw Dogs* (1972, a translation of the Western abattoir to the quiet English countryside for additional shock effect); a series of American novels, including those of Mickey Spillane, that mix sadism with erotic appeal, some of which were filmed but then eclipsed by the far more glamorous brutality of the English James Bond novel-film phenomenon. Lacking the filmic embodiment it "deserves," but undeniably paramount in this area, is Truman Capote's *In Cold Blood*, a "nonfiction novel" dramatizing a horrible, and real, multiple murder in a bland, factual style that is suited to the mindlessness of the act. In it, the step-by-step unraveling of the mystery of the perpetration is outdone, finally, by the mystery of the gratuitousness of the violence.

Parallel to the intrusion in the Capote novel of a destructive reality, a reality that could be assigned a monist basis in the absence of any metaphysics supplied by the author, there are interesting German studies and fictional representations of the outburst, breakthrough, or destructive intrusion of the evil of nazism. Thomas Mann's *Dr. Faustus* (1947) is a symbolic representation, in musical and artistic terms, of the state of Germany in the period

37 • *Murder as a Literary Art*

from 1933 to 1945, written from a viewpoint after the fact; his vision of a witches' sabbath that torments the dreams of the old German writer in *Death in Venice (Tod in Venedig*, 1929) seems an applicable analogue from before the fact.[32] As such, considering Hitler's activities in the 1920s and the proximity of the events of 1933–1934, it would be no more far-fetched than H. G. Wells's prediction of "The Second World War" in the 1936 *Shape of Things to Come*. Mann uses Freudian psychology and a popular view of early Germanic culture, along with Friedrich Nietzsche's opposition of Dionysian blood power versus the serenity and cerebrality of Apollonian civilization. Also dualistic, but not especially Freudian, is Heimito von Doderer's "first reality" and "second reality" in his novel of the submerging of post–World War I Austria in unreason and protofascism, *Demons (Die Dämonen*, 1956). "First reality" is truth, culture, civilization, and the idea of the city of Vienna; "second reality" is the demonic, including fantasies of sex and violence, culminating in Doderer's novel with the firing of the Palace of Justice in Vienna on July 15, 1927. Unlike the supernatural or the question of "others," these are basically materialistic projections of the concept that man bears within himself a destructive impulse. Doderer's fiction, like Mann's, may be seen as parallel to *Cat's Cradle* or *The Turn of the Screw* in that it has no dependence on the conventional religious supernatural[33] and in that the two realities exist side by side, like two worlds, allowing men to see their distorted and reversed mirror images across the boundary, as when, in Doderer's Vienna, as one critic has put it, "the very virtues of the 'first reality' turn out to be the vices of the 'second.' "[34] But the parallel is not finally sufficient to the demands of the subject; the magical evocation of the sinister in the films of Fritz Lang, especially the direct Nazi analogue *The Last Will of Dr. Mabuse (Das Testament von Dr. Mabuse*, 1932), is as memorable as any of the German artistic efforts before 1950, and as teasing in the removal of metaphysical certainties.

It is therefore possible to look to German literature today with some impatience, an impatience not entirely based on a reasonable view of history. For we feel that German writers should by now, 1976, a mere 31 years after the end, and 43 years after the beginning, of the Nazi horror, have produced works to explain convincingly to us what kind of a nightmare it was that dominated the first half of the twentieth century, have written a murder story, or a murder mystery with some solution, to fit this giant murder—to do for that murder as much, let us say, as *The Turn of the Screw* has done for the hole in the cosmos punctured by nineteenth-century science, or *Cat's Cradle* for the bombing of Hiroshima—not a final definition, in other words, but a fair start on one. This we can ask, though the list of the horrors of human history that have received literary treatment in any sense adequate to the challenge they provide is extremely small. This brings one to reflect, in a complaint that literature has failed to explain something that needs explaining, that the capacities of literature as "explanation" in general are possibly very limited. It is too familiar now to need restating that only science of limited kinds and application, and literature of the same, and inferior, nature, have ever allowed themselves the luxury of positive explanation. All great literature is finally "non-Euclidean" in the sense that it underlines the infirmity of human judgment and shows that to be able to explain, predict, or state with certainty the movement of one particle or act of the universe in all its ramifications is simply to be God, or the master of that universe.

GÜNTER GRASS

Murder then remains a mystery, and the proper form to an explanation of murder, whether or not that explanation is spoiled by an embarrassing surplus of corpses or a disorienting lack of a metaphysical frame, remains the murder mystery. And there is a good German murder mystery relevant to the problem of Nazi murder, incorporated in Günter Grass's *Tin Drum (Die Blechtrommel,* 1959). It is sufficiently complex to do at least elementary justice to its subject; the murderer is not caught or punished, as is fitting (as in *The Turn of the Screw*); and the identity of the murderer is both unknown and disturbingly involved with important metaphysical considerations, as in Ionesco.

The victim is a nurse who lives in the same rooming house with the dwarf-hero, Oskar Mazerath, in the years of his fame. This is in the postwar *Wirtschaftswunder;* Oskar's drumming brings such

39 • Murder as a Literary Art

painful delight to the memory-haunted consciences of the West Germans that a national movement has arisen, called Oskarism. Oskar could live and travel in great luxury, wherever he wished, but he prefers to stay just where he was before he became famous, in a converted bathroom at the end of the hall in the shabby rooming house. This is partly because of the nurse living across from him, with whom he is fascinated, and whose letters he intercepts, but whom he never sees until one night, inspired by the laying of a new coconut-fiber mat in the hall, he goes out naked, partly shielded by the leftover piece of matting he had in his room with him, and proposes himself to the terrified girl as she sits in the toilet. She flees the rooming house the same night, but Oskar still derives pleasure from visiting her room and looking about where her uniforms and dresses once hung.

One day Oskar feels like going for a walk in the country—with a dog, rather in the *Herr und Hund* manner. There is a nearby kennel that rents dogs for just such purposes, so Oskar is quickly outfitted, and off they go. When they have reached a suburban orchard, Oskar sits and rests while the dog moseys about in a nearby field. His reveries are interrupted by the dog's pressing its muzzle into his lap, and when he examines what the dog is offering he finds it is a human finger—a female human finger, wearing a ring. Oskar takes out his handkerchief, carefully wraps the finger in it, and puts it in his pocket—not, however, without being observed by a strange and curious man named Vittlar, perched in a tree in the orchard. Vittlar attaches himself to Oskar, and during a long conversation in which the finger figures, confesses that he is burning with jealousy of Oskar's fame as a drummer. Oskar kindly tells Vittlar that if he, Vittlar, would like to get a share of that fame he can turn Oskar in as the murderer of the owner of the finger (that is, the nurse). The resultant national publicity will bathe them both nearly equally. Vittlar goes off transfigured, and Oskar decides to flee, just to lend credence to Vittlar's story. He is caught in Paris, where he greets the arresting Interpol detectives by saying, "I am Jesus." After the trial he is confined to a mental institution, where he writes his story, *The Tin Drum*, and receives regular visits from Vittlar, who is now his disciple, urging him to go out into the world (he is thirty and soon to be released, and other clues are sure to turn up and require a reopening of the Ring Finger Case) and spread his message—take on, in other words, the burden of being Jesus.

Oskar has a history of assumed contact with the nature of Jesus. During the war, when he lived with his family in Danzig, he had approached the plaster statue of the baby Jesus in the cathedral and implored it to drum upon his drum. It had refused, but it relented and drummed for him when he made the request again, in 1944. Later that year Oskar, having become the leader of a group of rebellious youths, took them to the cathedral at night and had them remove the statue of Jesus and lift him up into its place, and then celebrate a mass to him. To the boys, whose crimes ranged from theft to murder, he was Jesus, for that was what he called himself, and he could perform miracles, breaking windows with his voice from far across the city and so granting them entrance to any building they desired.

The finger, or a finger, had also appeared before. When Oskar had worked as an engraver of tombstones, after the war but before his fame as a drummer spread, he had accompanied his employer to a Rhineland cemetery at Oberaussen to help place a headstone. As they busied themselves with this task, men in an adjoining plot disinterred the remains of a woman whose relatives wanted her dug up and reburied nearer home. Her body came out of the ground unwillingly, as it were, a piece at a time, and Oskar happened to pick up one of these pieces. It was the woman's ring finger.

From his hospital bed, a child's bed with high sides, tiny Oskar does not tell us whether he murdered that nurse or not. We know he has reason to feel somewhat antisocial in the erotic area, for no woman, including a nurse he had dated earlier, would take him seriously as a lover, and he wanted very badly to be so taken. We may doubt as well that Oskar *could* tell us the truth about the matter, for when he fell ill in 1945, with the affliction that caused him to become hunchbacked and gain a foot in stature, the doctor had predicted that whatever it was he had would surely reach his brain after a time. We cannot dismiss the possibility, therefore, that the whole later part of his narrative reflects the acts of a madman, and the whole of the narrative, from start to finish, reflects the narration of a madman. He has as well been placed in a hospital for the insane. Indeed, as with the narrator of Vladimir Nabokov's *Pale Fire*, we have to question whether anything narrated actually occurred, especially since there is more than one instance of the supernatural amid the rest—Oskar breaking glass with his voice, even inaudibly and at a distance of several kilometers; Oskar getting the statue of Baby Jesus to drum for him; the figure of the graveyard watcher Schugger Leo flying above the trees, and so forth.

So this murder seems unrelated to the new boundaries and conceptions of science, but it is hard to consider it as unrelated to the period of institutionalized murder in Germany. Oskar drumming in the onion cellar and as the purveyor of Oskarism enables Germans to let down their defenses, relive the past, and weep for what they have done and omitted doing. Yet Oskar himself is as well equipped with his little drum to lead them to hell as to heaven; he has defined his existence from his third year on by destruction—of glass, starting out humbly enough with the face of the family clock, leading on through *Kristallnacht*, when the grownups broke glass, to virtuoso performances in occupied Paris; of human lives, albeit on a small scale and indirectly, as when he led the boys' gang, gave his father his party pin to swallow as Russian soldiers watched, or told Roswitha to get her own coffee, thereby leading her directly into the path of an Allied shell, or—possibly—did something to the nurse who lived across the hall and would not accept him as a lover. Oskar is innocent of Nazi activity; he even broke up Nazi rallies on occasion by hiding with the magical drum under the rostrum. He has acted just as he has been considered by grownups; as an unfortunately handicapped and destructive child. The grotesque effects of *The Tin Drum* do not seem sufficiently welded together to give the whole a clear application and effect, but perhaps this is the way Grass wishes to describe Germany and the man who shaped its destiny from 1933 to 1945, the man whose voice could break things at long distances, whose magical charisma held Germans spellbound, who was deformed in mind, morally a dwarf, a child who never grew up, and who was called, in the early years before he came to power and was successful only in causing street disturbances, "Der Trommler."

FRIEDRICH DÜRRENMATT

Friedrich Dürrenmatt, the Swiss-German writer whose plays, most notably *The Physicists (Die Physiker,* 1962), have a certain fame for dramatizing contemporary issues, would hardly seem to be a literary artist capable of epitomizing any of the issues taken up in this chapter. His plots are unbelievable; his characterization stock-conventional; his penchant for the grotesque and macabre, along with the surprising turn of event, form a distasteful pastiche of Franz Kafka and O. Henry. Yet there is in one of his stories, *The Pledge (Das Versprechen,* 1958), a variation on the murder mystery that is indicative of changing contemporary conceptualization—if not illustrative of contemporary artistic accomplishment.[35] The subtitle of *The Pledge* is "Requiem for the Detective Story," and it is in this sense a murder mystery written to "end" (all) murder mysteries, to point out the inapplicability of the form, as conventionally written, to the complexity and unpredictability of reality. This reality is not specifically "contemporary reality"; like Robbe-Grillet, whose program for the *nouveau roman* can be seen as incorporating Dürrenmatt's rejection of the neat solution, Dürrenmatt only sees himself as making his fiction conform to tacitly generalized "things as they are" rather than to "things as they have become."

The Pledge has two narrators: an outer-frame narrator, an unnamed novelist; and an inner narrator who is also a participant, like Joseph Conrad's Marlow, in the story he tells. This is Dr. H., former police chief of Zurich, and it is his opinions concerning the relation of fiction to life that form the basis of our perception of the story. He compares, with heavy irony, the "duties" of the policeman and those of the writer: "Every audience and every taxpayer has a right to his heroes and his happy ending, and we of the police and you of the writing profession are equally obliged to supply these" (pp. 17–18)[36]—the policeman, or the detective, has the public duty of providing solutions to murders, catching the criminal, and the same thing is expected of the writer of detective stories or murder mysteries. Dr. H., as the policeman who cannot set up or control the conditions with which he works, reserves his greatest scorn for the writer, who can control the conditions by his own invention yet deliberately falsifies their true nature. In fiction, therefore,

> The fraud becomes too raw and shameless. You build your plots up logically, like a chess game; here the criminal, here the victim, here the accomplice, here the master mind. The detective need only know the rules and play the game over, and he has the criminal trapped, has won a victory for justice. This fiction infuriates me. Reality can only be partially attacked by logic. (p. 18)[37]

What the writer leaves out is just that element which decides whether or not the police do solve a case: *chance* ("in your novels chance plays no part"). When chance does occur in fiction, it is treated as something preordained ("some kind of destiny or divine dispensation"), rather than as what we presume Dr. H. to mean and what the tenor of his remarks indicates: a fickle and powerful erratic force that upsets, and prevents the application of, logic and its analogues—chess strategy, deductive reasoning, the Sherlock Holmes approach.

Dürrenmatt makes the application of this point to his murder mystery easy—all too easy, as is typical of him—by making his murderer insane. The criminally insane are, as we are accustomed to being told, either superhumanly accurate in their use of precisely logical steps, or wildly erratic and outside all human probability in their behavior. Either way they escape the meshes of a logical pursuit that attributes the "sense" of motive, means, and so forth to their actions.[38] Dürrenmatt's murderer, Albert, who lures little girls with candy and then eviscerates them with a razor, belongs to an existent type of sex murderer, but that does not affect the large gulf between his life and life in general. Dwight Macdonald has noted this of Alfred Hitchcock's celebrated film *Psycho:* Despite its firm basis in reality (the Gein case in Wisconsin) and its neat Freudian explanation delivered in the form of a pseudomedical epilogue, its hero is simply too far removed from our lives to be of interest to us.[39] His madness is like Albert's, clear, complete, and irretrievable, totally lacking in the teasing, borderline quality of that of Grass's Oskar Mazerath or Robbe-Grillet's Wallas (hero of *The Erasers*).

The critical role of chance in the plot of *The Pledge* is, like the narrative structure, double, and naturally it is in compliance with the sentiments of Dr. H. First, when Albert's most recent victim is found, the police (logically) conclude that a peddler who was in the area (a secluded spot at the edge of a forest) and who has difficulty justifying his movements is the killer, and they intensify their third-degree questioning to the point that he confesses. He then hangs himself in his cell, so the case is considered closed. Albert, unsuspected as before, is free to kill again. The police are defeated by their own logic, and by the unlucky chance that an innocent man incriminated himself.

The second unlucky chance is somewhat more complex in its effect, and as malignant, for when the sensitive and intelligent detective-protagonist, Matthäi, who feels uneasily sure of the peddler's innocence, pursues the investigation and lures Albert into a trap, he is defeated by chance just as victory, and justification, are within his grasp. For Albert is killed in a traffic accident on his way to meet, and to kill, the little girl Matthäi has set out as bait for him. Since Matthäi only knows that the little girl has met someone, and she, having been charmed by Albert (in much the same way that Ionesco's killer charms his victims), denies everything, Matthäi is left with nothing. His imagination and mental flexibility had enabled him to skirt the first logical trap, only to lure him into a second: The perfection of his plan to trap the killer, and its successful operation right up until the last moment, intoxicate him with the delight of ratiocination to the extent that the breakdown of the ratiocination breaks him, too. He becomes—with Dürrenmatt's usual flair for the melodramatic—a seedy, drink-sodden wreck, forever lost to his career and the world.

The logic of the murderer in this is hardly necessary to consult, either that he consciously seeks out little girls to kill because he hears a divine commandment to do so, or that he is unconsciously revenging himself on womankind for the humiliating treatment he receives from a wife who is his social and intellectual superior (as well as thirty-two years his senior). In combination with the accident that eliminates both Albert and his detective-pursuer, though, this logic can be seen to have a suitably "crazy" parallel to the situation of the real murderers in Capote's *In Cold Blood*. They set out, with a logic barely fitting to the feeble-minded, to rob a rich farmer about whom they know nothing, when the most superficial local inquiry could inform them that he keeps no cash whatsoever about him or in his house. They arm themselves, they plan their route in a carefully prepared vehicle, they set up an alibi. Then, at the last moment, they take into consideration the fact that, with their past criminal records, it is imperative for them to disguise themselves so that the farmer and his family will not be able to identify their faces from police files. Black stockings, says one, we must have women's black stockings to pull over our faces. What women wear such stockings? Why, nuns, of course! They then drive to a convent to ask for some old stockings, an effort so foredoomed to failure that the one who volunteers to go in and do the asking only pretends to the other that he has done so and been refused. They go on to invade the farmer's house, tie him up with the rest of his family, and are then faced with the "logical" necessity of killing them all to protect their identities. That all their thinking has served them as only the lightest covering for an inner desire to kill from the first is made clear by the boasts of one about killing at the outset, and the answering assurance from the other that he had killed in the past—this other, who had been treated harshly by nuns as a foundling child, being the one with the idea about the stockings. Finally, their desire to take some notable revenge upon society may be connected, by an outer and perhaps equally crazy logic, to the "chance" that *both* of them have been disfigured, and one partially crippled, by traffic accidents. If Dürrenmatt's situation is absurd, this is equally so.

The Pledge may correct the distortion that its Dr. H. complains of in novels, but in a way that Dr. H. does not seem to think of, for it freely employs the kind of chance we are used to calling strained coincidence. This is particularly evident in the murderer's own freedom from suspicion and observation, which stems from his wife's motherly protectiveness, which stems from her hatred and fear of an observing, ten-years-older sister, who has *also* married *her* simple-minded handyman. The novel closes with the figure of this fellow-to-Albert, who, we must believe, will be led to kill in the same way, presented for our consideration.

It is in this last, rather mechanical prediction of further horror of the same kind to come, parallel in this respect to the ending of Alexander Pushkin's *Queen of Spades*, that the novel departs from the "happy ending" of the murder mystery convention, for its use of chance (*Zufall*) is hardly such as to involve metaphysical considerations. That is, despite the powerlessness of the police, everything is explained and accounted for at the end by the deathbed confession of Albert's wife. And R. B. Heilman's intriguing comparison of it to *The Turn of the Screw* remains one of the very best demonstrations of the relevance of James's work to the themes of contemporary literature.[40] Not to modern literature, that is (the confrontation of James to Freud), but to postmodern: the dramatic assertion of the inadequacy of logic and the "lure of the demonic" (Heilman's characterization of the Jessel- and Quintlike power Albert wields over the children) that can be taken as its demonstration.

CHAPTER FOUR
Terror in Henry James

In their edition of Henry James's notebooks, F. O. Matthiessen and K. B. Murdock comment on James's *Sense of the Past*: "His 'hero,' translated in time, . . . is a source of 'terror' to the other characters as well as the victim of it himself, a man at once haunting and haunted."[41] This hero, Ralph Pendrel, is in this respect in a situation like that of one of James's most puzzling characters, Vanderbank of *The Awkward Age*, who is the source of the "sacred terror" (a phenomenon partly jocular) and also its victim, in that it is something undefined that sets him off from the others and puts him outside the normal course of life, sealing him off as well from its joys. This in turn is the situation of Marcher in *The Beast in the Jungle*, another metaphor of terror which in the fictional working is refined and abstracted in the same way as it is in *The Awkward Age*. Just how much of crude fear, physical fright, there was to be in *The Sense of the Past* we can only guess; there is, though, between it and the other two works, this strong link of a "terror" that has something to do with strangeness both in the consciousness, sooner or later, of the person bearing it, and in an effect visible or palpable to others around him, as if he somehow were "other" rather than one of them. *The Turn of the Screw* is, of course, linked too. James set out to reproduce its general effect with *The Sense of the Past*, and like *The Sense of the Past* it is a "ghost" story featuring the physical appearance of the dead and an impingement of the world of the dead directly upon the world of the living.

This matter may be likened to the time theory of J. W. Dunne, for James's terror, this common element in his late novels and stories, is primarily a matter of consciousness, specifically (since everything in James, even morality, finally relates to consciousness) *double* consciousness.[42] That term is used of both Pendrel in *The Sense of the Past* and Spencer Brydon in *The Jolly Corner* to describe a state in which the observer is aware of a surrounding reality that he shares with others, and also of another reality that he does not. It has undetermined dimensions and uncertain physical as well as metaphysical status, but it bears upon him and observes him nevertheless. The people with whom he shares the first or common reality, reality A let us say, cannot see into this other plane, that of reality B, but they can see that the observer—the governess in *The Turn of the Screw*, Pendrel in *The Sense of the Past*, to some extent May Bartram in *The Beast in the Jungle*—is in contact with something else, and this upsets them. To them (the housekeeper Mrs. Grose, the Midmores, the American ambassador) the observer is "queer" in some way, depending upon the extent and depth of the observation of the observer that James allows them.

Now Dunne posits a reality A of linear time, and the observing brain of the person in that time moving through reality A in a parallel linear path. But he also posits an observation on "time 2" or an observational reality B, open to the individual of ordinary life in "time 1" or our reality A. Insights into this superior status and time reality come to most of us in dreams, especially dreams of future events, which are breaks out of the A reality of past-present-future "as lived." To Dunne in his explanatory-inspirational mode, these are glimpses of immortality to come, proof that "nothing dies." To the average person, they are visions of terror, centering on the supernatural and death, on "the night my number came up." Double consciousness that moves one out of linear time is an agony of the soul; it is that aspect that Henry James explores.

This does not mean that Henry James finds all mysteries finally inside the human mind, despite his emphasis on consciousness: There is always the enclosing structure of interpersonal relations, and always the question of metaphysical agency in his work, the latter shown most clearly by the *revenants* in *The Turn of the Screw* and the appearance of the dead in many other stories. One can say, "Those are only ghost stories, written by a serious novelist as *jeux d'esprit*, to cater to a popular market," but that is like saying *Crime and Punishment* does not show the real Dostoevski because he wrote it in haste and great financial need. If we say, then, that the only reality in James is the mind of man, we must allow that the mind of man as conceived by James is free to move through space and time, beyond the boundaries of the life of the body. That puts James squarely into the supernatural.

The double consciousness is most clearly embodied when there is a physical re-creation of the observer that is visually identical but different, himself in some other guise, himself and not himself; in other words, when there is a double. As James worked it out in his notes to *The Sense of the Past*, "the thrill and the curiosity of the affair" was to be "the consciousness of being the other [Pendrel's double out of past time] and yet himself also, of being himself and yet the other also."[43] Where this thrill shades off into something more dire is in the inevitability of deadly enmity between doubles, a logical extension and intensification of that naturally existing between twins. Doubles, like matter-antimatter twins, have a poisonous effect on each other, as Poe's *William Wilson*, a classic of the literature of doubles, shows so clearly, for while the mind may delight in the achievement of a mirrorlike ability to "see from outside," it must finally revolt against, and try to destroy, a duplication of itself that shows any capacity to act independently. The strengthening of the imagined double is, of course, from one point of view, the equivalent strengthening of an acute schizophrenic condition.

As James noted to himself with some annoyance, for he did not want the planned *Sense of the Past* to repeat things he had done earlier, he had already "made use of a scrap of that fantasy in *The Jolly Corner*" of 1908,[44] by proposing a time fork, in which a man leaving the commercial bustle of New York to spend his life in European cultivation of sensibility also, in the sense of being double, *stays* in New York, and pursues a business career. Upon his return to the city, many years later, he revisits his childhood home and there wills to see the double, the man he would have been if he had stayed in New York. He looks across the ends of the time fork, and his successful vision is a nightmare, a man brutalized and morally debased, with missing fingers as an emblem of a scarred nature. His and the vision's mutual destruction is only avoided by a combination of chances—that a door closed by the double remains closed; that the man, Spencer Brydon, is not killed in his swooning fall down a flight of stairs when he sees the double advance upon him; that a telepathically sympathetic woman, Alice Staverton, is there to sustain him.

The use of the double, and its effect on the individual consciousness, in James's fictions, can be rewardingly compared with what has become the most common contemporary narrative of the double, the technological or science-fiction form. A rather well-written and representative example is James Blish's *Spock Must Die!* (1970), an incident or adventure inside the continuing, televised saga of *Star Trek*.[45] Its framework is highly technological and machine-dependent. In an effort to place an emissary on the planet Organia, the engineers of the *Enterprise* translate Spock, the brilliant Vulcanian-human second officer, into a beam of tachyons, while at the same time keeping him, the original, undisturbed. Unfortunately Organia has been sealed off by an enclosing thought-shield, placed by the Klingon enemy, that acts as a mirror to the tachyon beam, and the second Spock is instantly returned to place on board the *Enterprise*, identical in every way to the original except that he is mirror-reversed. His reversal is physically imperceptible, thanks to the symmetry of Vulcanian anatomy, but complete—that is, it includes his thinking, which is therefore directly hostile to the original Spock and all that he is seeking to accomplish. It is natural, therefore, that his first act is to claim that he is the real Spock, and the real Spock is the duplicate. Since he has all of the true Spock's memories and abilities, he is able to sabotage the *Enterprise* easily and to escape from it when his identity is finally uncovered—in that uncovering Blish treats us to a number of the puzzles described in Martin Gardner's *The Ambidextrous Universe* (see chapter 6), settling finally on the puzzle of the milk in *Through the Looking-glass* (Can a real—say, left-handed—cat drink reversed, right-handed milk?). The answer is no, pretty certainly, so Spock's double is stymied by the food on board the *Enterprise* and must give himself away by declining an invitation to eat some.[46]

As mechanically separate and "opposite" as such a double may be, Blish leaves room for the attachments of consciousness that give psychological interest, starting with the question that if one Spock is a re-creation and exact copy of the other, why should they not think and act exactly alike? If they did, "the replicate is simply a superfluity" (p. 19), as the false Spock puts it. In fact they do not. As the true Spock notes, "Even if we thought exactly alike at the moment of creation of the replicate, from then on our experiences differ slightly—beginning, of course, with the simple difference that we occupy different positions in space-time. This will create a divergence in our thinking which will inevitably widen as time goes on" (p. 19). In parallel, though Spencer Brydon may leave New York with a replicate of him remaining there to lead his "original" life, their twin courses grow farther apart, and more inimical to each other. A splitting of consciousness cannot produce entities that continue for long to share the original characteristics of the mind whence they came, we appear to be instructed by the literature of doubles; rather they express the extremes of a duality hidden in the original. It goes without saying that such consideration is based more on the "imaginable" than on the "possible": I for one consider the situation in *The Jolly Corner* a perfectly possible one, but I have no desire to engage hypothetical positivistic readers in a distracting argument over that possibility. In the same way, the machine envisaged by Blish for the duplication of Spock is imaginable and employs recognizable physical principles, but it is not even theoretically "possible." We may note, in a technological aside, that it is now theoretically possible to construct a machine to *grow* a double or exact replicate of any human being, but that leaves the time-space problem in even greater disarray than Blish's instantaneous re-creation. By interposing a mirror, Blish avoids as well the peculiar literary situation of having an identical double to begin with: The false Spock, by being a reversed, sinister (not "right") form, represents a duality as easy to plot as that of Dr. Jekyll and Mr. Hyde.

Enmity in itself is no certain source of terror; terror arises in proportion to the strangeness and unfamiliarity of the threatening force (the enemy as unknown) and to its menacing proximity (the enemy as having special knowledge of, and coming for, *me*). The double may appear familiar (as *Monsieur de Miroir*, I expect him to have my shape), but he potentially combines almost ideally the two sources of terror. That he is me but at the same time not-me makes him infinitely strange; and if he is an enemy, as he must in the end always be—his being robs me of part of my being, and there is no way for the question of "my being" to be resolved other than by the destruction of one of us (thus, "Spock must die")—he is an enemy utterly devoted to *me*, and he is armed with knowledge of me and my weaknesses that no other enemy could possibly have. This brings an intimacy to the struggle that is truly horrible; his octopus-like grip is so close that it seems impossible to break without doing myself as much harm as I do him (in the extreme case, naturally seized upon by Poe, the attack on the double is literally self-destruction).

James's story rather predictably dwells on the intimacy, it being amenable to the psychological method he employs. Spencer Brydon has a feeling for the old family house in New York, on the "jolly corner," that is not simply family feeling but a matter of near communication with the dead and with an almost corpuscular past:

> He spoke of the value of all he read into it, into the mere sight of the walls, mere shapes of the rooms, mere sound of the floors, mere feel, in his hand, of the old silver-plated knobs of the several mahogany doors, which suggested the pressure of the palms of the dead; the seventy years of the past in fine that these things represented, the annals of nearly three generations . . . and the impalpable ashes of his long-extinct youth, afloat in the very air like microscopic motes.[47]

To Alice Staverton, who thinks the house would attract him to stay in New York if it "were only furnished and lived in," he replies, "For me it *is* lived in. For me it *is* furnished" (p. 203), which suggests that he feels a part of his identity bound up in it. It is both what was, and what might have been, him; a "mystical other world" where he can hear "the scarce audible pathetic wail to his strained ear, of all the old baffled forsworn possibilities" (p. 209). By keeping the house, therefore, even though not living in it, Brydon keeps alive these "possibilities." They come to take the shape in his mind of an alter ego, his "other self" (pp. 211, 214), living in, or haunting, the house. The exploration of the house in search of "him" thus becomes a necessity for him, and as a task suitably undertaken at night, in silence and without the fear of interruption, it becomes more real to him than his daylight life:

> He was a dim secondary social success—and all with people who had truly not an idea of him. It was all mere surface sound, this murmur of

their welcome, this popping of their corks—just as his gestures of response were the extravagant shadows, emphatic in proportion as they meant little, of some game of *ombres chinoises*. He projected himself all day, in thought, straight over the bristling line of hard unconscious heads and into the other, the real, the waiting life. (p. 208)

It is typical of James that this equation proposes a "life" that is a matter of consciousness only (here set against the "unconscious heads" of people in the normal world); that is dangerous (in modern terms, productive of psychosis; in James's, risking death for an impalpably extended knowledge of being); and that is invisible, nonexistent to ordinary observers. The danger becomes progressively clear as Brydon gets down to his search. His method of insuring himself undisturbed contemplation of the "other" life also seals him off from outside help, for he constructs himself a time window in the middle of the night through which he steps and disappears. At his hotel they think he is at his club, and at his club they think he is at his hotel, while friends with whom he may have dined think he is at either hotel or club. At the same time he sees his "pursuit" as of "a creature more subtle, yet at bay perhaps more formidable, than any beast of the forest" (p. 210).

Brydon is ready to be frightened by a ghost, but what he sets out to do is to frighten a ghost. As he prowls through the dark house, with a half-formed plan of cornering the other Brydon on some back passage or stair, he sees himself as "some monstrous stealthy cat" enjoying a reversal "unique in the experience of man," for "people enough, first and last, had been in terror of apparitions, but who had ever before so turned the tables and become himself, in the apparitional world, an incalculable terror?" (p. 211). As the search progresses, night after night, and the realization comes over Brydon that the other, whose "wrath" now has grown to balance his "dread," is stalking *him*, the doubling of relation as well as being is complete:

It marked none the less a prodigious thrill, a thrill that represented sudden dismay, no doubt, but also represented, and with the selfsame throb, the strangest, the most joyous, possibly the next minute almost the proudest, duplication of consciousness. (pp. 213–14)

If Brydon is to end as the prey rather than as the hunter, he can take a queer pride in the fact that it is Brydon who has shown such strength: "If it was his other self he was running to earth, this ineffable identity was thus in the last resort not unworthy of him" (p. 214).

There is now a centripetal effect that draws the two "opposed projections" of Brydon into a rapidly converging path and into a meeting at something like a central still point—an effect that will have a multiplied reapplication in science fiction. Brydon feels himself in "the manner of a man slipping and slipping on some awful incline" (p. 214). Reaching the closed door of the small room on the fourth floor, where he senses the double to be waiting, he stands in strained concentration for as long as he can manage. Then, losing courage and unable to bring himself to touch the handle of the door, he looks yearningly down onto the dark street. He would climb down if he could, even hail a policeman, but "the life of the town [like that at Bly] was itself under a spell—so unnaturally, up and down the whole prospect of known and rather ugly objects, the blankness and the silence lasted" (p. 219). He grows desperate: "His choked appeal from his own open window had been the sole note of life, and he could but break off at last as for a worse despair" (p. 221). His "life," however he may have set it against the daylight world, is now matched against the "antilife" of the double; as he reflects that he has the whole house to traverse before he can reach the street door and escape (he has no thought of return and is ready to see the house razed now), he comes perilously close to jumping down from the high window. In an agony of dread he descends the stairs, incapable of looking to see whether the closed door is now open, and finds the double at the bottom, waiting, and forcing a meeting by blocking the way. When Alice Staverton finds him and revives him, he is sure that at the moment of meeting he had died, and that only through her efforts has he been brought back: "He had come back, yes—come back from further away than any man but himself had ever travelled" (p. 227).

Brydon's double is indistinguishable from a ghost, an entity approachable only mentally and by selected subjects—Brydon and the woman who loves him. As representing a life and fate that Brydon might have had, but cannot have, he is an outside and unknown influence threatening to the state or organism. Brydon's search for him is an attempt to master his own identity, and it could be that the search must be undertaken for Brydon to be able to retain his identity; but the resultant granting to the ghost of incorporation in space and time is very nearly fatal. The strangeness of the story is perhaps as close as conventional English fiction ever got to the strangeness of science fiction, and perhaps as well to the strangeness of human identity itself.

It is therefore fitting that, in the matter of the communication between the doubles, Blish's story should use terms that are very close to James's: The true Spock notes of his twin "that although his brain was essentially mine, its biases were opposite to mine. . . . I could never tell what he was thinking, but I was constantly aware of his physical sensations—and of his emotions . . . I found it very nearly intolerable" (p. 115). In the struggle for mastery, danger to others is as much involved as is danger to Spock, for the double is brought to an exactly equivalent existence, rather than being confined to a ghostly, midnight state. But the double is also a product of a technology, either friendly or inimical, and so the unknown in this story is very close to "unknown technology." That fact, and the nature of the enclosing, victoriously self-sustaining *Star Trek* saga, makes terror an emotion almost wholly inapplicable to *Spock Must Die!*, excitement and intellectual interest being more central to its effect. Projecting the mind of man against a background of galaxies can have a dissolving as well as an intensifying effect. It is this, along with other characteristics of science fiction, that I should like to take up next, before going on to a further look at the matter of doubles, under the special aspect of time, in chapter 6.

CHAPTER FIVE
Science Fiction

Ich fühle Luft von anderen Planeten.   •   Stefan George

There has been a faint but traceable contact between great writers and the questions central to the science-fiction imagination over the centuries. In English, Milton lends Adam, in *Paradise Lost*, the primary speculation that the multiplicity of visible stars is logically attached to the possibility of a multiplicity of planets and therefore a multiplicity of worlds; on a more mechanical level, Jonathan Swift, in *Gulliver's Travels*, predicted the two moons of Mars, their distance from the planet, and their periods of revolution, in a manner "uncannily close to the truth,"[48] although they were invisible to contemporary telescopes (they were discovered more than a century and a half later, in 1877). But while Swift, Milton, Donne, and Shakespeare all freely employed contemporary science, they did not write what we call science fiction;[49] while such minor work as Richard Broome's *Antipodes* (1638), with its London and anti-(matter) London, is only mentioned in the type of historical survey that starts out with Lucian of Samosata, straining to prove *nihil sub sole novum*.

For science fiction is properly a nineteenth-century phenomenon, a by-product of the triumph of the Industrial Revolution, which brought the machine into everyday contact with man. Nor could it have occurred until after the romantic movement, which codified and normalized the forms of imaginative projection. While it is possible to associate the romantic movement with the first general reaction against the machine and the power it gave the state, science fiction combined romantic forms with a romanticization of the machine, an exploration of the intoxicating possibilities it seemed to afford for extension of the hand and brain of man. It can be called the romantic literature of the machine, and insofar as it has always tended to posit further development, and subsequent capacities, of the machine, it can be called the literature of the future. At the same time it tended almost from the outset to move into two preexistent literary forms, which it has carried with it to the present day. These are, on the one hand, the boy's adventure story, wherein the airships and submarines of Jules Verne, perfectly adapted to the predominantly male interest in the machine, least curbed in youth, led on to Tom Swift's electric boat and flying motorcycle, Buck Rogers (with ray guns), and *Star Trek*; and on the other hand, since it has been difficult for the last hundred and fifty years to imagine the future of society independent of the existence and progression of machines, Utopian fiction. And that came quickly to include anti-Utopian along with Utopian fiction, for whether it be *Looking Backward* or *The Time Machine*, *Men Like Gods* or *Brave New World*, it is machinery and technology that make the projected society possible.[50]

Definitions of science fiction have only intermittently expressed these primary facts and tend on the whole to a narrowly abstract conception. Typical is that of Kingsley Amis's *New Maps of Hell*, the most comprehensive modern book on the subject: "Science fiction is that class of prose narrative treating of a situation that could not arise in the world we know, but which is hypothesized on the basis of some innovation in science or technology, or pseudo-science or pseudo-technology, whether human or extra-terrestrial in origin."[51] The "could not arise" upon which this definition hinges amounts to granting, at the outset, the irrelevance and consequent triviality that have been found in science fiction by conventional literary criticism and used as justification for its dismissal. Amis guardedly adds "in the world we know," but his reference to the reading of science fiction as an "addiction," which he compares throughout to the equivalent (and presumably rationally inexplicable) taste for jazz that is found in Western societies, further marks the tone of his book as a half-embarrassed apology for an interest in something rather *infra dig*, not to be treated with ultimate seriousness. But I doubt very much that science fiction could hold the contemporary interest it does if it were read as the description of situations that could not arise. What can or cannot happen may only be stated within a given statistical frame as far as we, and our technology, are concerned. About other technologies, we are clearly in no position to have much of an opinion at all; and equally clearly, things beyond our understanding may as well have happened in the past, as the result of extraterrestrial intelligence, as may happen in the future. We are in no position to require an innovation in extraterrestrial technology that could be, if it exists, a million years older than ours; nor is our technology apt to last a sufficient number of millions of years for us to discover whether our own past has been marked by such an outside influence. That a god came to earth two thousand years ago is no more or less likely than what Arthur Clarke specifies in *2001* actually happened deep in our past. Indeed, within the statistical frames we normally use, it is considerably more likely that the course of human history was altered by the interference of another planet's technology than by a divinity. Science fiction and religious fiction do not necessarily appeal to the same groups of people, but they share the same ontological basis. That is, they both describe things that are definitely *possible* and, in proportion to their imaginative truth, also believable.

A less narrow definition is given and then refined by Edmund Crispin (Bruce Montgomery) in the generally superior *Best SF series*, published from 1955 on by Faber and Faber in London: "A science-fiction story is one which presupposes a technology, or an effect of technology, or a disturbance in the natural order, such as humanity, up to the time of writing, has not in actual fact experienced."[52] This is still limited by the positivism of "in actual fact" and the tacit limitation to the future, but the continuing discussion of the genre that Montgomery has carried on in subsequent introductions to the volumes of stories shows a widening grasp of the issues. In *Best SF Three* (1958), he shifts from defense to attack, insisting that science fiction is actually returning literature to its pre-Renaissance concern with things larger than man, making the comparison of science fiction and religious fiction a matter of scale—the scale of the world:

> Thus, where mainstream fiction, thanks to the monotonously humanist bias of the last five centuries of our culture, has been almost uniformly catatonic in its withdrawal from environment, science fiction seeks to direct man's attention outwards once more—to mitigate the creature's

excessive preoccupation with himself and his society by throwing emphasis on the temporariness and precariousness of his situation within the macrocosm. (p. 9)

That "mainstream" fiction finds, in Montgomery's words, "greater interest and significance in the imagined adulteries of one out of 2,700,000,000 nonentities than in the death of a galaxy" (p. 9) is not entirely blamable; the agony of *Anna Karenina* is a pitifully small thing on the galactic scale, but to us other pitifully small things it is an intensely moving experience to share. And the experiences of a galaxy, dying or otherwise, are very difficult to share, Fred Hoyle's *Black Cloud* notwithstanding. There is a kind of encapsulation of the matter in a common difference between men and women: Women are far less interested in science fiction (and in science and technology, for that matter). Whether this is the outcome of the Fem Lib "centuries of brainwashing," or genetically determined, or a combination of both, need not be involved in the recognition of that fact or the fact that they are considerably more interested than men in adultery romantically presented, and in "matters of the heart." This goes with a type of "worldly" practicality—when I recently heard an intellectual mother say of her twelve-year-old son's interest in astronomy, "Oh, you know that stage, preadolescent withdrawal from the world," I could not feel she was *wrong* to see things that way, but only that she was devoted to a social world that she rather nearsightedly mistook for the universe. Boyish enthusiasm probably lets us in for most of our troubles, but for most of our discoveries as well.

Montgomery also takes up, in his *Best SF Three* introduction, the question of the "Other" that I have attempted to show as one of the critical themes of contemporary literature. He makes it clear that science fiction is that fiction which incorporates, and gives a perceptible being of some kind, to the Other; and for that reason it is of central concern to us:

> The aim is to make man look small; and the technique is to revalue him by showing him in the presence of some *other* thing over which his control is partial or uncertain or in extreme cases non-existent. As to the nature of the other thing, that varies very widely. . . .alien

civilisation . . . the definition or identification of "intelligence" . . . another space-time continuum . . . alternate worlds. . . . The Other Thing, then, is in some sense the definition of science fiction. (p. 10)

I am not sure I agree with the aim Montgomery posits here, and it is his "extreme cases" that I find both most interesting and most characteristic of science fiction, but otherwise I think this statement extremely apt.

Montgomery's introductions also testify to the slowly increasing recognition of science fiction, which has brought us to the point where, today, we can say that the world of literature and the world of science have come into a relationship that is recognized on both sides. A usable analogy is that of planets: The dark planet of science fiction, first heralded in the eighteenth century, was denied outright by a few and ignored by most, in the same way that astronomers dealt with planets outside our solar system in general—they could be there, but they are invisible to telescopes and must be hypothesized. They are so much smaller in mass than their mother stars, and the distances between stars at this end of our galaxy are so great, that discovering and recording the tiny disturbances of orbital configuration that make up their minuscule signatures is not only immensely difficult but hardly worth bothering with in the plethora of strongly distinct information, in the form of radio and light waves, streaming in upon our instruments from all sides. Literarily speaking, the same situation held: An indistinct body of literature, written by hacks, fanatics, and enthusiasts, almost none of whom had either scientific or literary credentials of any kind, therefore amounting to a group of pariahs, could hardly be taken seriously. Jules Verne and H. G. Wells might work out a kind of literary reputation on their own merits; C. S. Lewis could still be a "serious" writer and enter the field because he parodied Wells in order to undo what he saw as his baneful influence, and the baneful influence of science fiction. As for the rare scientist or astronomer who wrote science fiction, he could look to his scientific or astronomical colleagues for an audience and need not be bothered with by the literary establishment. If, indeed, a literary critic took up such works, how could he help looking foolish? It was not for him to gauge the scientific content of such fiction, and what else was there to it? The human situations involved were without interest except to the undemanding lover of fantasy, for they were impinged upon by imaginary situations overturning or contradicting the physical conditions of the life we know, the life that hums along unheard behind the scenes of every normal work of fiction, from the *Iliad* to *Ulysses*, with tiny superficial differences arising now and again, such as the form of vehicles driven or the chances in one hundred that the heroine might die in childbirth. For these and similar reasons, science fiction has been kept out of "fiction"; until recently, courses have not been given in it; and while there has been no conspiracy of silence about it, there has been a tacit agreement, critical and educational, to leave it to one side.

That situation has dramatically changed since 1960. Like all dramatic changes, it has run ahead of popular and even intellectual comprehension, and most people, along with most literary scholars, would ask even now, "What dramatic change?" Until literary scholars leave their present scientific illiteracy—a state they have only been in since the seventeenth century and so, one hopes, not to be regarded as more than a passing phase in their historical career—there will naturally be no change in one of the situations I have mentioned, the relative neglect of science fiction in universities. But a change in university policy is only a probable long-term side effect of the dramatic change I mention. The part of that change most of literary concern is that since 1960 a number of important writers in Western languages have started incorporating the themes of science fiction into their work, two of the most recent examples being Kurt Vonnegut's *Slaughterhouse-Five* and Vladimir Nabokov's *Ada*.

Behind that cultural fact is the truly revolutionary scientific "revision" of the world as we thought we knew it, from Einstein to Yang and Lee, and the accompanying historical fact that man, along with a portion of his science and his engineering, has entered space. So while science fiction has been given literary value by the fact that writers of major talent are taking it up, it has also been lent importance from a greater source: The expropriation of the "scenarios" or projections of reality by conventional fiction, thanks to the change in reality, leaves science fiction, for all its defects, the alternative, and inheriting, scenario source. That only a few men have so far entered the quarter-million miles of surrounding space into which we have extended our world is no more relevant to its application to the total human experience than that only a few people experienced mystical union with God in the Middle Ages, or that only a few explored the South Pole, directed the Spanish Inquisition, survived a Crusade, or fought in the critical battles that directed the course of history. Once such things are done and recorded, they become a part of every man's world; his world shrinks and expands in correspondence to them. That there is now outer space in human experience means that there is now to be a literature appertaining to that experience. Will it be parallel to the literature of polar exploration; that is, nugatory? The chances are it will not be so limited, for while the discovery and exploration of the poles was undertaken and accomplished with nineteenth-century tools and on the basis of physical principles that were the same for exploring the Niger, the Amazon, or the Louisiana Purchase (leaving to one side the alarming featurelessness of certain polar landscapes and the reduction of all compass directions to one at the poles themselves), there is now, along with the incorporation of space, the intellectual incorporation of space-time physics. It is as sure to remake our age as Newton's refinement of Copernican astronomy and hypothesization of gravity were to remake his.[53] As Teilhard de Chardin put it, "To us for whom new sciences have opened space and time with dimensions unsuspected by our fathers there are now new challenges. . . . the great affair for modern mankind is to break its way out by forcing some threshold of greater consciousness."[54] This means, too, that while the foolish battle continues between people who fancy themselves humanists but not scientists, and those they fancy scientists but not humanists, it is losing something of its necessary background. It has, of course, been going on since the outbreak of war between science and religion in the nineteenth century, has brought about the chasm in intellectual life most notably deplored by C. P. Snow, and is kept alive by what are, for the most part, acts of provocation by specialists in the pseudosciences, B. F. Skinner's preposterously entitled *Beyond Freedom and Dignity* (1971) being a recent case in point. But literature has been quietly approaching what these controversialists think should be its opposite, science, by entering a widening phase, bringing a wider view of human knowledge into the domain once thought to be private and specific to liberal humanism.

The dramatic change I speak of has not been accomplished without spiritual cost: It has brought all humanity who are unable to forget that fact into the dilemma of Faust, and it has given an edge to the harrowing of the soul that certainly more sensitive individuals have experienced in every generation involved in carnage. The situation is presented with both economy and ironic acuity in Vonnegut's *Slaughterhouse-Five*. The hero, Billy Pilgrim, has had a nervous breakdown and finds himself in the hospital next to a brilliant and omnivorous reader of science fiction, one Rosewater:

> Kilgore Trout became Billy's favorite living author, and science fiction became the only sort of tales he could read.
>
> Rosewater was twice as smart as Billy, but he and Billy were dealing with similar crises in similar ways. They had both found life meaningless, partly because of what they had seen in war. Rosewater, for instance, had shot a fourteen-year-old fireman, mistaking him for a German soldier. So it goes. And Billy had seen the greatest massacre in European history, which was the fire-bombing of Dresden. So it goes.
>
> So they were trying to re-invent themselves and their universe. Science fiction was a big help.[55]

Another way of putting this is to say that science has been reinventing the universe at a rapidly increasing velocity since Einstein's first publication of relativity theory, and that the only fiction we have had to put us into imaginative contact with this reinvention has been science fiction. It in turn has been for the most part a broken reed, thanks to its low status (quite on a par with erotic literature) and the hack standards of composition applied by all but a lonely few of its practitioners. They, the Asimovs and the Clarkes, are becoming less lonely now, with the company of such as Nabokov, Barth, Vonnegut, and Borges; they are coming into the tradition of Henry James, merging with "the novel" proper. That is going to bring us, the readers and the students of literature, into facing the same kind of harrowing self-reinvention that only a peek at the fire-bombing of Dresden, or a visit to Hiroshima, might have done previously. Vonnegut's imaginary planet, Tralfamadore, is one such heuristic device.

It is therefore that science fiction, for all its weaknesses and unrealized capacities, lies more directly in the path of twentieth-century literary development than a neosociological literature. Not that advancing technology is about to enable the banishment of simple human misery; human beings will continue to be miserable in numerous social situations, with and without having themselves contributed to their own misery; and considering the present increase in the earth's population it seems fatuous to imagine anything but a generally marked increase in human misery of the simplest and most direct kind, like starvation. And it would be a mistake, too, to imagine that social consciousness develops in proportion to social problems. In a 1969 Dublin address to a group of assembled Joyce scholars, the American critic Leslie Fiedler predicted an end to the egocentric, intellectually oriented, spiderlike literature that Joyce so quintessentially represented, and a shift to the literature of the bee—outward-directed, socially involved, coming to grips with the problems that affect man in the mass. This may be so, but I suspect that it is not. Too much of the development of education and technology lies in the opposite direction, toward the valuing of the individual mind that has the ability to employ the ever growing amounts of energy controllable by man.

Technology allows no retreat either, as each advance it makes becomes a part of the support of life; any "giving back" of advances over the environment would probably result in the extinction of the species, although it is hard to prove that from observation, there being apparently no animal that has ever done so. Advancing creation is the only viable alternative. In that frame, the current interest in staying home from space *so that* we can obtain racial justice and prevent starvation everywhere, as if we could buy those things and, further, buy them with the money we would have spent reaching space, that money itself having come out of the technology that got its drive and character from aiming at space, is as frivolous a gesture as that of Marie Antoinette and her court pastorals hidden within the bosky fastnesses of Versailles park would have been had it been meant as an economic model. It is improbable that contemporary literature will resist the force of the circumstances of expanding knowledge and, unfortunately, expanding power; it is most probable that it will be taken up with the new challenges man faces, the new dimensions of his existence.

This has no connection to the management of world society with an eye to justice and humanity; it is a matter of having or not having a literature that is imaginatively commensurate with the other areas of human thought and effort. Teilhard de Chardin may again be quoted with relevance to this matter, to show how the very same necessity of advance and discovery comes into the thinking of a man who presumably felt himself, as a Jesuit priest, already in possession of the central truth and mystery of the universe:

> We must put in the forefront of our concrete preoccupations the systematic arrangement and exploration of our universe, understood as the true country of mankind. Then material energy will circulate, and (more important still) spiritual energy, now corrupted by the petty jealousies of modern society, will find its natural outlet in the attack launched against the mysteries of the world. (*Building the Earth*, p. 55)

As a final note, it may be pointed out that this unification of science fiction with fiction in general yields a critical dividend. It enables us to keep to a single scale of evaluation, to treat a work of scientifically tinged imagination as a work of imagination, good fiction or bad fiction, rather than only within a special category of "science fiction." And it opens up avenues of comparison between forms that otherwise tend to be sealed off by genre boundaries. That between science fiction and religious fiction has been touched upon in this discussion; that between science fiction and the murder mystery, or detective novel, may also be seen in a converging relationship, brought about on the one hand by the maturation of science fiction and on the other by the disruption within the murder mystery of the positivistic outlook and the new experimentation with the "given" elements of the form discussed in chapter 3.[56] In a superficial way this is a re-creation of an earlier situation, for the two forms started together historically, and indeed both can be said to have been invented by the same man—Edgar Allan Poe. For Poe, the common basis of composition was "ratiocination" (the rational and logical attack on the unknown) and the "quiz" (intellectual hoax); for us it is, as Montgomery's revised definition helps us see (Montgomery, by the way, being a writer of murder mysteries who edits science fiction), the threat, or presence, of the unknown (the Other) setting a challenge of exploration and explication. The unknown killer, until discovered and exposed, is potentially a killer of any one of us, or all of us, who "enter" the world of the murder mystery by reading it; and insofar as that fictional world is successful in throwing out links of likeness to our lived-in world, our fear deepens, becomes more "real," leads us to lock the bedroom door when going to bed with the book, and so forth—to look at city hall or the police department or the man who waits on us at the shoe store with new, suspicious eyes.

In science fiction the same effects are thrown against a larger background, more like the murder mystery as it takes shape in Ionesco's *Killer*. If the Other exists at all in such a way that we can sense his presence, the chances are largely in favor of his being greater and stronger than we, so that the threat to us is, if he chooses, almost unlimited. He may as easily be nowhere (his source an error in our instruments, as when we were caused to think that the pulsars were sending irregular, and thus message-bearing, flashes)[57] as everywhere (the mayor, or the shoe clerk, may be his creature). He may be devil to us, or God, for the unknown may as well contain our salvation as our destruction. That the universe, like the murder mystery, is filled with violent death, is no guarantee that it contains the secret of our deaths.

And this element is more important to the definition or to the consideration of science fiction than is the originally accurate specification of technology or the machine, and the never accurate restriction of the action to a future time. For science fiction is primarily a matter of taking up the challenge of understanding, or at least exploring, the physical universe. Since imaginative exploration is, for human beings, a large step toward understanding, the outlook for science fiction seems promising.

CHAPTER SIX
Time and the Visible World

Relative Time

That time in fiction should more often than not be "relative" is natural; that it should be tied to space is altogether more difficult of comprehension and limited to the influence of modern science, for the most part, on contemporary literature. To deal first with the simpler conception, time for us is relative in that it exists as something we experience, and we experience everything in a constantly varying manner. Time for us is thus not naturally something independent grinding inexorably along whether experienced or not. Such time is, as an abstraction, the product of Newtonian theory; as a concrete presence in our lives it is the product of technology, especially of clocks, and is therefore often called clock time. Presumably a culture must reach a certain level in the construction of clocks before it can enjoy the concept of an independent, unvarying time. In Europe, clocks reached a high point of complexity, combining both mechanical and aesthetic self-assertion, in the sixteenth century; but it is classically the eighteenth century in which Newtonian theory and the use of clocks were popularly combined to produce an ascendancy of clock time, and clock thinking, that spread from Protestant Europe and its dependencies, in the ensuing centuries, almost throughout the earth.[58] The spread itself was greatly advanced by the fact that highly accurate clock mechanisms, built to withstand the rigors of sea travel, first made dependable and safe navigation possible.

Previous Christian ages were clearly more used to an infinite, and infinitely variable, time scheme managed by a God who was not primarily a clockmaker, who would stop the sun in the sky, or give Methusaleh 969 years of life. While the Greeks and Romans were able theoreticians and built clever stationary clocks, despite the lack of a technology able to provide them with accurate bearings, the ancient world ran for the most part by seasons and crops, and thus on the year, a crudely variant unit. Both the seasons, by artificial management of rain and high water, and the calendar, by addition and subtraction of days, required constant fiddling to insure the crops. Calendar and seasons are, of course, not separate; the calendar maintains the religious festivals which in turn mark the seasons. Egypt, the granary of the ancient Mediterranean, serves as a large-scale example of such practical time management, while the religious festivals of the Christian year served as the agriculturalist's timetable for many centuries to come.

A calendar of any kind is a product of human rationality, but it is a rational abstraction more akin to natural aberration than is its fellow abstraction, clock time. Clock time has a built-in tendency toward perfection, the goal of the absolutely interchangeable interval, that has involved technology in a long-term search—in effect, a search to "find" something on the basis of its being posited. The result has been that clocks have slowly crept forward in accuracy, currently employing the radioactive decay rate of certain atoms to refine their intervals to a variation of a second in 30,000 years. What is accomplished when this is done? In one sense, nothing, but that man now has a faithful companion to proceed in time alongside him, who can give but one assurance, that the rate at which he moves is very close to exactly the rate he was moving a year, or a day, before. That is all, for natural processes all have average rather than specific times:[59] It takes plus-or-minus so many hours for a chemical change to occur or a fly to be born, reproduce, and die, so many days for a tadpole to become a frog, so many years for a baby to learn to talk, centuries for a star like the sun to complete the main sequence and become a red giant, incinerating its planets. The sun and the planets are more like man than his machines, for they have irregular motions and do not keep exact time in their courses. The planets were assigned first circular orbits as a part of an assumed divine perfection, then elliptical ones, and finally elliptical ones with numerous irregularities and perturbations, their shapes, which turned out to be something less than spherical, undergoing the same process. Like men, they grow old and "die." The eternal sameness of a hypothesized clock time seems to interest man more than it does nature, or the matter that surrounds him.

And even man's most essential and proudest artifact, language, resists application to timekeeping in strangely relativistic ways. In English, for instance, time conception is considerably fuzzier than it need be, either theoretically or ontologically. The "present" is notoriously difficult to attach to the verb as a semantic feature, although the morphology of the verb has chronology as one of its functions. In "John reads Greek" or "Fred loves goulash," the verbs, like all such so-called present forms, are actually timeless —John and Fred have read and loved in the past, *may possibly* be doing so now, and presumably will do so in the future. W. F. Twaddell's revision of the traditional scheme in this area of grammar,[60] in which he asserts the modification of the verb by (*be* + *ing*) as "real present" ("John is reading Greek" but not *"Fred is loving goulash") is open to such counterexamples as that proposed by R. A. Jacobs and P. S. Rosenbaum: "Nagel is leaving town; I'm not going to let him ruin Agnew's campaign."[61]

So we may feel that those philosophers and writers of fiction who have asserted a relative time have asserted an idea too obvious to be visible, or to require statement, if it were not for the spread and triumph of clock time. What the tyranny of the clock has meant in Western life since the eighteenth century has been surveyed by many commentators:[62] Accurate clocks in factories made the hourly wage system possible, and the tying of men to linear time; and while the twin essential features of the Industrial Revolution, large-scale manufacture and the assembly line, were both possible without the clock, the analogy between their secret and source, the interchangeable part and the interchangeable interval of the clock, is a natural one. That workers object to being used as interchangeable parts and timed by clocks is also natural, although a demand like that of the United Auto Workers in a 1970 strike, that the punch-card time clocks be removed because they are "demeaning" devices, is a gesture of shirking work to the linear mind. To the United Auto Workers it may have been only a bargaining point, but to the philosophical view it is an effort, conscious or unconscious, to return the laborer to the more natural relationship he had to time, his day, and his work before the Industrial Revolution. Similarly, the office worker's 8:15 commuter train, the executive's 11:30 flight to Denver, the runner's "four-minute mile" set up artificial clock

70 • *The Hole in the Fabric*

barriers against which flesh and blood are pressed, or made to conform. It is not only a search for status that makes the office worker want to drive to the office, or be driven, and the executive to have the use of a company airplane. It is that he is thereby enabled to "set his own time," to take for himself the more natural boundaries of "between eight and eight-thirty," or "between eleven and noon." To the time-subdued twentieth-century mind, such gestures are nearly as dramatic as that of Jean-Jacques Rousseau when he renounced his watch, or the situation in Samuel Butler's *Erewhon*, where the possession of a watch was made a crime.

Legend and life can become strangely dislocated in time, as if cutting free to assert an existence independent of time. The nineteen-year-old girl, Ulrike von Levetzow, to whom an aged Goethe, in a flare of senile passion, addressed his *Marienbader Elegie* in 1823, lived on year after year, well into the modern world, dying in November 1899, spiritually aeons after the great poet had died and had become as well something like a demigod in European consciousness. In parallel, Mircea Eliade mentions an incident in Romania, where forty years after a true romantic tragedy the events had become embellished and celebrated in folk lore and song, including mythological material and supernatural beings, and the date set in the distant past, despite the fact that the heroine was still alive.[63] The opposite seems to occur as easily. One lends instinctive credence to the situation Kafka describes in his *Great Wall of China*, in which news travels so slowly across the vast extent of the celestial empire that in remote villages people wail and tear their hair on hearing of tragic events in the capital, which actually happened centuries before.[64] In 1893 at Rørbaek in north Jutland, the body of an Iron Age man was accidentally unearthed, its features so well preserved that the local people were convinced that it was the body of a peddler who had been murdered shortly before, according to rumor, by a powerful bad character in the neighborhood. Such was their fear of him that they hastily reburied the body and made no report to the authorities. And in 1952 the body of a man was found at Grauballe, also in Jutland, his general appearance, down to beard stubble, fingernails, and head hair, as if he had died (from having his throat cut) not too long before. An old peasant woman living nearby saw the corpse and claimed she recognized it as that of one Red Christian, a shiftless layabout and cutter of peat who had suddenly disappeared, when she was a young woman, in 1887. The old woman was wrong, however; when "Red Christian" was subjected to Carbon 14 testing, he was found to have died in approximately A.D. 300, or 1,570 years earlier than she and other local inhabitants thought.[65] Such are the tricks of memory, and the diaphanous boundary between past and present, in the stable surroundings of rural life, far from clocks and calendars.

We might say that a linear, constant-rate, anisotropic time (time with a dependable "arrow" or direction to "running down," or greater entropy, independent of human experience) has from very early in the history of literature been treated as counterintuitive, dispensed with or at least modified at will. But like the imaginative flights of the Danish villagers, these modifications are most often attributable, however tenuously, to a linear base; they are a matter of compression, expansion, or "trading of places" along a straight-line track leading from past to future—so Henri Bergson and Proust with the subjective experience of time and the past recaptured by memory, with "experienced" time versus clock time; William Wordsworth's "spots of time"; Virginia Woolf's and James Joyce's expansion of a few hours of clock time, a day, into a great deal of lived time (*Ulysses, Mrs. Dalloway*) and compression of multiple lived times into a small amount of clock time (*Finnegans Wake, The Years*); Thomas Mann's variations on both effects (*The Magic Mountain*). Lewis Carroll's *Sylvie and Bruno* goes further, to a presentation of simultaneous presents without "earlier than" or "later than" to relate them, a method possibly also used in Alain Robbe-Grillet's *Maison de Rendez-Vous*. Eastern literature does not lack the same effects. There is a case, for instance, for an assertion of psychological timelessness in such Chinese nature poetry as Wu-men Hui'k'ai:

> A hundred flowers are in spring, in autumn is the moon,
> In summer is the cool wind, the snow is in winter;
> If nothing is on the mind to afflict a man,
> That is his best season.[66]

All these cases, and all I have managed to collect, show in general a linear time scheme, even if only in the distant background, and a single state of consciousness. Such literary conceptions occur because, presumably, they spring from human psychology, which varies time in ways that include body temperature, distance, age, and vision of the future.[67] The "biological clock" of inner time is speeded up by the raising of body temperature, as in the fever of illness,[68] and slowed down by its lowering. In distance, H. Helson's *tau* effect shows that a person's estimate of distance is influenced by the time interval that delimits it—giving thereby a bodily demonstration of the Einsteinian wedding of space and time.[69] If three spots are marked equidistantly on a subject's arm, but with a longer time interval between the marking of the second and the third than between the first and the second, the subject, if he cannot see his arm but only feel the marking, thinks the space on his arm between the second and the third marks to be greater. J. Cohen's *kappa* effect also treats time and distance; combined with the *tau* effect it describes the phenomenon, familiar to most people, that happens on a journey: If the first of two fifty-mile stages is traveled at a slower speed, and therefore over a longer time, it will appear longer in distance, as well as in time, than the second leg, traveled at a higher speed and in a shorter time.[70] As to age, the older you grow, it may be the more you compress the farther past and expand the immediate past. And one's vision of the future causes alterations from small scale, like the gradient of tension leading up to an event awaited with trepidation (for example, an examination), to large scale, like one's view of an afterlife or the lack of it—the amount of time one feels one "has left" making a difference in one's perception of time in the present.

"Vision of the future" can certainly be expanded to include other types of visions that human psychology may experience. We do not need Joyce's *Finnegans Wake* to be reminded of the magical shapes time can assume in dreams, while Nabokov's *Despair* illustrates a rarer condition that is also amenable to psychological verification. In that novel, the hero experiences a kind of mirror-split of the personality, in which he can be making love to his wife in the bedroom while at the same time mentally sitting in the next room listening to himself making love to his wife. A specific instance of this has come up in the investigation of the effects of marijuana smoking. One of the effects upon the central nervous system caused by this consciousness-heightening plant, *Cannabis sativa*, is that:

> The sense of time is distorted: ten minutes may seem like an hour. Curiously, there is often a splitting of consciousness, so that the smoker, while experiencing the high, is at the same time an objective observer of his own intoxication. He may, for example, be afflicted with paranoid thoughts yet at the same time be reasonably objective about them and even laugh or scoff at them and in a sense enjoy them. The ability to retain a degree of objectivity may explain that fact that many experienced users of marihuana manage to behave in a perfectly sober fashion in public even when they are highly intoxicated.[71]

There seems to be a heightened sense of mastery over time associated with a mirror-split. Though marijuana users seem always to find time lengthening,[72] rather than speeding up, we have here a chemical analogue to Henry James's theory of the observer (he must be split to both act and observe the actions of himself with others), to Dunne's positing a time-2 observer of the time 1 of life and direct action, and to both Nabokov's *Despair* and *Pale Fire* of a reflected, split personality voyaging through time and space.

Science and technology took a great leap forward in the eighteenth century; physics took a great leap forward with Newton. But the linear time that Newton's physics required, which fell in so well with the Protestant ethic and the rise of the factory system, put science behind literature in the awareness of time as a natural and conscious entity. Literature cannot be taken as a totally homogeneous representation, of course, and it felt the weight of Newton too—there is a large literature of linear time between the eighteenth and twentieth centuries, with a heavy emphasis on chronological causality in human affairs, from postromantic naturalism and realism, the *roman expérimental* in France, the German *Bildungsroman*, to the modernized historico-bourgeois novel and *roman fleuve* of Jules Romains, John Galsworthy, and others. This fell in with logical positivism, Marxian historiography, and Freudian materialism: Whether by infantile trauma, capital acquisition, or chemical interaction, any human situation at point r is the product or outcome of another situation at point r minus time x.

Not until Einstein did physics supply a natural analogue to the human situation. Einstein's ideas are, of course, ideas like any others, until they receive physical confirmation. Most of them have; but there is little intuitive basis for testing them. To presume that the truth about nature is always in tune with human consciousness is at best a weak theory, since so much of nature eludes human consciousness—humans have no consciousness whatever about antimatter or electron rings—but humans are a part of nature and may be supposed to have a relation with the way things actually work. Unfortunately, though they are a part of nature, so are their speculations, some of which must be wrong for others to be right. Einstein's relativistic time is paradoxical because it goes beyond human consciousness (if time slows down as our velocity through space increases, we have, by definition, no way of ascertaining it, since any clock we take with us on our journey through space speeds up or slows down along with us). However, there are ways of confirming it: One is by observation of mu meson (muon) decay. It is known that at low, nonrelativistic speeds the time of the decay is such-and-such, say x, as observed in the laboratory. If it were x in the cosmic ray bombardment of Earth's upper atmosphere, no muon from outer space would be observable on Earth, for the decay would have run its full course long before the muon could reach the surface. It is known that these particles are coming toward Earth at near the speed of light, or relativistic velocities, and they are commonly observed at the surface. Therefore, the conclusion is inescapable that at such high velocities the decay is slowed down—from our point of view, of course; from the muon's, things are the same in outer space rushing toward Earth or in the laboratory at rest. This supports Einstein's theory that time slows in proportion to increase in velocity. In 1971, a sufficient standard of chronological measurement having been reached, actual clock transport was undertaken, and gave direct proof of the "clock paradox." Four cesium beam clocks were taken on airline flights around the earth, both east (with the earth's rotation, which should cause slow running), and west (counter to the earth's rotation, which should cause fast running). On the eastward trip they lost 59 nanoseconds; on the westward, they gained 273 nanoseconds. Einstein has not shown that Proust or Bergson was right to specify changing time velocity within human consciousness; he has rather shown that to imagine such fictional conceptions to be set against reality is an illusion, for time itself is dependent upon velocity. Most of us expect to live without appreciable alteration in our nonrelativistic velocity, though there is a marked physiological distinction between Earth velocity plus or minus the twenty-five-mile-per-hour top speed that Henry James probably ever traveled, and the same velocity plus or minus the speed of sound that contemporary writers might travel in a jet aircraft. The relevant fact is simply that relativistic time as an imaginative concept has a vastly different status when it is supported by evidence from physical reality, whether or not the conditions of that reality involved directly impinge upon man. Future space travelers will experience them directly; literary artists have experienced them imaginatively and described them; the mass of mankind has experienced them emotionally for unnumbered centuries.

But because time can change its shape and is only a factor of space does not mean that it is not relentless in its impingement, in nonimaginative ways, upon men.[73] The medieval figure of time as death, or death as time, is as perfectly adjusted to the facts of our existence now as it always was. We will not have changed time, in this sense, until we change death; and the space surrounding us is so vast that periods of time far beyond the life span we can expect for our own civilization must pass before we could get an answer from many galaxies to a query we sent, had it been possible to send it at the dawn of our history. The necessary differences in planet and galaxy time—time for each galaxy or star or planet being tied to some point when "things started" in the same way time for me started with my birth and will end at my death—has pushed both astronomers and novelists into representation of the fact that when communication begins with another culture (we could say with "another being"), it may already be long gone out of existence—or when it began, we may have been millennia before our own birth. In 1959 the Soviet ethnologist M. M. Agrest posited that many of the

Old Testament events, like the destruction of Sodom and Gomorrah, unexplainable by contemporary Earth technology otherwise than as "acts of God," were actually caused by extraterrestrial astronauts[74] (Arthur Clarke's "Third Law" makes the reasonable assumption that superior technology may be regarded by those who do not possess it as magic and supernatural). What would even eminent scientists of the nineteenth century have said if they had been placed in a boat in the mid-Pacific to see the Apollo capsule, with men aboard, arrive from the moon?

The linear time view regards the future as inaccessible, the past as irrevocably gone, and the present as a kind of time slot in which we move, think, and otherwise exist. It is as if we were confined to a small moving cage on a track, those points along the track we have moved past, and have yet to arrive at, being totally sealed off from us. The mnemonic aptitude of literature, along with the eschatological concerns of religion, often including a vivid projection of an afterlife, have progressed to the point where future and past states of an ideal observer are considered as open to him as his present state.

With Einstein these intuitions as well received a startling kind of physical confirmation. He pointed out that time is something that is tied to the position of an observer in space, which means that what is future to one observer is, at the same "time," past to a second and present to a third. Newton, on the other hand, had proposed absolute space and absolute time, a reality consisting of an infinite series or layers of "now" which come into existence successively. Einstein developed a Newtonian 3-D picture into 4-D, the fourth dimension being time, though the world still appears 3-D to (ordinary) human consciousness. For the three coordinates of classical mechanics, x, y, z, we have x, y, z, and t.[75] Each observer has his own set of "now's," and none of these various systems of layers can claim the prerogative of representing the objective lapse of time. Thus, for the dichotomy of Newtonian universal time (shown in figure 1a) we have a trichotomy (shown in figure 1b); for past-future we have past-future-elsewhere. For Einstein, "there is no simultaneity of distant events," for there is no worldwide instant, no "universal now."[76]

Time and the Visible World

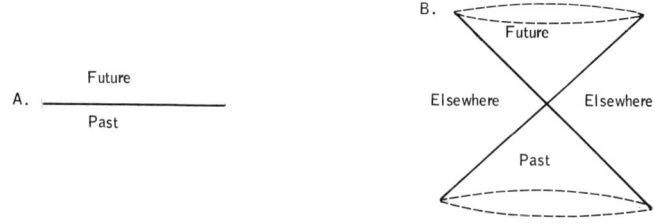

A. ────────────
    Future
    Past

B. Future / Elsewhere / Elsewhere / Past

Figure 1

An appeal to intragalactic distances and the visual images of stars gives a simple and partial example: In about 3946 B.C. the supernova explosion that we now call the Crab Nebula was five thousand years in our future, for it appeared as a bright star in the sky, visible by day and noted by astronomers in China and Japan, in A.D. 1054. But in 1054 it was an event five thousand years in the past of the star itself; it had exploded in one shattering instant five thousand years before, and for an observer at a few light-seconds away from that relatively close spot in our own galaxy, five thousand light-years from Earth, that blinding flash was just occurring in 3946 B.C., and so was "present." That means that our future, in the linear view as unknowable and mysterious as the immortal gods, is already past, from another, or another's, point of view. We may rear back here, and say, "Wait a minute!" Earth will only be destroyed, at the end of its planetary life, once, and that has not happened yet, so it is irrevocably future for us on Earth and will remain so until the arrival of one specific moment in time, *our* time. Thus, we can keep a grip on local landmarks of linear time that are, for us, of immediate and indestructible reality. That does not stop, however, the speculations of scientists—as Hilary Putnam of Harvard put it at a meeting of the American Physical Society, "The future seems to us unreal because we cannot remember it"; it is just as real as the spatial dimensions to which time is indissolubly tied; "the past and future are just as real as up and down."[77] What is apparently unknown is already known—elsewhere; inside the frame of relativity ours is the discomfort of what we imagine it would be like to be God in *Paradise Lost*, knowing the future, and yet required to act in the present according to a view to which the future is closed, going through the motions, for instance, of making a paradise for man to live in when he knows, and has planned, that man will fall and be driven from that paradise. Our future has already happened, when we take the potentials of the universe, or even a small part of it, as our frame of reference.

There is a parallel here to J. W. Dunne's aforementioned concept of Serialism, in which a hypothetical time-2 observer, who knows the future, moves back and forth over the linear track of time 1, the present as we live it. The time-2 observer is us, as fully a part of our being as the time-1 body-and-mind of present corporeality. Insofar as the time-1 part of us has contact, through dreams, premonitions, or otherwise, with the time-2 part, we know the future, the night our number is to come up. Whether we can act on that knowledge, or are bound by it, remains as much a problem to us as to God. How could God ever change his mind, from the beginning of all time, since at that moment he knows all the future? How can we act to avoid taking the fatal airplane flight once we have dreamed that it will crash, if that dream was a look into the future?[78]

But related to relativity in time are other concepts, such as reversal. Time, the mirror images of things, and the pairing of things with their opposites are not possible to separate in some cosmological models, among three of which the battle for acceptance has raged over the last several years—expanding, steady-state, and pulsating (or expanding and contracting). It is generally felt to be proved, by the red shift in spectography of observable stars, that the universe is now expanding. Time is one of the dimensions of this universe, so if we are to posit a contraction following the limits of the present expansion, a turning around and going back, it may very well be that time will be involved, will not go "on" independently, but turn around and go back as well, or run back "up" after having run "down." It depends, as P. T. Landsberg puts it, on whether the "cosmological arrow" (that of the direction of the universe) and the "statistical arrow" (that of entropy), run together or separately—a contracting universe, for instance, might be invisible as well as having backward time.[79] We might therefore imagine (even) such statistically disfavored events as our descendants rising from their graves, amid mourners whose tears run up into their eyes, growing down into helpless infants, and disappearing into the wombs that bore them; and as the progression reaches our century, American bombers rising slowly backward, laden with dead and wounded, into English skies, to move over France, where German fighters come to patch holes in their fuselages, as the hero of Vonnegut's *Slaughterhouse-Five* sees it on his reversed TV set.

A collapsing universe would be possibly the total reverse of an expanding one, from charge (the electron flow of "plus" or "minus") to parity (left and right, as when we see our double in the mirror) to time. It is quite certain now, since 1964, that if there are such things as galaxies of "antimatter," matter reversed in respect to ours in charge and parity (which is known to exist), they will have reversed time as well, running backward in relation to our time. Inhabitants of such galaxies will not see it that way, however; from their point of view their time will run forward while *ours* will run backward. Before 1957, CPT (charge, parity, and time) were considered invariant, the three being independently reversible. Then the work of Mme. Chien-Shiung Wu with the cooled Cobalt 60 atom, and that of Yang and Lee with further weak interactions, caused the "Fall of Parity": Nature was found to show a weak left-handed preference. Symmetry was restored by the theory of CP invariance—if you reversed parity *and* charge, identical reactions occurred. The 1964 Princeton experiments broke this down, showing that it is not enough to posit assymmetrical charge and asymmetrical parity; the assumption of asymmetrical time as well is the only way left to preserve overall symmetry invariance. This inserts the arrow of time more deeply into matter than does the second law of thermodynamics and requires matter of reversed charge (and thus CP) to have reversed time. In all cases, it is perhaps better to remember that the universe is always potentially stranger than any planetary fiction.

Finally, perhaps the central imaginative link between time theory and the other aspects of science in this discussion is the matter of movement, the gradual impingement upon the mind of man that he *moves*, that he and all the apparently static or stable parts of his environment are in a dizzying dance of change, a dance in which there is no finite measurement of steps, no finite prediction of what the next step will be, and in which, truly, you cannot tell the dancer from the dance. And in which there can be no stopping, cessation of the dance, insofar as it is possible, being death. H. G. Wells put this rather crudely and repeatedly in his fictional works, using those like *The Time Machine* and *Things to Come* to underline the moral that there is no safe haven from change and danger, that "either life goes forward or it goes back. That is the law of life";[80] in the fashion of a parable, with biblical overtones, the foolish hero of another Wells story who orders the earth to stand still causes instantaneous and total destruction.[81] Henry James puts the same thing rather subtly in his projection for *The Sense of the Past*, that the world of 1820 is a hideous trap for anyone to whom the world of 1910 is open, a backward step in the development of consciousness.

In the Ptolemaic cosmology the world itself was motionless, surrounded by fixed spheres; with Copernicus Earth leaped into motion around the sun; with post-Galilean astronomy the stars took on motion, carrying their world systems with them, like the sun, at vast speeds; with the application of cosmic spectrography all the star systems observable in the universe, including billions of whose existence man had been up to that time ignorant, were found to be rushing at increasing speeds away from one another. This has been a progressive breakdown in stability and fixity that could not have been better planned, by a malignant demon, to devastate the Ptolemaic, ancient, and traditional security of the world.

Henry James's Sense of the Past *and Some Analogues*

A sense of the past is given by many facets of human thought, most often in stable societies which buttress their stability with a sense of tradition and careful education of the young in values purportedly derived from the past, as in, until recently, China, India, and Japan; most dramatically by societies which make a reassessment, like Renaissance Italy with regard to the culture of Greece and Rome, or eighteenth-century Europe when archaeology got the start that led, with other factors, into the romantic movement. Cultures have different time scales as well: Those of great uninterrupted passage, like twenty-fifth-dynasty Egypt or Ming-

81 • *Time and the Visible World*

dynasty China, probably saw time as moving more slowly, and the past as closer and more visitable, than cultures like nineteenth-century France or twentieth-century America, in which social upheaval and scientific discovery make one period seem so different from another that it is difficult for inhabitants of a later period even to imagine themselves living in an earlier one.

It is easy to make inaccurate assumptions in this area, though. Twentieth-century America demonstrates a widespread yearning for its own past, to the extent that a distinct and flourishing minor part of its economy is the production of artifacts imitative of those of the past, or imaginative projections in the form of films, books, toys, and rebuilt towns in and out of amusement parks. A state as dedicated to the future as the Soviet Union spends millions of rubles on technicolor film re-creations of Tolstoy novels depicting the aristocratic life of a previous century, while the United States as unpredictably feasts upon the past of Britain, its own former oppressor. American TV audiences give rapt attention to BBC specials, some of them funded by American firms, of the life of Elizabeth I or of Henry James's *Spoils of Poynton* done in foundation-stone time-capsule style, embedded in amber, with no reference made or apparently desired to the time of the production. And the Egypt of the New Kingdom, with its capital in Thebes, was so unconscious of the great accomplishments of the Old Kingdom a thousand years before, a culture to our eyes very much similar, that it left the outer temples and the Sphinx at Giza untended and allowed them to become obscured by drifting sand. The young prince who later became Thutmoses IV (1406–1398 B.C.) would ride out on the west bank of the Nile past these magnificent ruins, and one day he lay down before the Sphinx to rest and fell asleep. He dreamed a dream in which the god of the Sphinx (to us, the pharaoh Khephren) appeared to him and said, "My state is . . . one of pain . . . the sand of the desert . . . presses upon me. I have been waiting to have you do what is in my heart; for I know that you are my son and my champion";[82] that is, instructed him to clear away the sand and to bring honor to the Old Kingdom, and the past, again. When Herodotus visited Egypt nine hundred years later, even knowledge of the past had largely deteriorated: The obelisks

82 • *The Hole in the Fabric*

of Thutmoses I (1525–1495) at Karnak were proudly identified to him by his priestly guides as the work of "Pheras," son of "Sesostris" (Ramses II, 1290–1224, he being about the only ruler in their past they knew anything of; "Pheras" was probably Herodotus' mistake for "pharaoh"). It is the Egyptian experience that has planted in the European imagination what we may call, in honor to Shelley, the Ozymandias theme. The diminution of the individual human being in a time frame of such extended linear dimensions is such as to reduce him to a cipher—or, as Kleist put it in another context, if he cannot attain the unlimited consciousness of a god, he is better off with none at all—that of a puppet. So we tend to view gods and men in Egyptian literature.[83]

Egypt and India may have only gradually lost their past; China has denied it at least three times, with the Maoist Red Guards, the Sun Yat-sen revolution, and, perhaps most dramatically, in 213 B.C., when Ch'in Shih Huang Ti, the self-styled "first" emperor, proscribed nonscientific books in scornful rejection of the heritage of Chinese culture. This legendary "destruction of the books" ranks with the probably more fabulous burning of the Library of Alexandria, whether by Romans or Arabs, and the iconoclastic excesses of 1789.

Akin to discoveries of the past are individual experiences, visions, and dreams, such as of the dead returned, which show a sense of the past generally limited, and literary creation, which can represent, with its usual freedom, a merging into, or trading places with, the past. In 1899 Henry James took up the idea of a novel in which the hero visits the past by exchanging places with a long-dead relative whom he resembles exactly. From 1910 he drops back to 1820, where he encounters, or lives, the life of his double, who is meanwhile thrust into the hero's twentieth-century life. This is according to a rather typical formula for James: to take up an idea or theme popular in contemporary literature and to introduce psychological and narrative complexity far beyond that of his models. The social phenomenon of Americans in Europe, and American-European intermarriage, surrounded by a flurry of light fiction, he incorporated into the aesthetic and metaphysical complexities of *The Portrait of a Lady* and *The Golden Bowl*; that of anarchist plotting and assassination, into *The Princess Casamassima*. As for time travel, H. G. Wells's *Time Machine* started its illustrious career in 1895, projecting a machine that could carry a man anywhere in time, but only to the same spot in space. Wells's hero, the Time Traveller, only goes ahead to the distant future, as had the hero of Edward Bellamy's *Looking Backward* in 1888; but since the turn of the century, time-loop or time-voyage narratives of every kind have become a commonplace in science fiction.

Wells's *Time Machine* is cheerfully stunted in its motivational and psychological aspects, in the same way that *The Invisible Man* and many other of his works are. It is written to give flesh to scientific speculation, and to warn of what a horror the future would be if the contemporary social arrangement of capital and labor were allowed to develop unimpeded.[84] Wells represents his hero, the inventor of the machine and the argonaut of the ages, very much from the outside and very sketchily altogether, since he uses him merely as a vehicle for action and for large-scale ideas. James, on the other hand, described with full psychological complexity (insofar as the unfinished state of *The Sense of the Past* allows) the effect upon a man and those known to him, including the woman he loves, of a shift in time. That it should be past time was as characteristic of James as the choice of future time was characteristic of Wells; James cared little for speculating upon the future of civilization—after 1914, he was not sure it had a future—while Wells, having what has come to be the mental set of the more creative science-fiction writer, like Arthur Clarke today, was fascinated by the future and probably saw little interest in science other than as a tool with which to alter the future.

Wells advanced no scientific analogue or basis for his time machine; none existed in 1895 and none exists today. He did have his Time Traveller sketch out an argument to his doubtful dinner guests for the existence of time as a fourth dimension, and in that, as Wells himself pointed out in a 1931 preface to a reissue of the novel, he can be said to have looked ahead to Einstein.

Now Einstein himself did not carry out many speculations about what experiences a man might have in time shifts, but in 1948 Kurt Gödel made an application of Einstein's field equations specifying a rotational velocity field that allowed an observer to travel along a path which would enable him to visit his own past and even to alter it. Gödel showed this in a diagram (see figure 2). The observer is posited as growing older as he proceeds upward on the right-hand (A) line; he could depart from A at x and travel along the different geodesic, B, for such a length that he would be brought back into his own past at y.

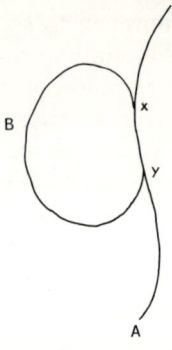

Figure 2

What looks like a fictional application of such a Gödelian loop is Alain Robbe-Grillet's *Erasers* (1953), a novel in which time and death, specifically a doubled day and a murder, are joined. The hero, Wallas, has been sent to investigate a murder that, unknown to him and the local police, but possibly known to his superiors in Paris, did not occur. The victim, one Dupont, was only nicked by the assassin's bullet and has gone into hiding, his death being announced to afford him protection from the political organization that sent the assassin. The government is taking steps against this organization, but Wallas has been told nothing of that. When he arrives on the spot he finds that his watch has stopped—at 7:30, the time of the supposed murder.

For the next twenty-four hours, Wallas wanders through the streets of the town as in a maze, losing his way, making and losing contact with people he wishes to question, and finding by degrees that his actions are falling into a parallel with those of the man he seeks as the murderer, but generally twenty-four hours later in time. The man, one "VS," has been seen at the café where Wallas is staying and was followed from the café by the same old drunk who follows Wallas from it. VS was at the post office for a letter; Wallas calls at the post office and a letter intended for VS is given to him, because of their physical resemblance; VS was seen loitering before the house where Dupont lived and was shot, and Wallas goes there to watch. When 7:30 P.M. comes around again, Wallas, by a complicated series of apparently minor and chance events, has hidden himself in Dupont's study to wait for VS, who he is quite sure is coming back to the scene of the crime. When a man with a gun comes through the door and apparently fires at him, he shoots, killing Dupont. At this point Wallas's watch starts up again, putting him back into time as the murderer he sought.

According to Subrahmanyan Chandrasekhar of the Enrico Fermi Institute, Einstein disapproved of such time schemes and felt it was impossible in the fashion Gödel described it, but perhaps not impossible in other conditions. That is not to suggest that Robbe-Grillet was using Gödel, of course; it would take a more thorough analysis of the novel than I have offered to ascertain what his conditions are. Chandrasekhar concludes, "The ability to visit the past does not seem to exist," and we must agree, certainly to the extent that recorded history bears no reliable evidence of anyone's ever doing it. Einstein did say, "We cannot send wire messages into the past," but Milič Čapek has claimed that he came around to approval of Gödel's trip on a curved path.[85]

Einstein barely existed for James, as important as he was to Wells, but there is an interesting temporal-metaphorical parallel in the narrative techniques of the two writers. Wells had his Time Traveller explain his fourth dimension with the following analogy:

For instance, here is a portrait of a man at eight years old, another at fifteen, another at seventeen, another at twenty-three, and so on. All those are evidently sections, as it were, Three-Dimensional representations of his Four-Dimensional being, which is a fixed and unalterable thing.[86]

The series of pictures records the fourth dimension, but they are records, not of something that *was*, but of something that *is*, the existence of a man. The picture as analogue of the man, with an independent existence, is a romantic trope that impinges closely on the subject here; Oscar Wilde's *Picture of Dorian Gray* features a transposition of man and picture, so that the man remains the record of a past event while the picture explores the future, changing as it does so. In *The Sense of the Past*, James has his hero enter the time of one picture, which is a portrait not of him, but of his double who lived a hundred years before. He thereby enters not his own past, but the past the picture had marked:

> Portraits of the dead are at best ironic things, but, unknown and unnamed as were these victims of fate, none had ever so affected him as after all reacting upon it. The general innuendo, as he felt himself take it from them, was quite out of scale with their general obscurity. . . . In presence of the single picture in which anything to call art had been appreciably active Ralph was luckily able—from the point of view of diversion—to treat himself to the sense of something like a prodigy.[87]

A difference between Wells's and most other writers' time-travel fictions, on the one side, and Henry James's, Lewis Carroll's, and some of our own contemporaries', on the other, is that the latter see time as a matter of different, but simultaneous, states, while the former see time as something to be voyaged through. This puts the latter closer to the speculations of physicists, on the nonlinear side. James put something of this viewpoint in writing: "I delight in a palpable imaginable *visitable* past,"[88] the past of Europe being as imaginatively close and palpable to his mind as its objects, houses, paintings, and gardens surviving from that past. There is no need for elaborate preparations, or machinery, for time travel in such circumstances; the clichés of travel brochures fit it perfectly, with phrases like "Visit the old potters' quarter, and take a walk through the past!" The borders between time zones in James are as close to the observer as they are in Gödel; it is a matter of walking from one room into another, or looking at a picture—a relationship not the less profound for its simplicity.

A nearly unknown writer, coming midway between James and our own time and a contemporary only by stretching the term, expressed the essence of it. This is Miles Breuer (d. 1947), whose short story, *The Gostak and the Doshes* (1930),[89] bears not only a thematic relation to Nabokov's *Ada* but a close parallel, in terms of the Einsteinian "fourth dimension," to the way time works in *The Sense of the Past* and generally, in a latent manner, in James's fiction. In Breuer's story a man moves from one university campus to another, quite similar, simply by a kind of misstep on a walk. The other campus seems more old-fashioned: The architecture is Victorian; the people more considerate and well-mannered. He joins their life, but his experiences there shade into nightmare—he feels trapped, like James's hero; he is caught up in a situation of embarrassment (finding his way about and recasting his mental landscape so as to be able to teach his subject at this university) which becomes one of acute danger. A war breaks out, and thanks to his "difference" and lack of successful conformity he is condemned as a traitor. By a mental effort born of desperation he manages to re-create the critical walk and escape back into his own time. He is left to ponder what it was he had visited, or where it was he had been. When he was in that old-fashioned place he was greeted as "from another universe"; when he is back he is asked by a scientist friend, making an effort to hypothesize what could have happened, to consider that "the section of a conic cut by the y plane looks different from the section of the same conic cut by the z plane. . . . Perhaps what you saw was our own world and *our own selves* intersected by a different set of coordinates" (italics added). This is possibly the basis of the difference between the different but strangely similar Terra and Antiterra of Nabokov's *Ada,* and the entire basis of *The Sense of the Past*. The central problem of the observer, whether he be cosmic or novelistic, is that of dealing with the terms of his own observation.

James never was, in the first place, given to chronological progression; not only do his novels lack the linear progression that was concurrently growing into the large-scale novels of George Eliot, Galsworthy, Romains, and Thomas Mann, they also lack chronological specificity. They are typically removed in time from passing events, for they make no reference, or reference of the most glancing kind, to such events. If you were given the task of dating the action in *The Golden Bowl* or *The Portrait of a Lady* or *Roderick*

Hudson you could do it generally, in that horses and carriages are used, the fever still reigns in Rome, there is no telephone, and so forth, but never specifically, for James did not intend that you should do it specifically. In *The Wings of the Dove*, the saga of Milly Theale works its way to Venice for its culminating stages—betrayal, death, promise, dedication—and once there, it merges with the Venice of the past. The palace in which Milly lives is a combination of the Gothic with Veronese's and Sansovino's imaginations; the *canali* are those of Guardi and Canaletto; the weather that of Tiepolo. This is nothing so magical as turning under a bridge and meeting a gondola filled with eighteenth-century revelers, but it is not the less time-warping for that. Milly leads her little group of admirers and betrayers into a historical continuum not qualitatively different from the Rome of Isabel Archer-Osmond's Palazzo Roccanera or from Hawthorne's stock Rome of the romantic Ruins of Time school, but less involved with clock time. James does not show his characters merging with the past here, or some "spirit" of the past impinging upon them; rather the past is *accessible*, forming an architectural and metaphysical frame for the present and the future. In that sense I use the overworked and kidnaped word *continuum*. In comparison, *The Sense of the Past* is as crude as *The Time Machine*; it is because *The Sense of the Past* puts James's ideas into a more easily described, and compared, form that I make it the subject of this section.

James starts *The Sense of the Past* with an unusual metaphor: His hero desires to "remount the stream of time" as he faces the eighteenth-century London house he has inherited, and he will do so as he forces the house to give up its "secrets" (pp. 47–48). That is so far quite conventional, the secrets of the past, especially surrounding an old building, being a well-used convention dating from the Gothic novel, more than a century old in European literature by 1910. But as James develops the metaphor, the terms change:

No man, he well believed, could ever so much have wanted to look behind and still behind—to scale the high wall into which the successive years, each a squared block, pile themselves in our rear and look over as nearly as possible with the eye of sense into, unless it should rather be called out of, the vast prison yard. (p. 47)

This is both strange and, as so often with James's central concepts, ambivalent. How can the blocks of the years make at once a wall and a prison yard? The past imprisons us in the present, or at least so Pendrel feels, for " 'present' was a word used by him in a sense of his own and meaning as regards most things about him markedly absent" (p. 49). Time, in a linear conception, also imprisons the observer in his "now" as if it were a cage moving along a railroad track, its speed and forward direction quite out of the control of the man inside. But here the metaphor allows two further extensions: (1) the wall composed of years grows larger as more of the present is used or as more time passes, and (2) the location of the prison is uncertain. From Pendrel's point of view it is clearly the present; like Henry's brother William in the garden of Lamb House, he wants to put a ladder up to the wall of his own world and look out and beyond. But from another point of view, one which we can discover here without pushing too hard on the fragile structure of the metaphor, "the vast prison yard" is not the present but the past, and by his explorations in time travel Pendrel may be exchanging relative freedom for real imprisonment. If a living man exchanges places with a man long dead, who is the gainer? Will there be a willing trade when the (once) living man, out of the present, wants his place back?

James's text as he left it stops short of that point, but the lengthy notes he left for the novel, as it was to be, make it clear that a growing sense of horror surrounding the appearance of the hero in the wrong time, 1820, and his own realization that he has no certainty of getting back to 1910, were to be the main effects. In the long first scene between Pendrel and his ancestral relatives, the "double consciousness" of the hero, "the consciousness of being the other and yet himself also, of being himself and yet the other also,"[90] is developed in a way, and to a point, that is to my knowledge unique in literature. Ralph Pendrel *is* his 1820 double in that he is in his clothes and in his place—at the door of the house, come to call for the first time upon his English relatives, one of whom he is more or less engaged to marry—but at the same time he is not entirely in his mind or in his body.

The matter of the body is uncertain. For all we can tell of the text of the novel, Ralph could be in the 1820 body, but in the notes for composition James toys with the idea that the perfection of Ralph's teeth might be one of the clues that strengthens the others' feeling of *wrongness*. On that basis, we could presume that James meant Ralph's body to move with his consciousness in time, if it were not for the fact that most often James refined in his text, and made more subtle, the relations and their objectifications he outlined in his notes. There are as well other relative crudities in the notes, like the matter of the teeth, that do not appear in the text, so it is finally impossible to decide whether or not James followed Wells in putting his hero in the past in total physicality.

But we can see that Ralph is not simply *in* his ancestor's mind, for he guesses and gropes as the conversation with the relatives progresses. Beyond that we do not know how much of his 1910 consciousness he has; he is so devoted to keeping one jump ahead of the questioning to which he is being subjected that the only thoughts revealed to us are concerned with what is going on in the room. In this claustrophobic situation, what happens is that the 1910 brain *intuits* contents from the 1820 brain (James posits in the notes that the ancestor has filled Ralph in somewhat about the 1820 situation; we see nothing of this in the text, but rather a constant process of the intuition). When Ralph feels there is something important he has to show the girl, he confidently slides his hand into his pocket, though without any knowledge of what he will find, and draws out the miniature portrait of her that was sent to him in America. When "Sir Cantopher" is announced and the others look at him questioningly, he produces "Sir Cantopher *Bland?*" without knowing as he opened his mouth that he would have the correct name to say.

These flights are, however, accompanied by drops, one of which takes us both to the center of the problems of interpretation of the novel as we have it, and to the center of its complexity. This is when the mention of another sister, Nan, leaves Ralph with no responding intuition at all, nothing coming to him as it had come when Sir

Cantopher was introduced and when he felt for the miniature and when, later, he feels in another pocket for gold, "knowing" that it will be there. He does not know who Nan is and he does not know whether the 1820 man knew. He is at a loss for words, and he notices that the others notice this. To clear the *impasse* he riskily admits ignorance: "You have then another daughter whom I hear of for the first time?" (p. 178).

We presume that he does this *since* he receives no information from the connection he has to the 1820 mind: If all is silence there, he may safely guess that the 1820 Pendrel had never heard of Nan either—at least on this day in 1820 time. The Midmores react with surprise, but all goes off pretty well and the conversation resumes a more or less easy flow. If we take into account James's notes, however, there is a very sudden drop and danger here, for in the notes James describes his plot as including a mistake made by Ralph on reaching 1820 time, of assuming that the Miss Midmore he meets first (Molly) is the girl his ancestor was to marry, while actually it was the younger sister, Nan. This is difficult to associate with the text, for in it Mrs. Midmore is present as marriage is discussed, and she certainly knows which daughter is which. We can also hardly imagine Nan letting Molly impersonate her, or Molly trying to do so, if letters about marriage have been exchanged. It seems necessary to posit considerable changes between the later (1914) notes and the writing, no matter how short a time may have elapsed. Pendrel could hardly have written to a girl and been sent her portrait and arranged a marriage and then have walked in the door and started making arrangements with another sister. But this *could* occur if the 1820 man had just seen the sisters, and/or given Ralph some wrong tip. The former is made unlikely by the clear impression the text gives that the American Pendrel is coming to the Midmores for the first time as Ralph walks in the door; and if Ralph is to have his own body in 1820 it must, of course, be at just such a juncture that he takes his ancestor's place. If the Midmores had already seen the 1820 man, they would have known immediately that Ralph was an impostor.

The interesting point is that in the text we can see a variation in this insight Ralph has, or is allowed, into the 1820 mind. If we borrow from the notes, we can see a direction in that variation to less and less insight, with the result of more and more fear on Ralph's part, in reaction both to the growing sense of alarm he sees in the others as they recognize his strangeness, his "suspicion of being suspected" (p. 337), and to the situation that slowly dawns on him, of being left alone and trapped in the past, with no contact at all to the brain he had drawn into 1910, and whose cooperation is necessary to effect a return to original places. Instead of sensing the presence of the other as an inspiration to do or say the right thing, Ralph comes to sense it as something malign, something powerful but inimical:

He is liable then say to glimpses of vision of the other man . . . to recurrences of a sense of that presence—which . . . *does* seem to him at times to hover and to menace: only not to the appearance or effect of reassuring or relieving him, but only to that of really quite mocking and not pitying him. (p. 305)

The effect of this is to put the story into the parallel James planned it to have to *The Turn of the Screw*, the sense of an innocent person dealing across the boundaries of life and time with another *will*, which is inimical to it, and which must be mastered on its own terms of purely mental communication. The likeness is not obscured by the fact that the governess deals with a mind of pure evil from beyond the grave and loses in the struggle, while Ralph has to do with a mind considerably less maleficent and wins, by returning, in the posited finale, to his own time. The notes repeatedly mention the "brutality" of 1820; James planned to have Ralph tell Nan, the 1820 person with whom he finds he can communicate, "of how poor a world she is stuck fast in compared with all the wonders and splendors that he is straining back to" (p. 331). There is no question here of the supposititiously European Henry James, so contemptuous of the vulgar present and the triumph of Americanism, projecting a yearningly sentimental return to the England of Washington Irving's Bracebridge Hall, the Cheeryble brothers, and Mr. Pickwick. Rather it is a situation that, by its free use of supernatural effect, casts the Jamesian equation into high relief: consciousness in a struggle with consciousness, suspended over a space-time infinity empty of every other feature but consciousness itself.

Time is subordinated to mind in this equation; linearity is replaced by a synchronicity of highly different states of being; the sense of the past is—a strange last analysis that is at once a central starting point for our age—a trap. At the same time, it seems true that James's novel depicts the state of being later claimed possible by J. W. Dunne in such works as *Nothing Dies*, and incorporated into such contemporary novels as Nabokov's *Ada* and Vonnegut's *Slaughterhouse-Five*. It could be called, after the latter, the Tralfamadorian principle: that we exist in another time or times (numbered by Dunne 2, 3 . . .) as well as in the linear progression from birth to death in time 1, "elsewhere" in Einstein's terms, as well as "now." Vonnegut's Billy Pilgrim is like Dunne's observer, and as well like James's observer, in that he has *freedom* even when in a German prison camp; and death is no frightful thing to him, for he has being above and beyond the linear sequence. James left the equation incomplete as it affects Ralph Pendrel; his time traveler could span the centuries but never came to tell us whether his moving from one time consciousness to another gave him personal freedom or exaltation as well as a profound sense of danger. Taken as part of its own period, *The Sense of the Past* remains a lesser thing than the complete and successful *Time Machine*; taken in terms of our era, it is a precognition of the subtlest effects of contemporary science fiction.

Ada

Je suis sur la terre comme dans une planète étrangère, où je serais tombé de celle que j'habitais. • J-J. Rousseau

Vladimir Nabokov's *Ada or Ardor: A Family Chronicle* (1969) is an excellent contemporary twin to Henry James's *Sense of the Past*, for it too springs out of the lowly science-fiction form. As James was inspired to work with the form of Wells's *Time Machine*, Nabokov was inspired to take up and, with his usual grace, scorn while taking up, the work of men like Clarke, Blish, Hoyle, and Borges. As unlike as the two novels, James's and Nabokov's, are, they share an important and perhaps unique characteristic, that they raise this science-fiction background to full novelistic status. Both men developed outstanding reputations as novelists before turning into the side lane of science fiction, and neither mastered any science to make the turning, but rather bent some of the material developed by the lesser, fully "scientific" writers to their purposes. In this sense—of being an unscientific work of science fiction, and of being a real novel with all the characteristics of the novel inherently lacking in the science-fiction form, from skilled characterization to subtle verisimilitude of motive—*Ada* is the first English work to fulfill the queer promise of *The Sense of the Past*, the first to make a circle of the incomplete arc it represents. Their subject is not machinery, or the obscure natures of extraplanetarians, but the human brain and heart, or the two together in one word, consciousness—James's that of a man of 1910 walking through a door into 1820 and becoming suspended between the two times and a double identity; Nabokov's that of a man living eighty-three years *out of* one summer, in a world he feels to be penetrated with double identity, and in contact with another world of a different time.

Ada takes place on the planet Antiterra, or Demonia, the action centering upon the years 1884 to 1922 of its chronology. The source of this chronology is unspecified; while most of what is unspecified in the narrative seems to depend upon a close resemblance to conditions on Earth (Antiterra has a moon, an apparently single sun, an oxygen-based atmosphere, oceans and continents like those of Earth, clouds, rain, wind, and so forth), there are distinct differences in Antiterran culture. Its technology had reached by 1850 of its time (I shall henceforward write Antiterran dates with an added "a" to distinguish them from Earth dates, so "had reached by 1850a") the level ours had roughly by 1950, when there was a "Great Reaction" against it and a banning of electricity.[91] As the story starts, there are no airplanes, telephones, telegraphs, or radio, but horses and carriages, bicycles with carbide lamps, cameras, balloons, cars with tiller steering (their mode of ignition diesel?), and railroad trains. As the story progresses, the forbidden technology reasserts itself—while 1884a has a generally late Victorian air, circa 1900, by circa 1890a the trains go one hundred miles per hour; by 1901a there are radio and telephone and electric light again; by 1905a transcontinental airliners and tape (voice) recorders; and by 1922a, when our lovers are reunited, and thereafter to the end of the story (1967a), there is a technology much like that we have had since 1950, with fast sports cars, trains, planes, television, motion pictures in color, abstract painting, and a tendency to replace men with machines. The situation is not exactly that of an Earth technology abandoned and then taken up again, though; there are flying carpets ("jikkers") left over from pre-1850a, and an elaborate system of water-driven substitute apparatus used in the nonelectric years, such as the dorophone (water-driven telephone), dorogram (water telegram), hydrogram (apparently the same), dorotelly (water-driven television)—all technically beyond any period of Earth invention, if they can even be considered physically possible on Earth. Among a few exceptions to the late-Victorian technology I have asserted is the "aerogram" of 1868a, presumably carried by the "petroplane" of the same date and thus a little ahead of its time.

Antiterran history and culture, like its technology, is a good deal familiar. So is its geography. There are Paris and London, Manhattan, Arizona, Texas, Mississippi, the Crimea, England, America, and France, along with Scott and Dickens, Musset, Rimbaud and his translator Wallace Fowlie, Dostoevski, Proust, Catullus, Atala and her Chateaubriand, Louis XVI, the painter Bosch, the *Arabian Nights*, the Sheik Nefzawi (of *The Perfumed Garden*, an erotic classic), Turgenev's *Smoke*, Marvell's *Garden*, Shakespeare. The literary and spoken languages mentioned are ours, too—German, French, English, Russian.

On the other hand, nearly as many places, persons, and works are mentioned in a distorted or altered form: "Russia" is the nickname for *Estoty*, a Russian-speaking land located in the place of our Canada; our Russia is *Tartary*; there is a town named Centaur in Arizona and one named Lolita in Texas; the poet John Shade, on Earth a character in Nabokov's *Pale Fire*, is real on Antiterra, while "Martin Gardner," on Earth the mathematical gamesman of *The Scientific American*, is on Antiterra a "fictional philosopher." Maupassant's stories are written on Antiterra by Ada's French governess, a nice satiric touch, while a popular children's book is *Palace in Wonderland*, which may or may not be related to another book called *Alice in the Camera Obscura*. A famous sex-oriented psychologist is Dr. Froid, or Froit; a Manhattan magazine is *The Beau and the Butterfly*, and so forth.

While the rulers of Antiterra are never mentioned, beyond an indication of an Anglo-American alliance ruling most of the planet outside of Asiatic Tartary (rather like a conservative's view of a successful outcome to our Cold War), their banning of electricity is apparently undertaken for the common good, more or less in the spirit of the American space scientist Carl Sagan's suggestion that "perhaps a sign of a truly advanced civilization will be the voluntary abandonment of technical pursuits for activities of another kind."[92] Any "activities of another kind" not familiar to Earth are absent, however, on Antiterra; its neo-Victorian world of arrested technology sounds just like our Victorian world of rampant technology and uninhibited individualism. The father of the hero and heroine, "Demon" Veen, an Antiterran aristocrat out of Edward Gorey with touches from the Victorian pornographers, spends his millions on maintaining troops of mistresses in jewels, furs, and villas; fights duels with a flair; is a wine and food snob; and prides himself on his sexual prowess—on one occasion at the theater, on a bet with his orchestra seat neighbor "Prince N.," he gets up at the end of one scene, goes backstage, has sexual relations with the actress starring in the play (a virgin, Marina Durmanov, later the mother of Ada and Van), and is back in his seat for the beginning of the next scene. Ho ho.

His son Van is cut from the same cloth, having millions to spend, and spending them on the same two things (or the same thing, ostentatious display, in the same two forms), conspicuous consumption of women (during his long periods of exile from Ada) and of less animate objects—villas, apartments, clubs, trains, planes, food, and wine. Van's life is dedicated to wrestling with much the same problem of love that his father's has been: Demon wants Marina, but Marina marries another man, his first cousin. Demon has sexual relations with her anyway, until he is obliged to desist. Van wants Ada, his cousin in the world's eyes but actually his sister; he has sexual relations with her anyway, until he is obliged to desist; she marries another man, and so forth. With the exception that Van takes up the study of psychology and the nature of time, he and his father share a cultural attitude that takes as of the highest moment, second only to matters of lovemaking, such questions as whether a man you have bumped into in a train corridor or who has stepped on your toes is of sufficient social status to be challenged to a duel, or should be horsewhipped instead.

The greatest weakness of *Ada* as a novel is that such an imaginary culture, a combination of Cyrano de Bergerac and a social paper's view of polite society before 1914, goes unquestioned, is in fact held up to admiration, in the hero's utter self-contentment and the absence of any point of view in or out of the narrative critical of his hedonism and social irresponsibility. That Van's comfortable world of money and country villas staffed by aged retainers and surrounded by the little farms of contented peasantry (poachers dealt with strictly) strongly resembles the fairy-tale Old Russia celebrated in other Nabokovian works, most directly, with the writer as hero, in *Speak, Memory*, is more or less immaterial to the purposes of the book—that Nabokov celebrates an unreal Russia on Earth is something we can complain about, but we are forced to allow him to do what he wants on another planet of his own invention. Yet the figure of his hero is presented for our serious Earthling attention; this man, Van Veen, is as we are. And he forfeits a good deal of that attention by acting, and to some extent thinking, like the hero of *My Secret Life* or of a pseudo-Victorian novelette written for Grove Press. He cannot do without sexual intercourse for more than forty-eight hours, for instance (the only reply possible to such adolescent fantasy is "Why not twenty-four?"), and we find that he is re-erect and ready for another go within seconds of orgasm, assures Ada he will possess her ninety times a month until he is ninety, drinks four bottles of champagne at a normal dinner (he drinks almost nothing but champagne), plays court tennis, fences with a French coach on a penthouse terrace twice a week, is so rich that no financial crash can touch him, is a crack shot and skilled wrestler and boxer, can identify the drugs administered, and the ailment they treat, by smelling a man's breath, builds for Ada one villa after another, over half the globe, abandons and gives away other villas after they have served their purpose as weekend pleasure nooks, along with the girl or girls involved. He can take any woman he wants almost anywhere, for no woman can resist his charm.

One feels there *must* be satiric intent in all this, rather like *Playboy's Oy Oy Seven*, but the closest we get to an exposure of the childish perspective that directs it all is when we find that Van solicitously patronizes for years an international "chain of palatial brothels" known as "Villa Venuses," whose extravagant offerings and fantastically varied architecture are indeed the offspring of a schoolboy's imagination, that of one Eric van Veen, translated after his demise at fifteen into reality by a doting (and fabulously rich) relative. Our author tells us that the boy derived the project (called "Villa Venus: an Organized Dream") from an overdose of erotic literature, but gives us no indication he is aware that the character of Van himself, the patron of such *Playboy* masturbatory fantasies, can only be seen to have the same source.

These, then, are *Ada*'s main weaknesses: a projection of sentimentalized preindustrial society and a hero who ought to be, but is not, a parody of the romantic-erotic excesses of third-rate Victorian fiction. I shall pass over others, such as numerous Thackerayan triflings with the narrative illusion and a whole crop of unfunny linguistic jokes (mainly bilingual puns) that are not even presented as throwaways, caviar to the general, truffles for the pedant, but *explained*—Nabokovian *tics douloureux*—and state that only the second, the characterization of the hero, is a serious weakness. It looks like a large-scale joke with a very successfully hidden point, but its intimate connection with the first matter, that of sentimentalized late feudalism (this is the way *gentlemen* lived in the good old days) makes that highly unlikely. So there are matters in Antiterra that have nothing to do with the theme I wish to develop and are wholly unworthy of the example of Henry James.[93]

What has most to do with *Ada* in the perspective of this study is that Antiterra has a twin planet, Terra, in turn quite recognizable as our Earth. The Antiterrans, Van and Ada included, are not sure of its existence, but we might say that we as readers are, for after all we live on it. This is what we do in reading the regular science-fiction story in which an inhabitant of cloud-covered Venus cries, "Bah! I hold no brief for a reputed twin planet to ours"; we reverse the point of view and gain dramatic irony. In Nabokov's Antiterra, so like Earth itself, it is easy to forget the dramatic frame and become confused, so that the speculation of a *terra ignota* becomes "Bah, I hold no brief for a reputed outer planet, beyond Pluto!" Antiterra is so believable in our own terms that it lures us into forgetting that we should doubt *it*, and into doubting ourselves. This is the first of the mirror traps in the land of Ada.

That one should have a mirror reflection is part of the basis for the derivation of an Antiterra, as well as for the Antiterrans' hypothesis of a Terra. Martin Gardner, whose writings are reflected throughout the novel, has cited one of the ancient Terran speculative bases for a twin: "Aristotle suggested that it was the Pythagorean cult's obsession with the triangular number 10 (the sum of 1,2,3,4) that led its members to add a tenth body called antichthon (counter-earth). It too [like the central fire that the sun reflected according to their theory] was always invisible because its orbit lay between the earth and the central fire."[94] This is something like Plato's speculation that the two sexes are split halves of original unified beings; the attraction in the concept of reciprocity and balance in nature (known in linguistics as the binary constituent hypothesis) leads one not only to propose pairings of diverse manifestations (like the two human sexes) but to propose missing members of pairs (like the twin to Earth). Mirror pairings, marked by superficial identity overlaying a reversal of left and right, are not confined to mirrors: one's left hand is very much like one's right and matches perfectly if placed against the right, which is much like putting it against a mirror, which means that it is very different from the right—as Gardner reminds us. Thus, Terran children have to go through a difficult period of discovering the difficulties inherent in mittens and boots, while adults, to whom such things have become unconscious, live comfortably in a predominantly right-handed world with a few nasty left-handed surprises like the axle nut that must be turned left to tighten, or the left-hand sink tap that drenches the inattentive hand washer when he turns it off "right."

Left-handers, the minority group, are more aware of the way right-handers have tilted technology to favor their statistical asymmetry; unless they develop a manipulative symmetry of their own (ambidexterity) they live in constant persecution by right-handed doors, levers, buttons, scissors, scythes, typewriters, golf clubs, hockey sticks, camera eyepieces, baseball mitts, rifle bolts, and gear shifts.

This is good philosophical training, it might be advanced, for their life on a resolutely asymmetrical planet, which persists in a one-way orbit, spins one way, and does not have interchangeable hemispheres. There are, of course, many planets; or let us say there are good reasons for imagining or hypothesizing many planets. Our local star, the sun, has nine planets, and several of these have moons, or little planets, of their own (Earth has one, of enormous relative size; Jupiter has twelve; Saturn, nine). There are anywhere from 1,500 to 2,000 billion stars in this local galaxy (the Milky Way), and there are probably hundreds of millions of galaxies in the universe—about 1 billion can be photographed by the Mt. Wilson 200-inch telescope, within the 10 billion light years of the universe we can observe. Now the number of stars in our galaxy, 2 million million, is 2×10^{12}, and if we multiply that by ten for the number of planets or satellite bodies to each, and then by 1 billion, or 10^9, for the number of galaxies, we derive a very large number indeed for planets in the observable universe (leaving aside what may be beyond the reach of present telescopes), 2×10^{22}, 10,000 billion billion.[95] Since there are approximately 3×10^8 seconds in a century, that would mean if we sat down to look over the planets in the observable universe with a view to finding a twin to Earth, and examined one a second, we would be at the task for 10 thousand thousand million centuries. Even if we drastically reduce the field of our hypothetical universal survey by assuming that habitable planets occur only around main-sequence stars lying between spectral types F2 and K5, so that we allow only 1 to 2 percent of the stars in a galaxy into our purview, there are still about 1 billion qualifying stars per Milky Way–size galaxy. The universe is as well violently alive, and it can be surmised that a million new solar systems

101 • *Time and the Visible World*

are formed in it every hour.[96] As the English astronomer V. A. Firsoff summarizes the situation,

> Far from being exceptional, the Solar System is rather a humdrum example of planetary configuration. There are multiple stars, each with an array of planets of its own; close binaries sharing one or more planets; superplanets that may have planetary satellites, which in turn may be accompanied by moons. Every imaginable variant of surface conditions will occur somewhere or other; and, since some stars are known to differ drastically in composition from the Sun, planets with exotic chemistries must likewise be expected, as well as millions upon millions of pseudo-Earths where life closely similar to ours is not only possible but probably inevitable.[97]

Could one of those billion billion planets be not simply a "pseudo-Earth," but a twin to Earth? At this point we necessarily pass beyond what is observable to what may be fairly or unfairly imagined. It is quite fair for Nabokov to imagine that there is a planet on which people very much like ourselves imagine us. That much we may certainly say, and pass on to what we may fairly imagine the relation of this imagination of Nabokov's to our own Terran existence to be.

Terra as twin planet to Antiterra combines two concepts, that of mate and that of opposite. Opposite is expressed by the "anti," as we know in the (unmentioned) Christ and Antichrist. On Antiterra this has mainly to do with a vision of Terra as equivalent to paradise, and life on "this pellet of muck" as a sort of hell, antiparadise (if Antiterra is to be taken as the equivalent to the hell we imagine on Earth, a planetary *Huis Clos*, it must be allowed that life on it is very pleasant, if not "heavenly" in the adolescent sense, for the Top People). The numerous twinnings and suggestions of mirror reflections in the Antiterran narrative are perhaps meant to support this major concept, to testify to the reality, otherwise doubted by the main characters, of doubled existence: Aqua and Marina Durmanov, twins, marry Walter D. Veen and Walter D. Veen, cousins born the same year. Both bear male children, Aqua's stillborn, which she planned to name Ivan, and Marina's the hero, Ivan (thus Aqua says "I have a twin sister and a twin son" [p. 25] and suffers from the delusion that her child lived and is actually Van, a fiction imposed upon the world in any case). Van knows of this "twin son" and refers to him as "my stillborn double" (p. 355), which double may be said to take an intermittent role in Van's affairs, as when faithless Ada calls to him to wait and he, disgustedly, "saw Van" obey her (p. 295), or when one who seemed "a pale, ill-shaven twin" (p. 481), delegated by Van, holds the crown over Ada's head at her wedding to Vinelander. Aqua's place in the bed of her husband, the Walter D. Veen known as "Demon," is taken by Marina, who is having an adulterous affair with the gay betrayer. Aqua senses this, in 1871a, as she escapes from a sanitarium and heads for home, where she stands unnoticed in the bedroom, finding there all her own things—clothes, cosmetics —just as they were. That is, she sees herself in the place of her twin, who has taken her place.

Ada and Van, the lovers, are not only intimately related, as brother and sister, but something like male and female twin-forms of the same concept of life: both of near-genius intelligence, proud and romantically inclined dispositions, both dedicated, for life, to the satisfaction of the other, like the mind and heart of one body. They share thoughts and dreams, and their bodies are, sexual difference apart, remarkably like a doubling: Ada's hands "are Van's in a reducing mirror," and "her plain Irish nose was Van's in miniature" (pp. 380, 58). Their teeth and birthmarks, those final signs of identity serving throughout literary and legal history, match. It may be noted that these resemblances are not so much identity as *mirror* identity, with the possibility of distortion (some guess Terra is "a distortive glass of our distorted glebe") (p. 18): In middle age, Van notes that he and Ada have the same tooth drilled and capped with gold, but on opposite sides of their mouths.

There is also the fact that Van spends several years perfecting and winning fame with a stage act in which he, as "Mascodagama," walks and dances on his hands, so costumed as to appear to be in normal rather than in reversed position. That this "magical reversal" has something to do with the Terra-Antiterra opposition is suggested by two passages in the novel, one in which a stranger, a fellow guest at a dinner in 1905a, when both Van's book on Terra and part of his study of time have been published, says to Van, "I'm delighted and honored to dine with Vasco de Gama" (p. 515; also in the invitation from Windsor Castle, p. 182). This is either a mistake for Mascodagama or/and a subtle reference to something else, more along the lines of exploration, charting of regions whose existence was before only suspected. Something to do with Terran exploration, in short, that could nearly be put in the peculiar thrill the reversed existence of Mascodagama gives Van, as he muses on the marks made on his hands (and thus also reversed) by the carpet, the lower world discovered by him, on which he dances.

In many small ways the relations of Van and Ada are "reflected" as well, especially insofar as those relations bear upon the innocent victim of their love, the second sister Lucette. During their 1888a summer, Lucette, who is watching them, seems "to peep out of every mirror" (p. 211), and when she steals upon them making love by a forest stream, Van is warned of her presence by the reflected image of Ada's expression in the water. When Lucette is later trying to get Van into a discussion of that summer, and is recalling a desk with a secret drawer by the end of a divan in the house at Ardis (the word *di-van* may be dismissed for its presumption), Van sidetracks her into a consideration of, or metaphorical digression into, the matter of the image of a hand on a transparent sign, which has either left or right identity according to the side from which it is viewed. Van wants to avoid Lucette, but at the same time he is powerfully drawn to her beauty in the absence of Ada—indeed, Ada herself advances the idea that Van console himself with this sister-eidolon, or insufficient double—and he finds Lucette's grown-up charms dangerously close to the original. Her voice "agonizingly" resembles Ada's (p. 366), and her kisses are just like her sister's ("she tasted exactly as Ada at Ardis," p. 467).

Elsewhere mirrors real and verbal occur with some regularity: Examples of the latter come when one of Van's psychiatric mentors, P. O. Tyomkin, is saved "from the dagger of Prince Potyomkin, a mixed-up kid from Sebastopol, Id." (p. 182), and when Ada writes Van to congratulate him on his book *Reflections in Sidra* (p. 503; realities in Ardis?); examples of the former occur when Van sees his father, Demon, reflected in a mirror at Goodson Airport, reading a reversed newspaper, and when Van remeets Lucette in 1901a he is revealed to friends of his father's by mirrors, but goes unrecognized.

Additionally, the motion picture film, with its doubling of characters real and imaginary, is associated at critical points in the story with mirrors and doubles: Marina waits for members of the film company by her pool with a mirror, having her hair dressed, and watching Ada and Van as they enjoy, in each other's company, "as they had never enjoyed before, the 'happy forever' feeling at the end of never-ending fairy tales" (p. 287), their passion the more hectically blissful for their knowledge of the falsity underneath it—Ada has been unfaithful to Van, and Van already suspects the truth. Ada leaves, "Marina and the mirror had gone," and Van takes a last dip in the pool while the butler stands "looking meditatively into the false-blue water" (p. 287). The afternoon is an ending, the end of the idyll, and in some ways an echo, or reflection, of an earlier afternoon by the same pool, with the film company, the director, and Marina going over a script while Van watched in disgust the poolside attempts of Herr Rack and hairy Pedro at flirtation with Ada. Van had stalked off and thereby walked into the film itself, partly by an accident of wording, partly as a revelation of double, and illusory, existence (p. 203).

As Marina, the actress, mistress of illusion and mistress of Ardis, sits watching her former lover, Demon, at a dinner that same summer, 1888a, her "screen-corrupted" mind flits over images of the past, placing Demon " 'between mirror and fan' " and in her only hit film, *A Torrid Affair*. She mixes that with a memory (an observation beyond her physical senses, perhaps) of Ada and Van, in an apparent denial of symmetry of two framed left hands, doing something puzzling. This leads her into a review of her life seen as a film, with the necessity of cutting-room work and studio retakes to put it in order—would Van and Ada thereby be corrected, trimmed, or cut altogether? Marina's mind is a sad confusion of insight and misinformation; she is right, however, to imagine Ada in a film. For Ada has a real, if short, film career, not only in the sense that her wedding seems, in Lucette's eyes, "like a badly faked episode in an old movie" (p. 481), but that she is given a role in Yuzlik's *Don*

Juan's Last Fling and is thereby preserved, in a way ordinary enough to the contemporary Terran mind but critical to the Antiterran plot, in a separate existence, indefinitely repeatable and thereby frozen in time. It is this Ada, the shadow-double of the screen, that appears on the ocean liner to insert itself between the fast-closing Van and Lucette—their chance viewing of Ada's film in the ship's theater causes him to reject Lucette's offer of a second-best liaison, and that rejection causes Lucette's suicide. *She* then passes into a permanent state of secondary reference, parallel to the status of the film image that set her aside in life.

Van pursues the shadow of Ada from the screen of one provincial movie house to another during the following years, in which the real Ada grows plump and middle-aged and the real Van, no longer the one who made love to the teen-ager of the film, becomes like its Don Juan, an "aging libertine." The reality of Antiterran life and the illusion of the screen are unquestioned; aging Van and elderly Ada, when brought together once and for all, are as much happier as we would be in real old age taken instead of an illusion of re-creating lost moments in youth. The Proustian doubt, however, remains, along with the question of whether the apparent life or the apparent illusion, the apparent real image or the apparently reflected one, contains more truth. While the novel *Ada* is almost bare of reference to the artist's role (in contrast to the equally reflective *Pale Fire*), a comparison of it to the artist as the one who "holds the mirror up to nature" is almost unavoidable; and if one holds up a mirror to two objects, one as it is in nature and one a reflected image, one's mirror will show the first reversed, distorted by a left-right trade, but the second true, as it is in nature. What is seen in mirrors in *Ada* may therefore be truer than what is seen out of them.

This is demonstrably true in the matter of the film of Van's *Letters from Terra* made by Victor Vitry (Fr. *vitre, vitré,* "pane of glass, transparent like glass, provided with glass panes") in 1940a. Vitry is a Frenchman, sounding like Roger Vadim in being married to his sex-star, and like Abel Gance in his reputation for genius, whose work, along with his name, merges true seeing with illusion and mirrors. Van wants to sue him for his distortions of "Terrestrial politics as obtained by Van with such diligence and skill from extrasensorial sources and manic dreams" (p. 581), and Vitry uses side-show tricks to give the film mass appeal—sadistic thrills (an accidental beheading), sex (a naked dance by his leading lady), and huge crowd scenes using, according to different accounts, a million extras, or five-hundred thousand, with five-hundred thousand mirrors, but Vitry's imagination provides Antiterra with the closest thing to real knowledge of life on Terra. What Van frets over as distortions include representations of the 1926 surrender of Abdel-Krim, an "Athaulf Hindler" taking over Germany in 1933 and starting preparations for something worse than a 1914–1918 war in which Germany invaded Belgium, Olympic Games in Berlin—the mirror held up to the mirror shows pretty true.

A return to the matter of Terra's being a heaven to Antiterra's hell, a reflection in a moral mirror, is possibly helpful here: Antiterra's first name is Demonia, and Van and Ada's father, Demon Veen, is named as if after it. *Ada* is close to Russian *ad*, "hell" from Greek *hades*; in the genitive case, as required, for instance, after the preposition *iz* ("from inside of"), it is just the same. Thus, Aqua's suicide note is signed "My sister's sister who *teper' iz ada* ('now is out of hell')" (p. 29), and Aqua dies with the hope that she will go to Terra the Fair, to live amid "a rainbow mist of angelic spirits" (p. 21). So Ada refers to "Terra, where they say our souls go" (p. 158); the doctor says the dying Rack "would be on Terra, ha-ha, in time for evensong" (p. 317). To a certain extent such reference fits Ada and Van's love affair in Terran (nineteenth-century romantic) terms; the love of brother and sister being tinged on Earth with the rosy glow of damnation and hellfire, Van could therefore say, along with Chateaubriand's incestuous lovers, that he'd make a heaven of hell, and swear

> Flesh of my Flesh,
> Bone of my Bone thou art, and from thy State
> Mine never shall be parted, bliss or woe.[98]

Demonia can then be, to such a guilty pair, "hell on earth," with a distant Terra as heaven, but the Antiterran cosmology posits no third place as (true) hell. There is either no hell at all (only *Ad*, Hades, place of lost souls, that may be Terra), or whatever there is to hell is on Demonia itself. Could it be our own (Terran) hell?[99] That would make the identification Nabokov applies to Van and Ada something of a problem, but it would also fit not only the names and references mentioned so far but a puzzling passage early in the book, in which Van as author comments on the religious enthusiasm that gave "Terra" life as a febrile fancy of a next world, an afterlife, confused with the real world "in us and beyond us" (pp. 20–21), and states that "our" demon enchanters are handsome creatures with fine wings and claws, not to be confused with the loathsome devils, offset to the angels of Terra, urged by religion.[100] Can "Demon" Veen be anything but one of these splendid Antiterran enchanters, decried by the religious enthusiasts of the day (reversed Antiterran equivalents of the Russian Old Believers)? But if Demon, then why not Van? He is another Veen, with all the charm, sexual magnetism, and love of self-gratification of his father. Whether or not they fit the religionist characterization of the devils as given especially to the torment of females, it is certain that both father and son have a cruelly powerful effect on the women around them. Demon keeps Aqua in a state only charitably described as torment, and as for Van, our author tells us that any woman coming into his proximity was lost unless (like Ada) an offspring of his father—his nurse and Lucette, his cousin, both commit suicide; only Ada, his sister, can withstand him. And the Veens are, at least intermittently and/or metaphorically, winged: Van's Manhattan penthouse apartment is called by a friend "your wing à terre" (p. 366); Van comments on Lucette's "black wings" (p. 486); Demon sets out for the hospital where Dan is dying "eyes blazing, wings whistling" (p. 433, albeit in an airplane). Van's tantrum when Ada tries to get him to visit the grave of Dr. Krolik ("I abhor churchyards," p. 297) could as well be taken as suitable to a demonic nature.

But Van, or Van and Ada, are not so demonic, in our sense or theirs, such fallen angels, or merely such natives of Demonia, that they do not share more of a link to Terra than is suggested by their own partial doublings and their apparently conventional use of Terran reference in a half-joking tone. We suppose Van to be a leader in the hypothetical study of the unknown planet; he holds university positions in psychology and has a special interest in Terrology—a combination of philosophy and "the terrological part of psychiatry"; he publishes a book on Terra grounded in the information he has gleaned from the testimony of people for various reasons clairvoyant. But throughout he holds back from belief or discovery, or possibly revelation: He puts the book in fictional form, and he never completes his dissertation, "Terra: Eremitic Reality or Collective Dream" (p. 182). In the acme of his youthful passion for Ada, he suggests that they, in their incestuously unmarriageable and necessarily clandestine state, are like "secret agents from another country" (p. 264). Ada delightedly takes this as an admission of his belief in Terra, but he withdraws under the qualification that he accepts the existence of Terra only as "a state of mind." It is Lucette, the frustratedly observant younger, and excluded, lover, who makes the accusation that Van and Ada had been on Terra together during their secret lovemaking expeditions at Ardis, or uses the expression "you'd been on Terra" (p. 371) as an equivalent for "you've been making love paradisically." And when we have what looks like the sole appearance of Terrans on Antiterra in the book, the strange group of a dozen "elderly townsmen" who intrude upon the "grand picnic" held in the forest of Ardis to celebrate Ada's sixteenth birthday, Van is at a loss—he does not recognize them; he cannot communicate with them; he retires baffled.[101] Ada has little to contribute here; as the fellow spy and Demonian of heightened consciousness she seems no better off than Van. Knowledge of us, of our world, seems to elude them systematically. Is that a mirror reflection of the fact that knowledge of them eludes us, or a matter that can be clarified with information available on Antiterra? The separation of Earth and its twin, the world of Ada and Van, seems so hopelessly complete and yet so tantalizingly imprecise and variable. At one moment Terra is a matter for scornful reference as exploded myth, dematerialized fairy tale; at another it looms enormous and solid over the Antiterran horizon like a vast moon. Be that as it may, this separation may be founded on physical and psychological matters of near finality, on the basis of which we can decide that Terra and Antiterra not only do not touch each other, but never will.

One of these matters has been put by Einstein in the form of a little fable and made the subject of a pair of fascinating books, Edwin Abbott's *Flatland: A Romance of Many Dimensions* (1880), and Dionys Burger's *Sphereland: A Fantasy About Curved Spaces and an Expanding Universe* (1965). Einstein's fable pictures creatures living in one dimension, on a line.[102] Since their world is length only, they would know nothing but that line, and if they traveled along it they would decide that their world was infinite, since it went on forever. From the point of view of an added dimension, though, this is a pitiful little world—limited in fact to the line tracing a circle. The two-dimensional savants who made this discovery might themselves decide that their world was infinite, because it went on in "every" direction forever—but they could themselves only be living on a sphere. Could it be that we three-dimensional people are in the same situation with regard to a four-dimensional viewpoint? Our world goes on forever, as far as we can surmise, yet that is no indication that it is as we think it is. It could be like the circle to the one-dimensional existence and the sphere to the two-dimensional—"infinite" but finite, a finite space that also has no space beyond it.

Abbott's book and the sequel to it by Dionys Burger are essentially the same idea spun out into fictional story form, with people, animals, houses and—to a certain extent—passions and dreams in the worlds of different dimensions. There are incidents in both books that illustrate somewhat more fully, and with fictional relevance, concepts possibly at play in *Ada*. One such is that a gentleman in Flatland has the shape of a square, a lady a line, and a priest a circle, which makes them easily distinguishable from our point of view, but not from theirs, for theirs is two-dimensional and they are only visible to each other on their sides.[103] They have color, though, and color coding and a freedom of movement that enables them to interpret shapes as they turn. A square and a line moving at right angles to the observer might seem identical, but on turning to come at the observer the square would show another side, while the line would shrink to a point. A circle seen from any angle looks like a line in two dimensions, and when women take on the colors of the priests, the situation in figure 3 arises.

110 • *The Hole in the Fabric*

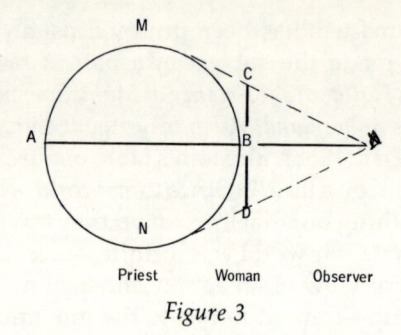

Figure 3

With AMB and CB, half each of the priest and the woman, red, and ANB and DB, the other half, green, there is a constant source of identity confusion that is both dangerous (to run into the pointed [tail] end of a woman causes puncture and death) and productive of social disorder until it is corrected.

Again, when the gentleman square of Flatland visits Lineland, where all is one-dimensional, he causes universal consternation by speaking while invisible and by taking leave into sudden invisibility after appearing to the Linelanders—as a dot. These situations are shown in figures 4a and 4b. In 4a, the Linelanders can accept the Flatlander as one of them, for he too appears as a line (from their point of view, a dot or point). But they have no conception of his real shape, nor any way of understanding it. He can cross and recross their line (as in 4c), take any position in their world, but to them he is always a point, just like any one of them. In 4b, he is a dematerialized voice, Hamlet Senior, a source of terror; when he

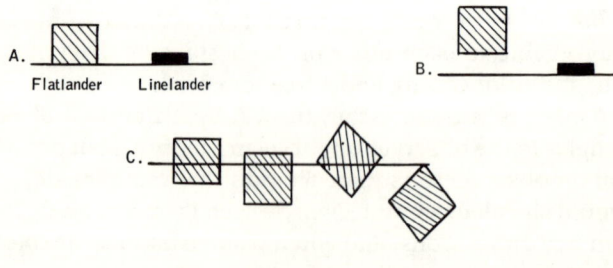

Figure 4

takes his leave and disappears, moving from a to b, they have no alternative but to decide, until he speaks, that he is dead. When he does speak, he appears to be in telepathic communication with them from another world.

The square, in turn, is put into the position of a Linelander when he is visited by a sphere (figure 5). When the sphere wishes to appear in Flatland, he allows its plane to intersect his being, as in figure 5a. There he appears identical to a typical Flatland circle, and his movements in the Flatland dimensions leave that appearance unaltered. But a movement on his part at right angles to the plane of Flatland (using the third dimension) causes a dramatic alteration in his size—it may become a point, as in 5b, which would be equivalent to a woman seen head on by a Flatlander, or a circle of varying diameter (a to c), and so forth.

In the story of *Sphereland*, the further concept of symmetry is introduced, the dogs in Flatland, for instance, being either mongrel (facing right) or pedigree (facing left). They are in all other respects

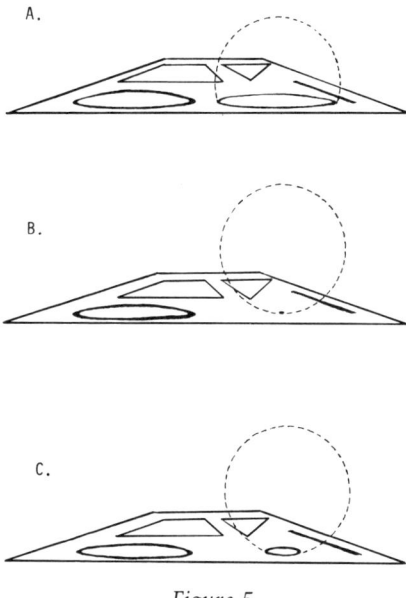

Figure 5

identical, but in their own world there is no way of making one into the other ("no matter how a mongrel is turned, he cannot be turned into a pedigreed dog!").[104] Unless the sphere lifts one of them into three-space, that is, and sets him down reversed, which makes him into the mirror image of what he was before (what he saw himself in the mirror as), mongrel if pedigree before, pedigree if mongrel before. A problem is that from the point of view of the one turned, be it dog or citizen, nothing has happened to him. Rather his world has changed, been reversed from left to right. If the king of the Linelanders were turned to face the other way on his line, he would only think that his world had turned around him. A reversal in individual being is in this geometrical sense too much of a change to be realized, and as such must be projected into the unchanged outer world. The hypothetical reversed Flatlander, Mr. Vertato ("turned about"), who has been turned through the (to him) inaccessible third dimension by a visiting sphere, finds nothing wrong with his handwriting when he goes to the office in the morning, but it turns out that his secretary cannot read it—to her, but not to him, it is reversed.

This problem—From whose point of view are you speaking?—applies not only to the Einsteinian clock paradox, where it is soluble, but to the question of heaven and hell as well. In Sartrean terms, how do we know we are not in hell, here on Terran Earth? Or could it be we are in heaven? Unless it be granted that there exists what no Flatlander, butterfly, or human can be demonstrated to have, consciousness of more than one state of being at once, there is no way for us to know, or for him to know, that he has undergone a metamorphosis. That is, from our point of view, unless he writes for us! We could tell a heavenly being, were he to enter our world, by his capacity to change his shape at will, to see beyond us and around us, and to partake of a being in space and time denied to us ("immortality" having the pragmatic meaning "not tied to our clock time"; "heavenly being" as well being equivalent to "being not tied to our existence in space and time"). But we cannot speak for him, or the feeling he may have of being equally outstripped by creatures in other, further, modes of being, denied to him and putting him in our place—a Terran hell opposed to a hypothetical heaven.

Einstein and Abbott and Burger do not enable us to see through all the mystery surrounding *Ada*'s world-antiworld, but they do enable us to see that Van and Ada are in "our" heaven but do not know it, for they succumb to the temptation of placing "their" heaven in a further dimension that they cannot reach.[105] Their Antiterra is Flatland to them; but we can see, from our deprivation, that it is Earth as it might have been, should have been had the Industrial Revolution not gone wrong, causing by its uncontrolled expansion the revolutions of 1905 and 1917, the rise of fanatic nation-states, a half-century of terror, totalitarianism, and devastating war. On Antiterra none of the mistakes of Terra are made; each time the concentration of energy reaches the danger point it is defused, set back, by a partial dismantling of technology. Nevertheless its inhabitants tease themselves with the concept of heaven, unable to see that they are in it, or at least another dimension along toward it.

Besides this possibility of a difference in dimension separating Terra from Antiterra, there is also the possibility of a difference in the structure of matter on each planet, a difference parallel to mirror reversal. The matter we know on Earth is composed of atoms with positively charged nuclei, their unit the proton, and one or more negatively charged electrons. The proton is "heavy" (having a mass 1,840 times that of the electron) and positive in charge; the electron is "light" and negative in charge. The asymmetry here indicated between mass and charge would be balanced or canceled if these particles had mirror twins of reversed qualities—a light particle with positive charge, and a heavy one with negative charge. In 1932 the first of these was discovered and named the positron, and in 1955 the Berkeley accelerator gave evidence for the second, the antiproton.[106] If a particle of ordinary matter collides with one of this reversed or "anti" matter, they mutually annihilate each other. Put another way, antimatter has little chance of existing inside our "world of matter" (whose boundaries are unknown) because its contact with matter would destroy it instantaneously, along with the matter it came into contact with. In a state of isolation from matter, however, antimatter is simply matter of reversed charge and can hypothetically exist as normally as matter does for us: Antiwater would be as wet as water, antisnow as white as snow, anticarbon and antihydrogen capable of combining to form the whole range of molecules, plant and animal life that we know on Earth. An antisun would shine the same way as the sun; the planets circling it would be antiplanets, "normal" in every way except that they would instantly vaporize any body or being reaching them from a universe or planet composed of matter.

On the small basis of the fact of existence of reversed particles, a large amount of cosmological—as well as philosophical—speculation can be imposed. As Thomas Gold of the Cornell Center for Radiophysics and Space Research puts it:

If there is no law of physics that can distinguish matter from antimatter in an absolute fashion, then the perfect symmetry of matter and antimatter implies that we have no way of defining which of two possible kinds of universes we live in. The description of our universe should not involve the statement that there are two different possible universes and that we happen to live in one of them. As we cannot make a distinction between the two kinds of universes, we describe only what our epistemological position allows.[107]

How do you tell Tweedledum from his brother? If you live on Antiterra, how do you know it is Antiterra you live on and not the Terra you imagine to be elsewhere but opposite?

Again, Hannes Alfvén notes, "Assuming that antimatter exists in some part of the universe, we feel convinced that it would contain a world similar to our own";[108] this might be said to follow in the same way that it follows to have a mirror image of oneself. It *is* possible, as Gardner speculates, that "antimatter is nothing more than ordinary matter with its entire space-time structure down to the last detail, reversed as by a looking glass"—a looking-glass image very dangerous to come into contact with. Gardner cites a suitable picture from C. H. Hinton's description of symmetrical charges in matter:

115 • *Time and the Visible World*

We must conceive that in our world there were to be for each man somewhere a counter man, a presentment of himself, a real counterfeit, outwardly fashioned like himself, but with his right hand opposite his original's right hand. Exactly like the image of the man in a mirror. And then when the man and his counterfeit meet, a sudden whirl, a blaze, a little steam, and the two human beings, having mutually unwound each other, leave nothing but a residuum of formless particles.[109]

There is a well-established but distant literary analogue to this imagined physical process in the homosexual and heterosexual pairs, often lovers and always twins or very similar, brothers and sisters, of European romantic fiction. They form the pedigree of Ada and Van, who, in the conventional moral terms of society, are bent upon each other's destruction. Their "unwinding," or undoing, is a matter of incestuous love, that ecstatic union that plunges its communicants hellward. But is their world so opposed to its heavenly twin? Here we see several themes brought together: the double ("other"), the existence on separate time tracks, matter and antimatter, and mirror reversal. In those *Doppelgänger* narratives, like Poe's *William Wilson*, Hawthorne's *Monsieur de Miroir*, or Dostoevski's *The Double*, the narrator and his twin travel for some time along parallel paths, to the narrator's wonder and distress, the "other" being either his conscience, his good half, or the opposite, a satanic temptation come to steal his soul, and in either case a "supernatural" entity. Then their paths converge and come into direct opposition. There is a violent discharge or *undoing*, generally the death or disappearance of both figures.

In Nabokov there is a good deal of such twinning, most directly in *Pale Fire*, but also in *Despair*, where a false twin is constructed by a deranged protagonist, and to some extent in *Lolita*, where a mad Humbert and an equally mad Quilty revolve as two antithetical "planetary" wanderers about the doomed sun represented by the girl, meeting, or colliding, at the end to bring about each other's death. In *Pale Fire*, the mirror and the theme of self-destruction are most directly employed: The hero has one being, or disguise, in the world we know, and another, possibly imaginary, in the reflected world of *Zembla* (semblance). He moves from Zembla into our world but finds himself pursued here by the reversed image of what was there faithful Gradus, worker in glass and crystal (and maker of mirrors), here the evil Sudarg, dedicated killer. The reversed nature extends to other members of his terrorist organization, "for example, Nodo, Odon's [Odon is a loyal citizen] epileptic half-brother who cheated at cards, or a mad Mandevil who had lost a leg in trying to make *anti-matter*"; and it may be that it dooms Gradus from the start—in a mirror image, he "is to meet, in his urgent and blind flight, a reflection that will shatter him."[110] The murder is bungled, may indeed have been committed by someone else pursuing a man whom the hero greatly *resembles*, and the hero ends by suicide, taking over the job of destroying himself.

In Henry James's work the double has much the same existence, an existence that again derives from European romanticism. In *The Jolly Corner*, as we have noted, the double is the hero as he would have been had he remained in one of two worlds, the unknown one, represented by the New York of aggressive materialism he left as a young man for Europe. On his return many years later, the double represents a physical threat to him, and their meeting in the old family house on the jolly corner is fraught with danger for the hero, who must seek out, see, and know, risking at the same time the unraveling that physical antipathy can effect. He sees, realizes the nature of his enemy, and loses consciousness. But he survives and is free to assert his identity and power by ordering the old house to be torn down—so that he may construct a profitable apartment house on its site. Which leaves us with the question, Whose identity does he have?

In *Pale Fire*, one of the central images of the double enmity and danger is that of a game of chess. The hero is, or was, or imagines himself to have been, king in Zembla; he compares himself to *solus rex*, the endangered and unprotected king on the chessboard. But the name he takes in our world is Kinbote, which means, we are told, "king murderer." In other words, as we may reconstruct the game, although Kinbote is playing defensively, as king in flight, the king across the board is himself, too (the two sides of the chessboard are mirror reflections of each other). There are no other kings but Kinbote, king in exile, and Kinbote in his former avatar of king of Zembla, Charles the Beloved. So no matter how the game ends, as long as it is not a draw, the hero will be involved in the going down of one part of himself. Winning a game of chess is by "checkmate," a folk-etymologized form of the Persian phrase applied to the same situation, *shah mat*, "the king is dead." Ernest Jones, in a 1930 study of the career of the American chess master, Paul Morphy, advanced the theory that this questing for the death of the king in chess is a concealed form of attack on the father and a reflection of a wish for his death.[111] Chess is satisfying to a certain kind of mind (the "anal-sadistic") because it is complete, final, and yet socially approved. If the winner can derive satisfaction from a murder at such a symbolic distance from the real act of murdering his own father, he finds himself well served inside an activity that gains, in many parts of the world, the highest approval. With whatever skepticism we may wish to treat the good doctor's hypothetical and doggedly Freudian analysis of the unfortunate Morphy, long dead by 1930, and Rimbaud-like in his meteoric rise followed by an abrupt decline into obscurity, we can accept the idea that a game is a way of adumbrating, and even working out to a state of empathic fulfillment, acts of violence. In a game like football the symbolic violence and that which it shadows forth are so close as to be difficult to separate, and in many other games also called sports there is a possibility of doing real physical harm. In bridge or *go* or chess, however, the physical imitation of violence dwindles away completely (you do not touch, often do not even look at, your opponent, and there is no tool used in the game with which you can touch him), and patterns of abstract, intellectualized violence are the only ones that can exist.

For all Nabokov's apparent fascination with chess, he has never gone so far as to put the violence of his plots entirely within such an abstract pattern—a pattern as abstract, say, as that of *The Jolly Corner*. *The Defense*, a novel that pits a grand master of the game whose mind is deteriorating against unknown enemies, comes the closest among Nabokov's works; but at the end, Nabokov inserts a sudden shift back to physical reality and has the hero fall to his death from a high window. And there are not many other writers who have experimented with the chess metaphor, despite the fact that it has great heuristic value for this struggle with the double in postromantic terms. Besides the work of Nabokov, Lewis Carroll, and a few others, there is not enough literary background to refer to as a given or parameter. It is necessary to go outside conventional fiction for clear examples of what might be done—the example I have in mind is a chapter called "A Game of Chess" in an unusual work of literary criticism, *Words in the Mind*, by Charles Davy. Davy tells of a childhood friend, the school chess champion, describing to him his thoughts as he played the game. The champion first described the pieces as having, in his mental view of the board, tail-like appendages that indicated their possible moves onto other squares. These appendages formed a network of lines of force, a map of possible moves that Davy calls a "relations-pattern." The boy's concentration upon it became so acute that he would lose all sight of the physical board, moving over into a pure contemplation of the abstraction, where the mystery was laid out before him. At one critical point in a game he lost consciousness, falling back into the arms of Davy, and never played again; for from that experience he developed a fear that he would go over into the relations-pattern one day and be unable to return. He would be "abstracted."[112]

There is a parallel here to the mirror story: The land through the mirror brings knowledge and power not obtainable here, and sometimes an inner knowledge of the workings of things on this side, but there is a danger that once there, fully across into the other world, perhaps antiworld, you will find it impossible to return. The idea so teasingly advanced by Tweedledum and Tweedledee, that the Red King's awakening from his dream will cause Alice to disappear, since he is dreaming of her (*Through the Looking-glass*, chapter 4), is a humorous example; the danger the visionary feels, that it would be as easy for him to return never as to return before the water in the pitcher has evaporated a drop, is less humorous and has become an equally real threat to those contemporary visionaries who set off on chemically induced voyages—take too long a trip, embark on an orbit more cometary than planetary, and you do not get back, at least not within your own lifetime. Finally, it is the Faustian dilemma: If you post your soul as bond for a journey through all times and places and a knowledge of the inner workings of things, how can you be certain you will be able to reclaim it, along with your original time and place, at the end?

This doubt results in a *fear* of the other, or other side, something naturally analogous to the threat posed by the other side of the chessboard, the game opponent who shadowly embodies the assailant. The antipathies of *Ada* seem to embody it: It is Aqua on Antiterra, with her vision of Terra, who commits suicide; it is from the insane and hospitalized that Van gathers his notes on Terra. We may consider that Terra and Antiterra can never come together, finally, in the same way that the man in the mirror can never meet his double, one side of the chessboard become the other, the chess player enter the abstract field of relations behind the board, matter meet antimatter, or past time meet future time. Ever *physically* meet or come together, that is; that *Ada* makes a claim for a subtler connection is made most probable by a chess reference, admittedly in the supersubtle mode, in the scene of reunion between Van and Lucette at Kingston University in 1892a. Lucette wishes to draw Van's attention to a remembered desk at Ardis, whose secret spring, when pressed, shot open a hidden drawer (the whole is a metaphor of inducing female orgasm). Her curiosity over it was doubly aroused because it stood by a closet in which Van and Ada locked her on more than one occasion, under the pretense of play, so that they could escape her observation of their lovemaking; in Lucette's terms, they locked her up when they went together to Terra. The way to Terra was, in this case, managed by finding the spring that released the drawer, and in the drawer, which Van professes to remember as "empty," was "a minuscule red pawn" (p. 374), that is, on the one hand the clitoris, on the other the changeling of the chessboard (Alice is a pawn until she is changed into a queen), and a hint of the invisible world (does the caterpillar know of the butterfly?).

Now the dimension of time is naturally adapted to fit such conceptualization. We all know, and most of us feel, the attraction of a visit to the past or the future as a key to knowledge and power, whether it be so trivial as to look at the racing results in tomorrow's newspaper and then return to place bets accordingly, or so profound as to answer the question Borges poses in one of his stories, whether Christ really died on the cross. A visit to "the other side" by means of a time shift is most often less abstract than the view through the chessboard, but that is not necessarily true; and it is probable that time is most commonly used (clearly enough in memory) as the permeable dimension to bring together what we have just described as physically un-unifiable. In the spiritual sense, time is the least concrete and most frangible of barriers; this applies as well to *Ada* as to any other novel in the large modern literature of psychological time.

Time in the planetary sense seems in general as forbidding a barrier as those of matter and reflection; if there were, for instance, antimatter planets twin to planets of matter, it is possible that the time of the antimatter planet would be reversed with respect to that of the matter planet.[113] Then a message from one to the other could never be returned, for the answer would go into the past of the sender. Nabokov specifies no such reversal; insofar as he specifies at all, he encourages us to believe that Terra and Antiterra move in the same time direction, fifty to one hundred years apart. Such a gap can be, of course, just as impassable a boundary as a reversed direction in time. When it is associated with the possibility of Terra being less physical than metaphysical, a situation arises quite parallel to one imagined by Samuel Taylor Coleridge in his "Time, Real and Imaginary":

> On the wide level of a mountain's head,
> (I knew not where, but 'twas some fairy place)
> Their pinions, ostrich-like, for sails outspread,
> Two lovely children run an endless race,
>   A sister and a brother!
>   That far outstripped the other;
> Yet ever runs she with reverted face,
> And looks and listens for the boy behind:
>   For he, alas! is blind!
> O'er rough and smooth with even step he passed,
> And knows not whether he be first or last.

This is subtitled "an Allegory"; its terms are presumably that the girl, who runs ahead with clear (if reverted) sight, is Time real ("real" in God's sense, ideal in ours), heavenly Time, the Platonic ideal, the time of the inner workings of the universe. These workings are unknown to man, who gropes blindly; he is as a child —more childish and pathetic, though, in that he is blind. He cannot see what he pursues: Though he goes forward "with even step" (the regular intervals of man's time), he can only intuit by indirect evidence (the evidence we have in the world of time's arrow). We are sure of the reality of the "Time" we imagine, but we are incapable of describing it with surety and finality, even after over a century of dizzying scientific progress since Coleridge's day.[114]

Without making an attribution of influence of Coleridge on Nabokov, we may fairly use this poem as an analogue to *Ada*, I think, if we entertain the possibility that *Ada* itself is an allegory of time, or at least partly allegorical, in that its characters may be used to represent not only their fictional beings, but intellectual concepts as well. We may then see the "fairy place" of line 2 as Demonia, the imaginary planet Nabokov must specify to give himself an observation point, an ideal from which to view the real, a metareality—as Coleridge gives himself with his "wide level of a mountain's head." The sister and brother are Ada and Van, winged in Nabokov as in Coleridge so that they may be both human and more than human. We meet Ada and Van as "two lovely children" at the beginning of their narrative, which is in turn an "endless race" on the part of the brother to capture the sister, on the part of Van to capture (literally, recapture after losing) Ada. Ada, the ideal, the beloved, in being eager for that pursuit and that prospect of capture, runs looking backward, watching and listening. The backward look is in one sense the look into the past, the look back to the idyll of their childhood love; while Van holds this image as well, he is the pursuer, the longer-after. He is "blind" in that he does not know the ideal along with the real; the full picture is not open to him. He pursues knowledge of Terra, which is real in the sense discussed earlier, that it is *us*, but cannot reach and grasp it beyond the fragmentary and unreliable testimony of visionaries and lunatics. Ada shares his interest in Terra but not his efforts. Her research is confined to butterflies; she rests secure, we may imagine, in possession of either the knowledge he seeks or in a feminine quiet assurance of inner knowledge. Van *catches* Ada at the end of the novel, but he can never catch the ideal (with its special reality), for it is always ahead of him by being locked in the past. Thus, the race is endless. When he finally grasps the remembered reality, it has become something else (the Coleridgean schoolboy's vacation, when it finally comes, cannot be just the dream he constructed out of past vacations); the remembered body has grown plump and corseted, and he doubts his own potency. So when, in *Lolita,* the remembered body is found, another person is inhabiting it.

Those of Van's researches not concerned with Terra (which I am here using as equivalent to the image of Ideal Time) are concerned with time in its own terms. The two studies are linked in that to entertain the concept of a Terra involves for the Antiterran theorist the difficulty of explaining a chronological "crossroads" where past and future markers, like scrambled road signs, overlap. This difficulty is so great that it is abandoned to the deranged mind for solution. The "crossroads" is very possibly a reference to the crossing lines of relativistic time inside Minkowski space, commonly shown as in figure 1 (p. 77), between "past," "future," and "elsewhere." While the "now" of the left-hand, Newtonian diagram extends throughout all space, the "now" here is at the crossroads, with no determined relation to any other point in space-time. Here the "no-longers" and the "not-yets" of any two places are not all the same; if the places are distant enough, none are the same. From the point of view of Demonia, Terra is "elsewhere" and not capable of the same "now."

The impulse for Van's study of time is given both by his loss of Ada and by the loss of Aqua, his presumed mother, who describes her suicide (in a note addressed to her husband and to her son) as an attempt to know what even the hands of a clock must know, "where they stand" (p. 29). Reading that note, Van determines that a life well lived is one that gets "life's sundial to show its hand" (p. 29); similarly, when cogitating with Ada whether he and she might have been borne past each other, either in parallel or in crossing paths along the Riviera in 1881a, by respective tutors and governesses, Van is drawn into an intellectual snarl of time-space and space-time relations (p. 153). It is noticeable that Van here sees time and space combined, and both in the perspective of death: He views the past as a "mirror-lined" maze where the paths (time tracks) cross with or without contact (in the same space frame, or different); by the time of his showdown with the rival suitors of Ada, in 1884a, he uses time and space to deny death, allowing a spot of limited space equivalent to the being of a man, but not an equivalent in limited time, for from that little space the narrow slot between past and future extends infinitely in a laterally extended present. This gives the basis for Van's mature speculations as we see them developed in his books and lectures and aging thoughts: the refusal of a time-space analogy, which develops into his denial of a time-space relationship; the equivalence of time to human awareness of time; and the assertion of such awareness as the basis for immortality.

In this last, Van's thoughts merge with Dunne's claim of personal immortality on the basis, roughly, of the fact of human awareness of time, the human capacity to view it from above and beyond, the "beyond" taking the concrete form of accurate vision of future events in dreams or states of heightened consciousness. Dunne saw no reason to link such consciousness to the physical and limited existence of the human body (Van's "space"). In the Jamesian sense, Dunne constructed a religion of consciousness, for he used human consciousness, specifically its moments of finest, metaphysical (metatemporal) awareness, to arrive at the central time doctrine of Christianity, personal immortality, without the help of that or any other religious framework, revelation, or the agency of a divine being. Like James and Nabokov, he replaced religion (faith) with awareness, or faith in awareness. Van cites Dunne on the matter of the capacity of dreams to break out of linear time, their time, by a precognitive "reverse memory" (p. 361). Van's own experience is marked as well by glimpses, hints, revelations, of nonlinear paths of time that amount to separate existences (comparable to those in Borges's *Garden of Forking Paths*), "time forks" flirted with, rather than pushed to the nightmare horror of self-revelation of James's *Jolly Corner*, that lend support both to Van's view of the insubstantiality of space and the capacity of the human mind, along with the human *being*, to deploy or to dominate time.

These narrative forks look like minor errors, wrinkles in the folded carpet of fiction (an image Nabokov takes from James), when they are left unexplored; an example is the 1884a farewell to Ada, which Van effects by leaving the butler Bouteillan with the car and plunging into the forest at a prearranged spot, beyond which the girl waits. The farewell over, he returns, not to car and butler, but to horse and groom, and gallops off. In the passion of the moment Van moves himself into a more romantic setting, or a more romantic time. The shift is not one of space; Bouteillan does not wait *now* with the car "in another part of the forest"; the place, the Forest Park, is the same, so the "fork" is one of time. The principle is clearer in other examples. It is effectively *stated* when Van, determined to commit suicide when his relationship to Ada has been discovered and he has lost her "forever," loads his pistol, puts it to his head and squeezes the trigger—at which he finds the pistol is a comb and he is alive, having either left or entered a dream state, as well as a fork, that the author informs us is only one of many that stems from the "dream-mind" (p. 446). The "dream-mind" is both that of Dunne's traveling time-2 observer, and the mind of the artist—like Tolstoy with his alternative endings to *The Devil*, Nabokov is offering here an alternative, tragic ending to the story of Ada and Van, with a double suicide. The dream concept gives a general background of interchange of realities, the experienced or "lived" reality and "unreality," or dreamed reality, a formula most consistently applied to fiction before—at least in English—by Lewis Carroll. On his 1888a return to Ardis, Van does not recognize Cordula de Prey when she greets him and tells her they are *both* dreaming; after a conversation with Ada over the lovers each has had and a bad dream about sordid betrayals he lies dozing at thè poolside with the thought "was he dreaming now that he had been dreaming?" (p. 198). When this summer comes to a tragic end with the sordid betrayals become "real," Van leaves the house half in a dream of desired death in an Alpine avalanche, finding himself now skiing in a snowstorm, now descending the staircase. Ada catches him up, to tell him of her dream, that they were in the Alps together.

The dream element and the fork in time are brought together by the assertive, creative force of the mind of Van as character and as author. Dreams, like everything else in literature, are finally a matter of language, of words and word associations; and from the point of view of the author as arranger of words, an alternative event or a fork in chronology is a matter comparable to a slip of the tongue or pen—in the terms Van uses when he sees Lucette unexpectedly at the Hotel Alphonse IV in Paris in 1901a, comparable to "something replayed by mistake, part of a sentence misplaced on the proof sheet, . . . a wrong turn of time" (p. 460). It is to be expected, therefore, that Van, like his creator (we presume), dreams about words; playing the alphabet game ("Flavita") gives him a chance to glimpse "the lining of time." In 1888a he falls asleep on the library divan reading Rattner on Terra, just as the butler touches the globe, which is dusty, and complains of the lazy and shiftless maid Blanche—she must be sent away. Van sleepily translates the butler's remark to get "The world is dusty," adding to it a visual image of Blanche wiping the globe where the butler touched it, and in his overlap of dream state and real state he is led to reflect upon "the confusion of two realities, one in single, the other in double, quotes" (pp. 231–32) as a symptom of impending insanity. This is parallel to Barth's "Menelaiad," with deepening layers of quotes (fictional artifice) marking deepening layers of illusive reality.[115] So he cries out to Ada in suspicion and despair upon her return a short while later, and to her reply, "What?," answers with a single-quote speech inside his own double quotes, taking a refuge in literature from his literary reality. He speculates that dreams are randomized restaging of the past, grotesque and only intermittently plausible, as he recasts the women he embraces in the years of separation from Ada into Ada herself.

The literary quality is heightened by the fact that Van writes himself—about time for the most part—and muses over his writing in a fashion that underlines the interchangeable character of fictional reality and irreality: If he were blocked by traffic on the way to a lecture, he reflects, he need only alter his manuscript where it refers to the density of the traffic. In his dreams, Van gets the freedom in and control over his life that his creator has over him. So Nabokov ends his book with Van working over the manuscript of his book, stating that his hero and heroine, flat-lying, racked by time, would go, if they needed another world of afterlife, into an Eden or a Hades composed of the text of their own book or the text of its blurb. Their red pencil corrections on the text look infernal; they lie flat in making love and in that they are Flatlanders both in a special sense, being on Antiterra, and a universal sense, being like all of us denied the full vision of the divine completeness and multidimensionality; Rack is the name of the musician who broke things up between them.

Van's own Antiterran time theory shows this composition and direction tendency (similar to the requirement made upon the reader by Alain Robbe-Grillet in such novels as *Marienbad* and *Maison de Rendez-vous* that he select and compose, as Van does among his dreams and forks in time), along with another kind of literary quality, that of the celebration of time-in-memory and the Proustian "time captured" or capturable of the moment of heightened experience. The idyllic summer of 1884a at Ardis, in which he and Ada discover and merge into each other, is that large spot of time that Van labors the rest of his life to re-create. Suspended between this ideal past, in which, as a boy, he held and possessed his beloved Ada, and the doubtful future, which holds only an uncertain hope of recovering an Ada who will no longer be the child he loved but an aging woman, and which holds finally death, Van chooses to build his time theory on an insistence on the sole reality of time in the present (a present built on the past, as we have seen, or a present expandable to include those moments of the past which are privileged and from which one derives one's being). He tells Lucette with abrupt certainty that "time . . . is motionless and changeless" (p. 482); in the carriage, you and the carriage remain still while the roads move. Clocks, as external to the reality of lived life as roads and stones, are therefore meaningless. This time, "individual, perceptual" (p. 536), naturally allows an individual and perceptual denial of death—"That I know others die is irrelevant to the case" (p. 535)—since denial of the clock's fictitious universal moment denies at the same time the necessity of a universal chronology. By the heightened present of his theory Van can claim he has "given new life to Time by cutting off Siamese Space and the false future."

In Van's contempt for space, the rejection of "the artificial concept of space-tainted, space-parasited time, the space-time of relativist literature" (p. 541), we can hardly find a basis for interpretation, in its own terms, of a book that takes as its setting a puzzle of space, the alternate or dual existence of Antiterra and Terra. Its assertion of an independent time is an unconscious Newtonianism, quite insufficient to the larger (authorial) scheme of reality. This makes Van an "unreliable narrator," for, as Einstein put it, "the four-dimensional mode of consideration of the 'world' is natural to the theory of relativity, since according to this theory time is robbed of its independence."[116] Van is here finally as trapped in a partial perspective as he is in his cumulative disparagement, in his old age, of the nature and reality of the twin planet about which he as a young man actively speculated. While his time theory applies quite well to other Nabokovian books and thus can be imagined as close to Nabokov's own, its concomitant rejection of what we contemporary Terrans know to be a fact, our own existence in a space-time matrix, and its preference for a personalized Newtonian model, reveal its inadequacy. We presume Nabokov himself to know about Flatland and Terra, but we find that he keeps the information well concealed.

Thus, the main philosophical speculation of *Ada*, and its hero's consciousness, are represented by a time theory that seems much the same as that of Proust, heightened in its unrealistic aspects by an almost obsessive insistence on the hero's part that the "lost" time was never lost at all, that Ardis and his romanticized incestuous idyll were anything but what we as readers know them to be, with or without the warning given by other works of Nabokov like *Speak, Memory*, suffering from so clearly parallel an idealization of a lost past of country *estates* (a pun Nabokov should recognize), servants, governesses, horses, and grooms, all in a state of enforced suspension preventing progress onward to industrialization, class warfare, and revolution. Van's time philosophy, "Veen's time," fits in with all else mentioned so well that it makes Van as a character unappealing, to say the least—his totally self-centered existence (his interest in Ada can hardly be called altruistic, any more than Humbert's in *Lolita* can be; Van would have her if he had to destroy her in the process), his pursuit of pleasure at all times, his life of savoring expensive pleasures. Veen's time is the time lived by Walter in *My Secret Life*, being in effect another tie to the element of Victorian pornography in *Ada*. Van's refusal to relate to any other time but the present he himself is experiencing is of a piece with his refusal, and his lack of need, insulated as he is by money and social position, to relate to other people, places, or affairs that he does not choose to allow to concern him. Van's thinking is a perfect example of what the psychologist John Cohen has posited as a type given to a long-range "mirror effect" in psychological time, in that "there is a sense in which one's psychological future mirrors one's subjective past. In this sense, the further ahead one looks, the more the vision of a millennium resembles the golden age of a mythical past."[117] The mirror doublings of *Ada* relate to time seen in such a perspective:

> Alice! A childish story take,
>   And, with a gentle hand,
> Lay it where Childhood's dreams are twined
>   In Memory's mystic band.
> Like pilgrim's wither'd wreath of flowers
>   Pluck'd in a far-off land.[118]

Whether Ada and Van exist in a reflected present here, apart, and are together there, in a reflected past, the past and present corresponding to a real Terra and an imagined Antiterra, or a real Antiterra and an imaginary (in the Berkeleyan sense) Terra, the key source is childhood. Whether it be Van or Vladimir writing the oneiric celebration of the last page of *Ada*, Van come into a realization more suitable to an author than to a character, or Vladimir extending his various elbow-nudges of this parody-blurb-that-is-also-a-blurb, it makes little difference in the end.

At this time it may be pointed out that there is in literary theme the same type of economy that Claude Lévi-Strauss has found in society and Noam Chomsky in language: No matter how complex and superficially variant structures may appear, they derive from a finite core—finite and potentially markable. Here is Lévi-Strauss quoting from a myth of the Andaman islanders in the conclusion to his *Structures Elémentaires de la Parenté*:

> The future life will be but a repetition of the present, but all will then remain in the prime of life, sickness and death will be unknown, and there will be no more marrying or giving in marriage.[119]

The basic elements noted are those of most all projected "after" lives—freedom from care, disease, and the threat of death. It is entirely different from the life we lead, but necessarily very much alike, too—if it were not recognizably our own life again, it would have no link to us sufficient to make it an ideal (for this reason, Buddhists demonstrate little interest in the actual conditions, the physical feel, of their future lives in metempsychosis, by the very fact of the transition without memory into another body and another being). Therefore paradise loses its appeal, both literary and psychological, if it is too rarefied and abstract; if we are to have the world again, it must be our world, the same only "in the prime of life," we must not have disease, pain, and death, but we must have life.

We are now ready to see that the "after" part of afterlife is something outside the finite core, which itself contains only the necessities—to be alive without the dangers and trouble of life, to be without fear, to be secure, to have and not to want. The space-time location of this life is part of the surface complexity, infinitely variable. But *it is the same thing*. It cannot be two things at once, of course; at one time, for one derivation, either literary or cultural, a single path to surface structure must be taken—to the afterlife, to the anterior life, or to one of the parallel lives, to speak in the time dimension. James's *Sense of the Past* deals with the anterior life, the mounting of the stream of time within one's gens, to live in the body of an ancestor; Well's *Time Machine* deals with afterlife, in the sense of speeding downstream to the final periods of the whole human gens; Nabokov's *Ada*, like his less ambitious *Pale Fire*, depicts parallel lives of the same consciousness, or the same person. In each case there is no corresponding alternative life in another time dimension. That is, you may believe in a heavenly reward in a Christian sense, but you may not concurrently believe in metempsychosis or Platonic transmigration or in the idea that you have an antimatter twin whose path is converging with yours. Multiple belief of this type is *possible*, but almost never noted, owing to the economy of the structure. The elemental mirror-yearning in us all, we might say, seeks ideal structures, but only one at a time. Our faulty life here will be redone, but without faults, in the hereafter, ideally mirrored in the future, or it is now being mirrored by imaginative duplicate creation (the marriage of souls), or by . . . and so forth.

A writer may, of course, re-create any belief or conception he wants, but he too has a natural, system-dictated tendency to re-create one at a time; and to vary the ideal content, as we do ourselves. We can imagine the new life of the future to be either a heaven or a hell, and that the alternation is dictated by certain acts committed in this dimension; we can conjure up twin life, that of the mirror directly gazed upon, as a source of terror as well as an entry into and area of experience and knowledge that doubles what we have. There is probably no accidental connection between fictions such as James's and Nabokov's and the general collapse of the Christian world view in this century; speaking in structural terms we can say that the Christian view has been regenerated or rederived from deep structure into concepts like Antiterra, the Sirens of Titan, and the Sense of the Past, to give us back in a framework of twentieth-century physics and astronomy what we had in one of tenth-century metaphysics and astrology, and lost.

In a certain sense, the derivable conclusion of *Ada* is a disappointment, disappointingly literary. The book folds into itself, the characters Van and Ada die, if they do die, "into the finished book," a solipsism that fits uncomfortably well the modernist fascination with mirror literature, novels that are being written as they are told, fruitless games along the lines of *The Counterfeiters* and *Point Counter Point* in which we never get beyond the easily amazing discovering of the unreality of unreality. Nabokov, like James, takes refuge in a metaphysical silence. Nabokov's silence is annoying in a way that James's is not, because Nabokov seems to toy with approaches to answers and to discard solutions frivolously, or fly in the face of those solutions, like relativistic time and the relation of space and time, that are offered by the contemporary world view. But Nabokov's very teasing makes his book put the matter—the possibility—of multiple worlds into the serious novel just as Milton put it into the English epic poem; while James's use of a science-fiction trope for its dramatic possibilities, without open consideration of its metaphysical consequences, stops short of the same impact.

Ada's presiding scientific philosopher, Martin Gardner, makes an apt quotation from Ludwig Wittgenstein in his *Ambidextrous Universe*, to the effect that "the solution of the riddle of life in space and time lies outside space and time" (p. 149). This is the same old problem that Dunne demonstrated with his picture of the artist painting a picture containing an artist painting a picture, Archimedes with his call for a place to stand, Velasquez by looking puzzlingly out at us from among his royal subjects in *Los Niños*, the problem of analyzing language using language. You cannot treat a concept from inside it; you need a metaspace, a metatime, a metalanguage—in all cases, a position outside the frame. In a sense, *The Sense of the Past* gives us a metatime, or certainly the movement inside time that makes you aware of the frame and the need to get out of it; *Ada* attempts to give us metatime and, in spite of all inner disclaimers, metaspace. This is not of itself the answer, though; it is just the place from which, or the time in which, the answer can come. For who, after all, could give the whole answer in this early stage of the development of knowledge, even with the extrasensory help of the artistic imagination?

CHAPTER SEVEN
The Erotic

The Awkward Age *and* Lolita

In *Ada*, as well as in other Nabokov novels, such as *Lolita*, where the hero is the "father" of the girl he loves, there appears another theme out of the romantic tradition: the erotic titillation derivable from incest. Making love to one closely related, forbidden in almost all societies, still retains a powerful shock value, as well as an iconoclastic thrill. It is an act among very few that combines physical innocuousness—even innocence—with a generalized effect of *damnation*. When the reader is presented with it, he feels something like "that's it, they're doomed now"; a border has been crossed that is like dying or the loss of virginity, in that there is no known way to recross it, or undo what has been done. It is a tribute to the power of sexual taboo that incest is certainly more powerful an act than murder in this aspect of unforgivability, although murder, in both literature and life, is its closest rival. For murder, while physically the *ne plus ultra*, remains a social necessity of sorts under various names—execution, military action, crime-fighting, and so forth. Novels written to construct elaborate scenarios in which it is justifiable are always popular—witness James Dickey's *Deliverance*.

But incest is not allowed any such defense, social utility being built into its prohibition rather than available as a justification. The forbidding of related women leaves them free for use as gifts to unrelated men, the combination of exogamy and incest taboo assuring regular outward ties and the adaptive basis of a society, according to at least one anthropological theory.[120] The human social need may perhaps be imagined as great enough to explain some of the unconscious or preconscious force exerted by the taboo; otherwise, on the conscious level, modern man, as a citizen of a superstate, might well contest such social utility. There is at the same time, and even today, a widespread belief that children born of incest are monsters, half-wits, and so forth—"fruits of incest." This remains a potent supplement to the fear of bastards.

The change in contemporary sexual attitudes has almost necessarily changed the view of incest as well, though to nothing like the degree it has changed the view of intercourse otherwise irregular, like premarital or adulterous. If we distinguish two sexual revolutions in our century, or two peaks of sexual revolution, a "modern" one in the 1920s and a "contemporary" one in the 1960s, there is a large distinction and physical difference to the latter, thanks to science: the availability to women of an ovulation-suppressant, a chemical agent (taking the popular Ortho-novum as an example, a combination of norethindrone, progesterone, and mestranol) that simply does away with the possibility of unwanted conception. That a woman would employ such means, however, to clear away the difficulties attendant upon an incestuous relationship is a *grotesquerie* more typical of life than of literature.

The notation of taboo made so far about incest is quite insufficient to explain the excitement it engenders. There may be an intellectual side to this, not yet mentioned. For while incest may consist of little more than a man lusting after female flesh and taking what's in the vicinity (more or less the case, if there is ever a pure case, in Ralph Ellison's *Invisible Man*), in more rarefied surroundings it may amount to a kind of physical solipsism, with a claim to such self-sufficiency that from one's own self, with only the barest minimum extension, into the being of the closely related woman, all things can spring. In Nabokov's Van and Ada, as more disguisedly in the Shelleyan *persona* seeking a sister and spouse in such poems as "Epipsychidion," such intellectual hubris, metaphysical arrogance, is clearly adumbrated. Typically, the background against which it is cast is diabolism, or at least militant atheism: If one is so assertive of one's own self-sufficiency as to admit no need to go outside one's own self, or twin self, for anything, then there is no place in one's view of the world for a superior and transcendent being. He must be either denied or attacked. Like a Ptolemaic monarch or an artist whose relation to the world has grown totally inward, the incestuous lover—and thinker—needs and tolerates nothing but his own creation.

While incestuous sexual behavior is not much of a modern problem, incestuous sexual thinking might be so called, if we allow that it is an exotic bloom, a late and poisonous flowering of Renaissance humanism. In its heritage, science is equally (but less obviously than the ovulation-suppression trick) the dramatic proof of the extension of man's control over his world. And Nabokov's fiction is the first since Sade's to bring together sexual action with a metaphysics of insolence. The mixture in *Ada* of sexual intercourse between a brother and sister who are near-twins, and a philosophy of time that insists on the reality of only the passing moment, is a very startling thing. It is built upon turn-of-the-century Victorian decadence, the apex of a society world-powerful and self-satisfied, but no longer energetic or morally sure of itself—a situation and time spirit beautifully captured, in a German milieu, by Thomas Mann's *Blood of the Walsungs* (1905), in which a Siegmund and Sieglinde of the modern era, bored and pampered children of a rich mercantile household, enact a listless parody of the heroic and divinely guided incest of their like-named Germanic forebears. But *Ada* goes beyond this to the assertion of a world, an *anti*terra, in which such a relationship can achieve—admittedly not without social disapproval—a perfect union of physical act and intellectual perspective.

But *Ada*, for all its narcissistic diabolism, neatly sidesteps the question of incestuous offspring, Van being assured that he is as sterile as he is potent. And if the perfect incestuous union is not to be the source of a nobler progeny, as when Siegmund lay with Sieglinde, then where lies the necessity of the partner? The necessity, that is, if it is correct that "intellectual" incest is the work of a profound self-satisfaction? Egotistical self-satisfaction can, of course, extend itself to include a twin to itself (a twin equal in beauty and wit but acknowledging a secondary status), or even a "little co-soul," just as commonly in the normal marriages of society it will extend itself to another member of a "set," but no further. When not faced with the problem of self-reproduction, it is most fully developed when incapable of extending the circle of its affections beyond itself, when its sexual expression is as solipsistic as its thought, when it can no longer abide even the mirror twin across the chessboard but must have itself alone as companion and dummy adversary, with the *game* replaced by the *problem*.

Problems have been called the onanism of chess. From that point of view, a scene that can be called a "key" to one of the most remarkable novels of the past several years, Nabokov's *Lolita*, is that in which the narrator-hero, Humbert Humbert, masturbates while sitting on a couch in fond contemplation of his desired object, a twelve-year-old girl, whose legs are, in a mockery of physical contact, thrown carelessly across his pajamaed lap. As he reaches the plateau phase, sure of the orgasm, he feels "Lolita had been safely solipsized";[121] incorporated, that is, by his own phantasy *solus ipse* of memory and desire (with a parallel, in its seraglio imagery, to the *solus rex* of the chessboard), which makes Lolita over into the young girl he had loved and lost when himself barely adolescent. Imaginatively, and to the limit of physical spasm, he has mastered a child, stranger to him and his thoughts, who represents the accident of the physical world. The world, to this large extent, is thereby his own creation and subject realm:

The least pressure would suffice to set all paradise loose. I had ceased to be Humbert the Hound, the sad-eyed degenerate cur clasping the boot that would presently kick him away. I was above the tribulations of ridicule, beyond the possibilities of retribution. In my self-made seraglio, I was a radiant and robust Turk, deliberately, in the full consciousness of his freedom, postponing the moment of actually enjoying the youngest and frailest of his slaves. (*Lolita*, p. 62)

Only the absolute monarch (generally mythical), the masturbator, and the artist have this total control of sexual phenomena, and of the phenomena enclosing them. The artist and masturbator, who are real, are necessarily only dealing with shadows—the same shadows that obscure and highlight the act of incest, so peculiarly a real act, and crime, based on an imaginary, unreal distinction. Partly illustrative is one of the better jokes collected by the indefatigable G. Legman: "The dreamer keeps his secret close, but he is not averse to letting on that the illusion is preferable to the reality, or at least safer: The boy who would rather have a wet dream than a woman, because 'You meet a better class of women that way.' "[122] The possibility strikes the observer that our contemporary tolerance for the masturbator and the incestuously minded (does Legman wish to show their interconnection by listing the above joke under the heading "incest"?) may be linked to our like tolerance for fiction of incestuous and masturbatory inwardness, both as regards plot (*Lolita* being an example) and as regards the manner of writing (all of Nabokov's work; several combined examples in the modern pantheon, *The Counterfeiters*, *Point Counter Point*; the descriptive obsession of Robbe-Grillet; the full-blown, even terrifying, language obsession of Joyce; the "real" masturbation-as-theme in Burroughs; the identity of the writer and the written in Grass, etc.).

In those cases I have chosen to view through a sexual *grille* there is the same withdrawal from public view, solitude or secrecy, the imagination feeding as if upon itself rather than upon external reality, and solipsism. The sexual-creative object is either fully internalized and worshiped by masturbatory writing-about-writing, or partially so, marginally externalized (as in incest, where she is of the same stuff as oneself), and the writer *disguises* the centrality of the creative act. This latter situation is clearly that of *Ada*, where the two main characters are coeditors of the book's manuscript, and it hovers as a nagging possibility in several of Henry James's novels. There is a great deal of heterosexual intercourse in *Lolita*, and the hero satisfies himself with the person of the young girl far more often than he does in the act of masturbation, but the masturbation remains, it seems to me, the key to the plot and, for that matter, to the style.

Now Henry James's career ran right through the erotic decadence of the European *fin de siècle*, and it is in that decadence that we might seem to have the closest parallel to those aspects of contemporary eroticism I have been discussing. James was forty-seven in 1890 and did his best work from 1897 to 1904; he knew Swinburne, Wilde, Whistler, and Beardsley; he wrote for the *Yellow Book* (or published in it); he adopted a personal catechism as strongly derived from Walter Pater as that of any of his contemporaries. Yet his work is as unmarked by their popular flirtation with diabolism and the challenge to a God-ordered world in erotic extremity as if it had been written in another century—as unmarked as it is by the examples of Joseph Conrad and Thomas Hardy, with their more convention-respecting assertion of blind forces in life. James's scorn for the crudities of a Wilde or a Swinburne, his natural existence in an atmosphere of greater subtlety and deeper challenge, sets him quite outside the narrow equations of works like *Salome* or *Lesbia Brandon*—and apart from the time-spirit that makes them now seem so dated, so dependent upon the certainties they mocked. Wilde may have exploited the sexual and aesthetic factors of *Lolita* (as in *The Picture of Dorian Gray*) far more openly and luridly than James ever dreamed of doing, but it is James's work, not Wilde's, that has the quality of prevision of the situation that has made *Lolita* such a key work of our own time.

James's *Awkward Age* (1899) may seem a strange choice to illustrate such prevision—if not a willfully perverse one. It is the most strictly constructed of drawing-room novels, with the entire action kept rigorously down to scenes of conversation—middle-class conversation, of a fearful social self-consciousness, at that (which led Edmund Wilson to call the characters a "gibbering disembowelled crew").[123] It takes place, almost without exception, around a tea table. The plot is as domesticated and comfortable as we might expect from such a setting, in its main outlines. Should a girl, Nanda Brookenham, too old to be treated as a child and kept off in a nursery, yet too young to be properly part of the "world," a virgin, inexperienced and (it is hoped) to be so kept until she marries, be allowed to approach the tea table? to join, that is, in the conversation of her parents' set? Nanda's age is awkward, and so is that of her time (*it* is an awkward age), suspended between the old-fashioned confident seclusion of young maidens and the vague portents of a new day of social libertarianism, with the young turned loose. A subject to inspire William Dean Howells, if not Louisa May Alcott. The extremely pallid question of which suitor this virtuous but unexciting girl will choose from a field of eminently suitable—more suitable than passionate—candidates, becomes the main matter of suspense in the plot, once the tea table question has been decided.

The domesticity is, however, only a surface matter, there being a large amount of sordid and adulterous by-play going on at the same time. Little of it is expressly stated, but it appears that Nanda's chief suitor, and the one she loves, Vanderbank, has been her mother's lover—in the not-too-distant past. The vaguely incestuous and sharply disagreeable nature of the situation is one James employed as an expression of evil hidden beneath the fair social surface: In both *The Portrait of a Lady* and *The Golden Bowl* the innocent heroine is brought into admiringly close and/or sexual contact with people whom she trusts but who are concealing a sexual relationship between themselves that is of indecent proximity to one that she has undertaken. Maggie Verver finds she has married her father's wife's lover; Isabel Archer, introduced by a dear friend to a handsome widower living alone with his little daughter, marries him, only to discover that he and the dear friend were lovers, and the child is theirs. When Vanderbank finally jilts Nanda, after a long tacit courtship, he jilts her mother, too. This action is paralleled elsewhere in the set: Mrs. Brookenham's friend, the Duchess, brings up her ward, Little Aggie, in secluded innocence while carrying on a liaison with a gentleman named Petherton. Petherton, it may be, has a concurrent liaison of another kind with Mitchy, a rich but lower-class suitor of Nanda's. At Nanda's urging, Mitchy marries Aggie, and Aggie, now out into the world with a vengeance, takes Petherton as a lover, and the circle of queasily analogical incest is complete. There are other complications as well, hardly more presentable. One such is that Nanda's brother Harold apparently becomes the lover of Lady Fanny, Petherton's sister, whose marital infidelities are a major item of talk among the set, and whose husband, Cashmore, becomes a regular visitor of Nanda's at approximately the same time her brother is cuckolding him. It is understandable that the London *Spectator*'s 1899 review of the novel expressed distaste for its "wealth of sinister suggestiveness" and "atmosphere of mental and moral squalor," calling its characters "smart degenerates."[124]

Despite all this, and the critical speculation it has caused in the years since the novel was published, it has been left relatively unnoted that the main "other" character, the one outside the set, elderly, conservative, country-living Mr. Longdon, is potentially the very solipsistic artist-creator we have been discussing.[125] He comes up to London many years after figuring there in society as a young man, Rip van Winkle-like, to peer about him after his long country exile, and—What does he see? (In our terms, What does he project and create?) He sees the young girl, Nanda, and in her the exact physical image of the girl he loved and lost in London past. The lost girl was, in fact, Nanda's grandmother. This lends a tightening and domestication to the situation Nabokov used: The lost girl reappears, but in a crowd of strangers, and it is years later, and she is in fact another person, and the age of the enraptured discoverer-dreamer, tied to the former time, is grotesquely out of phase with the magically restored youth of the apparition. James puts it all in the family, so to speak: Longdon has been known to the family over the years and is a welcome guest. James's narrative contains none of the threatening, beyond-the-law atmosphere of *Lolita*, nor does it contain that novel's primary mystifications, whereby Humbert is willingly drawn into the girl's proximity by a mother all unconscious of his motives, while he in turn is unconscious of his proximate and powerful rival, Quilty. Nanda's mother, contrastingly, makes a calculated use of the old man's attachment to her daughter toward the end that he will leave the girl his money. Because this brings Longdon into the group of Nanda's suitors and widens the net of relations, it provides the Jamesian *desideratum*, "complications almost beyond reckoning."[126]

But the amiable tone of *The Awkward Age*, with the group of friends all volubly conspiring for Nanda's good, does not altogether conceal the fact that Mr. Longdon is devoted to an *idée fixe* and burns with the same fires that consume Humbert Humbert, comical sadist. We see into Humbert's mind, while we do not see into Mr. Longdon's (the method of *The Awkward Age* requires that we see into no one's mind) but reality external to the *abhijñāna*-nymphet exists no more for him than it does for Humbert Humbert. Once they discover the girl, both dedicate their existence to her; indeed, Humbert's existence has more flesh to it outside the critical relationship, for we know the details of his marriage and exile from felicity, while Longdon seems risen from the dead to appear, *dybbuk*-like, in London at the dramatically required time. The dedication in Humbert's case sets itself the end of physical, sexual possession; in Mr. Longdon's it is more diffuse and complex, but ends—possibly—in the same way. Mr. Longdon has little fictional existence outside his

Nanda-obsession, and hardly any physical life inside the fiction either—he has been, so far as we know, in retirement and obscurity in the country since he was refused by Nanda's grandmother, who then married another man. He is like the Man of Feeling, in his most popular form of one of Dickens's kindly old bachelors (Mr. Boythorn in *Bleak House* is a representative example), who had one great love, and when that was denied him, dedicated himself to a dignified and solitary existence. In Longdon's case, the revolving years bring the girl back to him, to pay court to once more; his passion, asleep for two generations, is alerted as if by some inner signal, or trick of time. He rouses himself, goes back to the city, and at the end of the year chronicled by the novel, when all the set's games over Nanda are played out, he goes back to his country retreat and obscurity —taking her with him.

Most of the uneasiness the reader of *Lolita* feels comes from the youth of the heroine; the uneasiness of the reader of *The Awkward Age* comes from, if not his perplexity over plot and motivation, the incestuous closeness, confidence-sharing, and interrelation of the characters—the Brookenham set is too much like an extended family for all its intercourse to have a sexual term. Lolita is unknown and unrelated to Humbert and Quilty, up to the point of their connection; Nanda is known and watched over from childhood by the set. Vanderbank, her chief suitor, has celebrated her birthdays and noted each of the stages of her development for some years before the action of the novel starts, at which time she is nineteen and he, thirty-four. Mitchy as well is of an age with Vanderbank, and his devotion is parallel, avuncular yet sexual, with the difference that it is apparently real, while Vanderbank's is sterile.[127] Mitchy's devotion is productive only of a foolish chivalric gesture of self-abnegation toward Nanda, however. Mr. Longdon makes the third fairy godfather: While Vanderbank's "fatherhood" takes the form of making love to the mother, and Mitchy's that of providing money, Mr. Longdon's combines love and money—he falls into the role of the one who will pick the husband for the girl and fund the marriage. The intensity with which he plays this role becomes progressively more like the elaborate play-acting of Humbert and has the same result—all barriers between him and the girl fall away.

Inside the distinction of style between James and Nabokov, the discovery of the girl in the two books has a dramatic likeness. Humbert narrates his experience with passion and, at the same time, a self-conscious literary flair:

> I was still walking behind Mrs. Haze through the dining room when . . . without the least warning, a blue sea-wave swelled under my heart and, from a mat in a pool of sun, half-naked, kneeling, turning about on her knees, there was my Riviera love peering at me over dark glasses.
>
> It was the same child—the same frail, honey-hued shoulders, the same silky supple bare back, the same chestnut head of hair. A polka-dotted black kerchief tied around her chest hid from my aging ape eyes, but not from the gaze of young memory, the juvenile breasts I had fondled one immortal day. And, as if I were the fairy-tale nurse of some little princess (lost, kidnapped, discovered in gypsy rags through which her nakedness smiled at the king and his hounds), I recognized the tiny dark-brown mole on her side. With awe and delight (the king crying for joy, the trumpets blaring, the nurse drunk) I again saw her lovely indrawn abdomen where my southbound mouth had briefly paused; and those puerile hips on which I had kissed the crenulated imprint left by the band of her shorts—that last mad immortal day behind the "Roches Roses." The twenty-five years I had lived since then, tapered to a palpitating point, and vanished. (p. 41)

James's treatment of Mr. Longdon in the same situation is characteristically muted and indirect (the girl's photograph is seen before the girl) but portrays an emotion as great. When Vanderbank tells Longdon he has a photograph of the girl, "the old man was all eagerness" (p. 10), as if subject to premonition. He takes the "child's" picture up, and studies it intently, puts it down, moves about the room, returns to it, "as if accidentally and absently, he bent again over the portrait of Nanda" (p. 15), keeping his face concealed as he does so. He then quietly announces the resemblance to the girl he lost: "She's much more like the dead than like the living" (p. 16). As he tells Vanderbank, "There was nothing after Lady Julia," (p. 20); now the nothingness has been replaced with the double.

When Mr. Longdon actually meets Nanda, Vanderbank is again

the observer. After the introductions are made and the girl turns to making the tea, Vanderbank has "a strange sense that [Mr. Longdon] was so agitated as to be trembling in every limb" (p. 91). Compare Humbert at the first sight of his Lo ("my knees were like reflections of knees in rippling water," p. 39), and his imagined shaking of limb before a group of adults surrounding the girl ("playing safe, I kept away, for I was afraid that the horrible, insane, ridiculous and pitiful tremor that palsied me might prevent me from making my *entré* with any semblance of casualness," p. 41). Vanderbank starts to speak to Mr. Longdon in alarm, hearing the "low gasp" the old man gives, "but even as he spoke, Mr. Longdon's face, still white, but with a smile that was not all pain, seemed to supplicate him not to notice" (p. 91). Humbert: "My heart beat like a drum as she sat down, cool skirt ballooning" (p. 60). Both Humbert and Mr. Longdon experience the stock romantic faintness, stopping and racing of the heart, weakness in the limbs, pallor—all as true as it is conventional—with the difference that Mr. Longdon seems to go further with it, to the verge of something like a swoon. He is incapable of speech, like T. S. Eliot's narrator in "The Burial of the Dead":

> I could not
> Speak, and my eyes failed, I was neither
> Living nor dead, and I knew nothing,
> Looking into the heart of light, the silence.

Mitchy and Vanderbank later apply to the scene, in the language James used to express the most powerful projections of sexual feeling in his work, the conception of "sacred" terror or awe before the woman on the part of a man who worships rather than possesses and who is struck into a condition of impotence by the emotion (compare Humbert's dream of a gun that shoots feebly dribbling bullets and his experience of such embarrassment when attempting to execute Quilty). Mitchy says gleefully, "He knows that he's pierced to the heart! . . . [He's] the victim done for by one glance of the goddess!" (p. 94).

Mr. Longdon has meanwhile found it necessary to withdraw to another room to pull himself together. When Vanderbank goes in to him he moves about, tears in his eyes, "as if with a sacred awe" (p. 98), and says

'I'm too absurd to be so upset'—Mr. Longdon smiled through his tears—'but if you had known Lady Julia you would understand. It's *she* again, as I first knew her, to the life, and not only in feature, in stature, in colour, in movement, but in every bodily mark and sign, in every look of the eyes, above all—oh, to a degree!—in the sound, in the charm, of the voice.' (p. 97)

In such scenes there is the problem of the contrast between what the character feels and what the reader, or the imagined present observer, can feel. To the hypothetical observer, the nymphet psychology of Humbert is curious but unappealing, and the actual Dolores Haze of the miraculous re-creation is perilously close to an ordinary twelve-year-old, a spoiled American one at that. Nabokov is not so crude as to transform this twelve-year-old into a romantic vision of loveliness, through and for Humbert's perception *and* ours; rather he includes the apparently disadvantageous verisimilitude:

Very infantile, infinitely meretricious. Humbert Humbert is also infinitely moved by the little one's slangy speech, by her harsh high voice. Later heard her volley crude nonsense at Rose across the fence. Twanging through me in a rising rhythm. Pause. "I must go now, kiddo." (pp. 43–44)

In the end this makes it easier for us to share Humbert's passion.

Nanda, similarly, is *affectively* goddess, actually child. Indeed, the talk James gives her, in this first scene, is painfully childish, childishly winsome, even for an upper-middle-class London girl of the 1890s:[128]

'I can make tea beautifully,' she said from behind her table. 'Mother showed me how this morning. . . . I haven't yet done it this way at home—I usually have my tea upstairs. They bring it up in a cup, all made and very weak, with a piece of bread-and-butter in the saucer. That's because I'm so young.' (p. 90)

This as the life and soul of Lady Julia is comparable to Dolores Haze of Pisky, Ohio, and Lawn Street, Ramsdale, Mass., as the life and soul of Annabel Leigh, of the princedom by the sea—a deliberate sidestepping of the objective correlative, a deliberate presentation not of beauty but of *awkwardness*. "The Awkward Age" is a title equally applicable to both novels, for while Lolita is a child unsuitably and unnaturally made adult, Nanda is (physically) an adult made unsuitably childish, held back by a mother who fears her competition. Nanda's social being, and in particular her speech, is as meretricious to the doting observation of Mr. Longdon as Lolita's is to Humbert:

> 'Well,' said Nanda, looking away again, 'he has come into my life.'
> 'He couldn't have come into a place where it gives me more pleasure to see him.'
> 'But he didn't like, the other day, when I used it to him, that expression,' the girl returned. 'He called it "mannered modern slang," and came back again to the extraordinary difference between my speech and my grandmother's.' (p. 143)

This difference in culture Nanda mentions, in her rather mannered profession to Vanderbank here, shows in both cases, more subtly in James's, another aspect of the unnaturalness of the older man's interest in the girl. Mr. Longdon expresses doubt to Mitchy that "any real contact is possible" (p. 323) between his age and hers; the equivalent point in *Lolita* is made, typically, by more metaphoric and roundabout means. To Lolita, Humbert looks like a movie star, and he benefits from the resultant crush she develops on him. That is, the physical gap between them is reduced by the empty illusion of the screen and overcome only by flight, duplicity, and transcontinental mirage, the whole as unstable as that in the book's early, and premonitory, film image, of youthful Humbert's relation to an "American kid, the son of a then celebrated motion-picture actress whom he seldom saw in the three-dimensional world" (p. 13).

The disproportion and the sense of unreality give both novels a strong comic element—pathetic-comic. Mr. Longdon, like Murnau's film figure of a sadly by-passed age, gets "The Last Laugh," but in a way equally removed from the normal and verisimilar. He is to have the girl, but at the cost of withdrawing himself and her from the real world, for her the world of passion, sexual love, and, potentially, motherhood (perhaps the last vengeful projection of Humbert-Nabokov's imagination is that Lolita dies in childbirth). If the girl is not to be a child, she is not to be anything. If Humbert at the end is left alone in a landscape of horror and emptiness, having "used up" the child who was to restore the past to him, James's quiet rounding off of his novel is in the end at least as jarring. More so, in the sense closer to life, its disquiet stemming not from lurid event—capture, enslavement, death—as from what does *not* happen, the final "awkwardness" that shuts out life for Nanda as surely as matters more clear-cut do for Lolita.

Mr. Longdon's first conversation with Nanda has a comic side, turning on the question of her being "down," or allowed in the drawing room, a situation that has a Wonderland aspect:

'Mother thinks she's more at home than almost any one. She does it on purpose: she knows what it is,' Nanda pursued, with her perfect gravity, 'for people to be disappointed of finding her.'

'Oh, I shall find her yet,' said Mr. Longdon. 'And then I hope I shall also find *you*.'

She appeared simply to consider the possibility and, after an instant, to think well of it. 'I dare say you will now, for now I shall be down.'

Her companion just blinked. 'In the drawing-room, you mean —always?'

It was quite what she meant. 'Always. I shall see all the people who come. It will be a great thing for me.' (p. 100)

Mr. Longdon's sincerest wish, we have no reason to doubt, is to find Nanda a more suitable partner, husband and lover, than himself, but it could also be, we have some reason to believe, that he is as successful as Humbert in the process of self-deception. Equally insidious is the possibility that the scenes of the novel, and thus the actions and speeches of the characters, are infected—colored—by Mr. Longdon's (outside) opinion of them. This would mean that we see the Brookenhams, Vanderbank and Mitchy, Nanda and the Duchess, not only from "outside" in the sense "from the author," as they speculate over the motives of Mr. Longdon, the mysterious stranger who has entered their lives, possibly to change their destiny with the power of his example, his moral seriousness, and

—above all—his money, but we see them also in a perspective that becomes slowly, more and more sharply, his. That is, from "outside" in the sense "from Mr. Longdon." This despite James's announced plan of a "circle of rounds" for the novel, without authorial "going behind," the characters all sharing the role of lighting a central situation.[129] By that plan Mr. Longdon is one of the circumferential figures, but, possibly because he has close ties to the author, and definitely because he is the outsider who judges the others, he becomes dominant. We know that for Mr. Longdon to hover about Nanda as part protector-and-guide, part wooer, is unnatural and ridiculous, but it would not of course seem quite the same way to Mr. Longdon himself. We know that it is harmfully foolish for Mitchy to marry Aggie, for Vanderbank to act as if he is saving himself for some higher fate and, once he is locked into this stance,[130] for Mrs. Brook to attempt to force her daughter to take Mr. Longdon instead; but on the whole the members of the set are not so aware. They are adept at backbiting, and several of them join in mockery of the strange paralysis of Vanderbank, but it is only from the point of view of Mr. Longdon, granted the surmise of his controlling tendency, that all this falls into a meaningful pattern. Or if not meaningful, eminently satisfactory. The suitors eliminate themselves one by one, and the group is so spellbound by its own social pattern that it can feel there is no other suitor possible besides Mr. Longdon.

In the same way, blindly occurring events, social conditions, accidents (Mc)Fate, *seem* to close around Lolita, driving her into the arms of Humbert. Humbert's own consciously laid schemes backfire; it is only by the accidents of the highway (cunningly hit upon by Nabokov, the foreign observer, as central to the conditions of American life) that he both gains and loses the girl. From Humbert's point of view, which is the controlling one, the girl is his natural prize and right. To make him as much the fool of fate as Lolita, or to make Mr. Longdon as much so as Nanda, is to miss something.

Note, for instance, Nanda's innocent talk of herself and Mr. Longdon as lovers, something perhaps almost to be expected of her inexperience and naiveté, but something too that must be given fuel to supply it:

The Erotic

She showed somehow that she wouldn't flinch. 'You weren't asked till after he had made sure I'd come. We've become, you and I,' she smiled, 'one of the couples who are invited together. . . . Why, don't you know?. . . . The Duchess and Lord Petherton are like you and me. . . . They're one of the couples who are invited together. . . . Mitchy really oughtn't. . . . He has his ideas—he thinks nothing matters. He says we've all come to a pass that's the end of everything.' (pp. 153–54)

In this cheerfully corrupt world, the irregular couples are invited to country weekends together, so as to do them the favor of making their arrangements easier (so the Prince and Charlotte maneuver themselves in *The Golden Bowl*). Mr. Longdon not only allows this, but encourages the girl, even before the question of her suitors has been settled, to turn to him for something the others cannot give her, and to stay with him in the country (this is the first segment of the visit that by the end of the novel has taken on a permanent character):

'You mean then that I may come alone?'
'I won't receive you, I assure you, on any other terms. I want to show you,' he continued, 'what life *can* give. Not, of course,' he subjoined, 'of this sort of thing.'
'No—you've told me. Of peace.'
'Of peace. . . . I think that when we're alone together—'
He had dropped for so long that she wondered. 'Well, when we are—?'
'Why, it will be all right,' he simply concluded. (p. 150)

The matter of what society did and did not allow, regarding the disposition of teen-aged girls, we need not inquire into at length here. Suffice it to say that Nanda's parents are selfish enough, and sufficiently taken up with their own narrow concerns, to allow the girl to be carried off by the Grand Turk if they could see an advantage in it. They, and their set, are pretty much content with whatever goes on, short of murder or disfigurement, provided there is no scandal.[131] Whatever social code may be applicable or accepted by author, character, or reader, the simple physical facts of the situation remain eternally the same: The "Temple of Peace," with its overtones of vestal virgins and with Mr. Longdon posing as a mere doorkeeper, is a cardboard stage set, awkwardly thrust in front of the real sexual mystery that is being celebrated. Once he has her staying with him, he stops talking about Lady Julia, having made the transference from the dead to the living (as Humbert ceases further mention of Annabel Leigh once Lolita is in his grasp). And Nanda, once established, seems to withdraw from her former contacts, even from that with Vanderbank:

> 'Do you expect to be here long?' he asked.
> It took Nanda some time to say, 'As long as Mr. Longdon will keep me, I suppose—if that doesn't sound very horrible.' (p. 229)

Mitchy and Mr. Longdon can agree, late in the novel, that Nanda "has nobody else" (p. 325) but them. Since Mitchy is now married, Mr. Longdon need only appear at the Brookenham house, where Nanda has been temporarily taken back, and collect her:

> 'You say you *will* come then?' he asked. . . . 'You understand clearly, I take it, that this time it's never again to leave me—or be left.'
> 'I understand,' she presently replied. 'Never again. . . '
> 'Well!' He raised his hands and took her face, which he drew so close to his own that, as she gently let him, he could kiss her with solemnity on the forehead. 'Come!' he then very firmly said—quite indeed as if it were a question of their moving on the spot.
> It literally made her smile, which, with a certain compunction, she immediately corrected by doing for him, in the pressure of her lips to his cheek, what he had just done for herself. (pp. 366–68)

Such are the outlines of two novels of the incest of the imagination, two novels that present what James called the "labyrinth of mere immediate appearances," beneath which the "fine meaning" lies, with cross-references "as thick as the green leaves of a garden!"[132] The metaphysical *noise* present in Lolita is in contrast to *The Awkward Age*, which has the metaphysical silence of Shakespeare, but the resulting impression is the same: a man, and man, much alone in the cosmos, analogically an outsider in the social microcosm, spinning out of his own being a "recaptured" love. Without knowing it, what he is actually attempting is to turn time around so as to recapture his own past, and his lost youth. He thinks he has succeeded, that a chronological anomaly, willed or granted for his own private benefit, has returned what he lost; but the present plays him the trick of proceeding, and being, behind the illusion he projects, so that the girl is only a mirror replica of the one he seeks, and at the same time a different, real girl, whose life he can only lay waste by his intrusion. The combination is one that may fairly be called contemporary if at the same time one recognizes its roots in both Renaissance and modern. It is romantic, and twentieth-century, fantasy, with the difference that the girl, *la prisonnière*, is real, while in *Remembrance of Things Past* and *The Story of O* she is not.[133] It is the story of Faust and Gretchen/ Margarethe, with the difference that there is no Mephistopheles. That means that the loneliness of man—once his last illusion, that of love, has been broken—is real, too.

Sex and The Turn of the Screw

One of *Ada's* jacket blurbs, quoting *Book Week*, tells us, "Nabokov is immensely sophisticated, learned, witty, and self-aware, a complex master of technique far beyond the Jamesian dimensions, and as openly sexual as James was repressed." This puts popular wisdom as neatly as we could wish, right down to the obscurity of language—both unintended, with "complex master of technique" for "master of complex technique," and intended, with catchwords to conceal logical shoddiness. The elision of "as James was repressed" gives us armchair psychology: "Henry James was sexually repressed" is in turn apparently derived from the general truth to which we all, as enlightened Freudian moderns, subscribe—"The Victorians were sexually repressed"—from which it is possible to proceed syllogistically to "Henry James was a Victorian," Q.E.D. Additional evidence is a matter of tacit reference; we all know that Henry James did not include openly sexual scenes in his novels (any more than his contemporaries did), neither did he tell dirty jokes, chase girls, or, for that matter, get married. My comparison of *Lolita* with *The Awkward Age* has certainly failed to fault *Book Week*, in that it has shown no open sexuality in the latter novel, but I hope that it has shown something else as obvious but more often forgotten: that sex does not go away for being hidden, and there is as much of its essence—that is, of passion and imagination—in one master of the novel as another.

For no one can be a master of the novel without including the terrible power physical love exerts, and while the power stays the same, popular opinion as to its manifestation varies widely. A few years ago we found James Joyce obscene; Joyce, a fastidious man, found Wagner obscene;[134] James, whom we now find overdelicate, made no such complaint of Wagner, and he was no Wagnerite; while there were those of his contemporaries who found several of his novels, among them *What Maisie Knew, The Awkward Age*, and *The Golden Bowl*, shocking for their open retailing of sexual exploits. So it goes. What a blow *Ada* must have been to those who sat down to read it for its open sexuality!

Like *The Awkward Age*, *The Turn of the Screw* is a story in which a large amount of sexual passion may be assumed to exist underneath the surface of the narrative, its pattern of adumbration on a scale that makes it easy to miss. Like the figure in the carpet, it is everywhere, yet seems to be nowhere. Unlike *The Awkward Age*, however, *The Turn of the Screw* has of recent years been subject to a sexual (or "Freudian") interpretation that has not only identified the sexual element but made it the whole spring and source of the action. According to it, the governess exceeds her authority with the children because she is in love with the master and wishes to impress him. Since he is not to be impressed by the ordinary course of governessing, she must concoct some grave danger to her charges, from which she can then rescue them and receive his love as her reward. This danger must be grave indeed, for he has told her he wants to be bothered as little as possible over the children—in effect told her he cares nothing for them. The governess is unconscious she is doing this, because she is sexually repressed and cannot admit her sexual motives to herself. She therefore thinks she is protecting the children against an actual, outside evil, which happens to have come along providentially to supply her with the occasion she needs to demonstrate her heroism and devotion to the master. She overdoes it, unfortunately; with the ghosts she has conjured up she frightens one child into fits and kills the other, putting him in such terror that his heart stops. What the master's reaction is, we are not told.

Such is more or less the outer limit of assignable, sexually derived action in the story. Its existence is a tribute, if not much else, to the capacity James developed to incorporate fictionally the feminine as well as the masculine point of view. The governess is a vessel of consciousness inside a fictional frame that demonstrates peculiarly sharp awareness of the limitations of human communication—that is, of the difficulties of maintaining, being, consciousness itself. In this respect the governess is a modern Cassandra, fated to see and understand what others cannot, and to fail to get them to see and understand, and representing in her state not the anger of the gods with men but the state of her creator, the artist, and the hopeless irregularity of the medium of human communication in which he works. The use of gesture and the unspoken in James, for instance, is presented as a matter of social *reportage*, with little or no acknowledgment that important parts of it are James's own creation. That is, James assigned gesture and unspoken content while representing it as observed social reality, and there is as large a gap in this area, between the practice of the individual artist and the social reality, or shared custom, in James's case as in that of Joyce or Beckett. Daisy Miller's fault, for instance, in going out in a carriage unchaperoned and then abandoning that vehicle for a walk in the Roman streets with a relative stranger, was instantly recognizable to a contemporary of James's. It was established as a gesture of daring unconventionality and challenge. But there is no consciously known convention for the transmission of the narrator's opinion of Daisy Miller to the girl herself, in the instance that he is in love with her without being aware of it. Here James operated with something close to his "own" code.

The same independence occurs in the speeches James assigns his characters. They are his, not theirs, and not simply in the trivial sense "written by James," but apart from the speech of contemporaneous people in the real world, with the admitted exception of certain high-frequency "in" words. The normal vocabulary of English, the high-frequency words neither "in" nor "out," is of course shared by James's characters with the world of real speech; but how little that has to do with the matter of perceived communication we are only now being shown by linguistic theory.[135] And that an artist should deviate from normal code patterns is also unrelated to the extreme sensitivity to semantic differences the normal patterns demonstrate—if he wants sensitivity, it is there already, but if he wants a divergent form, there is room inside the code for him to have that, too. Remarks of extreme banality, like "I don't know why it is, but Bridget doesn't respect me," represent subtleties of perception of speech and gesture not at all banal in their number and complexity. The eye of the fly remains a wonder of nature. Common speech is also productive of *formulae* (folk wisdom) that economize on, by discarding, the subtleties of experience: "Touch the spot and they'll come round every time" as advice in courtship, for instance. The choice of a governess rather than a tutor, then, for James's story, was not so much dictated by a Flaubertian desire to seize upon a feminine consciousness as a focus of irresponsible imaginings as by something nearly the opposite—as a vessel of (fine) consciousness *per se*, and as a focus of love. By George Eliot's phrase, which James approvingly quoted, "In these frail vessels is borne onward through the ages the treasure of human affection."[136] Among women—of sufficient breeding, education, or experience of adversity to sharpen their receptivity and analytical powers —James found his analogue of life lived to the highest.

It is therefore, in *The Turn of the Screw*, that James willingly made use of a stock romantic-gothic "woman's" novel, with the female protagonist so dear to Mrs. Radcliffe and the Brontë sisters, sufficiently clichéd by the beginning of the century to be satirized in Jane Austen's *Northanger Abbey:* the inexperienced, young, and not especially beautiful girl, deprived by the accidents of fortune or social status of the suitors girls dream of—rich, handsome, and aristocratic ones—who *meets* such a man and is given by him a difficult and dangerous *task*—one from which the delicate and highborn ladies in whose company he moves would shrink. Notice the identifiability this girl has for the female reader, something of a *bovariste* in the majority, who is not getting the social attention she deserves, who is prevented by bad luck, lack of money, being born at the wrong time and to the wrong parents (who oppress her), or being married to the wrong man (who has pulled her down to his level), from taking her place in the full round of balls, parties, receptions, and other exciting events put on by more fortunate people elsewhere. Further, this fictional girl has had a hard time of it and is, supremely, an orphan (like Esther in Dickens's *Bleak House*); she is "ready for love"; the task she is set calls her to a castle or a forbidding great house, emblem of the social world denied to her and at the same time empty, or half-abandoned, a place of sorrow where unspecified dark and even criminal events have taken place. It is owned or presided over by the task setter, a darkly handsome but fiercely masculine and unapproachable man, separated from the normal course of human affairs by some more or less terrible criminal onus, and/or emotional and physical scars that he bears. Because he is outcast from, or has given up, his own social world he is a believable match for the little Cinderella-governess or Cinderella-housekeeper, and in the end she does marry him, expressing thereby a masochism of her own—being a poor thing herself, she will take on the lifelong task of serving the needs and sharing the downcast condition of a once proud master. At the same time, the union satisfies another masochistically derived adolescent female fantasy, partly born of ignorance and shyness, that of having for a husband a loving creature in need of tender care, like a puppy dog, responsive but not overmastering or terrifying. Better if this animal shape portray more clearly the terrific aspects of maleness, as in *Beauty and the Beast*, while at the same time acting passively. So the Beast savagely rends the animals of the forest but is diffident and gentle with the beautiful and innocent girl, wanting from her not the savage use of her body but her *pity*, which will, once received, transform him from a monster to a Prince Charming, the sugar-coated bridegroom.

Meanwhile, the threatening passion and the brutal sexuality are coded into wind and weather and violence of external event. There is not direct carnality, but storms, fires, a madwoman held captive in the attic, falls from horses, rumors of war. The fire that consumes his house and ravages his person expresses the master's dangerous love, while he and his house express together the imaginative passion of the timid girl and her reader. James, while bound by a sexual censorship nearly equivalent to that pertaining to the Brontës, was unable to use this coding of external effects. He was sensitized to its triteness and aware of its delineation by John

Ruskin as the pathetic fallacy. His restraint left him with the choice of leaving the sexuality out, which would have been original but clearly impossible, or of refining the code somewhat, so that a distortion of external event would not be necessary and the historian's pose he sought, that of reporting actual event and real world, could be maintained.

The French answer to the problem set by realism was not one James felt he could use. The problem is, How do you represent the sexual side of life once you have lost the referential freedom, in a bourgeois age, of the Renaissance novel, and wish to eschew romantic symbolism and transformationalism, the mapping of sexuality onto the landscape? By the end of the century the French novel had developed a veiled allusiveness that can be called the technique of role statement with omission of facts. Thus Emile Zola could wax hyperbolic on the coarseness and hugeness of the sexual appetite of *Nana*, show her in the company of lovers, including one Lesbian friend, and show her vulgar manners in public, her self-assertiveness, and so forth, but never show her making love to anyone, or directly discussing making love to anyone. Such role-naming, the inclusion of prostitutes and profligates, the demonstration of sex by a transference from the hyperbole of the inanimate to that of lurid roles and debased actions, was hardly open to James. First, he apparently believed as firmly as the majority of his English and American readers that the inclusion of such matter in the French novel was at best embarrassing, at worst indecent and degraded, a saddening example of the French predilection for matters unclean. Second, the career of a Nana or the predicament of a *Boule de Suif* was alien to the normative realism James upheld in fiction, for the lurid is by its nature a matter of taking the highly unusual (and thus unrepresentative of life as a whole) and making it the assumed reference of fiction and the boundary of its purview.

That James wrote, in *The Turn of the Screw*, perhaps the most successfully lurid story in English fiction does not obviate this point, for the life-setting of a governess taking care of children in an English country house is, as a matter of surface representation, rather more normative than the *moeurs* of a whorehouse *de province*—a subject one of the Goncourts told James he was taking up (as James put it on another occasion, "What won't the French write about next?").[137] That the deep structure, the concealed events beneath the surface, are of the utmost horror and damnation in the narrative of the governess with the children, and of the most quotidian predictability in the case of the whorehouse, is not of deciding importance here. The "horror beneath" had become something like a staple of English fiction by James's later career; as for the French way, he could not have chosen it if he had wanted to, given the censorship accepted, and applied, by his audience.

Sexual representation in the story of the governess of the children is therefore doubly muted: The Rochester figure is removed off-stage and remains there after his initial meeting with the girl, where he sets the task and she feels first the pangs of the love she will carry throughout the narrative. But this first muting does not cause the romantic reality transformation we have noted, directed by the sexual frustration of the governess. So much has been established as definitely as anything in literary criticism can be, over the past ten years or so. There is then a second muting in the story, the subtler coding mentioned above, that leaves exterior reality, including such potentially metaphysical events as a mysterious stranger suddenly appearing on the roof of the house, untouched, so that events are perceived by the governess-narrator realistically, as any equivalently intelligent and sensitive person would perceive them. And the personality of the governess is subsumed to her role of observer, to "keeping crystalline her record of so many intense anomalies and obscurities."[138] Her insights, rare enough to be questioned by the dull-witted and thick-sensed, are such as are derivable from a human being in her place and time, but not such as to allow her thoughts about other things—her hopes for romance, for instance—to intrude upon that role of registering consciousness and its proper concomitant emotion, protective love for her charges, the children.

If she eludes our grasp, then, because of the formal requirements she serves, the same cannot be said for the characters she observes. The problem remains of what Miles did at school. What he said, or told about, is very possibly connected to what he was told by Quint, or what he did with Quint, and this is given a sexual overtone. And the relation between Quint and Jessel was clearly of a scandalous nature and therefore, for the woman at least, a sexually "compromising" matter. While it *could* be stated, as an illicit pregnancy, for instance, Miles's crime could not. In his preface James indirectly described the matter, bringing a psychological principle to his aid, as the question of "evil":

Only make the reader's general vision of evil intense enough . . . and his own experience, his own sympathy (with the children) and horror (of their false friends) will supply him quite sufficiently with all the particulars. Make him *think* the evil, make him think it for himself, and you are released from weak specifications.[139]

In this way James chose the Miltonic over the Dantean hell, and made the choice as well, we may note, for the grand style (of what Hugh Kenner calls linguistic autonomy) that so often goes with lack of specificity, the language of high abstraction and low specification. This was not so at the beginning of his career, and it may be noted that his plots changed at approximately the same time that his language changed—noted for it provides another indication of the failure of the theoretical independence of code from message in literature to materialize. *The American* (1877) and *The Portrait of a Lady* (1881), for instance, both present a mystery concealing evil in human relations, bearing strongly on a sexual element, but once the plot has reached the climax of its development that mystery is cleared away and the worst, the truth, is known. Newman learns that the Bellegardes have committed a murder, but he fails in his attempt to use it to get the girl he wants. She refuses him, enters a nunnery, and that is that. Osmond smuggles his paramour, and the mother of his child, into the company of young Isabel Archer in the most insidious way; not until they are married and Osmond has gotten her money does Isabel learn of the plan into which her life has been so neatly fitted, but when she does she can act with full knowledge. Even by the time of *The Bostonians* (1886) this has changed. The central and possibly determining relationship of the book, between the heroine and an older woman, is most probably a Lesbian one, but it is left undefined, put into the reader's hands for him to decide on the basis of his experience; and the style of the novel has changed to a kind of exhaustive cataloguing of Boston events and interiors, meetings and conversations public and private, on a scale hitherto unused by James. By the period of the final novels, circa 1900, we are given the outlines only of the evil, its form once more sexual. In *The Golden Bowl* there is no way of telling whether the Prince and Charlotte were lovers either before or after the marriage of the Prince to Maggie and Charlotte to Adam Verver, yet that love is the flaw in the bowl, and without its resolution there is no resolution to the novel. At the same time, the language of the book has become all indirect allusiveness, circumlocution, and abstraction.

That we should find an analogue for the suppression of sexual detail in James in his suppression of the details of evil may sound ironic in a way familiar to our criticism of the Victorians and Edwardians, "sex" in that rigidly dualistic time being close enough to "evil" on any terms, unless qualified by motherhood, the family, bringing children into the world, and so forth. There would seem to be nothing but a gain for all concerned if what is missing is supplied—the "seem" in that statement being the product of the (mainly American) flowering of the pragmatic tradition, which treats "evil" (a term not really of its working vocabulary) and sex as what they *are*, what they occur as in the real world: behavior. James fails to specify behavior, to name the specific acts of his characters upon which his fictions turn—in their absence. There is no way to supply what is missing from *The Turn of the Screw* in any literal sense, that is, by any effort of critical detective work, any more than there is a way to equate Milton's "hideous obscure" with any set of behavioral parameters. But that impossibility does not reduce the potential of considering the omission in an abstract way. Granted that *The Turn of the Screw* would no longer be the story we have if its missing sexual acts and thoughts were supplied, would such a *Turn of the Screw* be a better one? My own opinion is that any work of fiction purporting to delineate human experience that fails to demonstrate its sexual component is inferior; that a work with a less clearly specified sexual component is inferior to one with a clearer specification. But such a principle may be too coarse-grained entirely to apply to the point here.

A critic who has given consideration to this point is John Bayley, author of *The Characters of Love*, who notes that the absence of sexual physicality in the great literature of "personality," or full human range, is not always an absence that can be filled by the addition of physical scenes. The masters of the novel, like Tolstoy or James, are not so easily brought to book. He concludes that *"The Golden Bowl*, for all its obvious artificiality, is yet a far more physical and less abstract novel than *Women in Love."*[140] The peculiar vices of Lawrence's style apart—his abstract tendentiousness is what Bayley sees as most debilitating in it—along with the question of whether Bayley would say the same thing about *Lady Chatterley's Lover*, the thought naturally arises, Might not the method of non-specification, in the hands of certain writers, have represented (in the sense "outlined") an element in sexuality that there is *no other way* to approach, with the linguistic tools we now have? Writers not like Stendhal, Balzac, or Tolstoy, who see and project like gods, with Apollonian clarity, to whom the affairs of men are confidently interpretable; but like Gogol, Dostoevski, or James, writers with a vision of troubled sensitivity, to whom what is simple to other, superior or coarser, humans is of infinite complexity and insoluble mystery. As far as the tools are concerned, a paramount question of the contemporary period is, after all, whether we are going to be able to represent sexual physicality with the subtlety and beauty that we have managed to apply to most all other attitudes and functions in life. For now we are free to turn the resources of novel, theater, and film on this hitherto forbidden subject—one not always forbidden to representation in other times and cultures, but forbidden to us in the West during the period of the development of the aesthetic forms we now use. The progress marked by D. H. Lawrence, James Joyce, Philip Roth, Luis Buñuel, Jean-Luc Godard, Edward Albee, Fernando Arrabal, and others leaves us still a long way from the goal.

If this is true, *The Turn of the Screw*, like *The Golden Bowl*, may turn out to be ahead of us on our path of progression, rather than behind, in its assigned place of "typical Victorian repression and censorship." On the one hand, there can be no deciding the matter until we have reached the end point and goal, and can look back with both scientific knowledge and aesthetic accomplishment. While present scientific knowledge has shown us, for the first time, what sexual physicality, beyond its most elementary aspects, *is*, the scientifically aided aesthetic progression may already be faced with diminishing returns. On the other hand, if sexual attitudes and sex "life" do inform the whole of human existence to the extent that has been claimed in our century, the subject of sex could easily turn out to be too large to handle at all, indivisible from such questions as the purpose of life and death, impenetrable to more than reflection or echo by art.

The Feminine Psyche

We have now, in the 1970s, a great Western upsurge in consciousness of the status of women. Given the synergistic development of events by contemporary communications, it may even become a worldwide upsurge. It combines consciousness on the part of males that females are now considerable for roles hitherto exclusively male, and consciousness on the part of females that they are ready for such roles. Whether this has much to do with "consciousness of being a woman" (as against "consciousness of being a man") is debatable; indeed, to the extent that the concept of sexual equality is part of the new consciousness, the division of being and thinking as a man, versus being and thinking as a woman, is rejected as part of the baggage of male chauvinism, just as every male-female difference but the actual physical morphology is denied. "Thinking as a woman" is, then, only a matter of thinking within a male-imposed inferiority whose characteristics are passivity, quietude, receptivity, acuity, sympathy, and other "feminine virtues."

It would then follow that literature featuring women characters who are pious, kind, passive, etc., and males who are dominant, active, and vigorous, is part of the same old male chauvinism and has the conscious or unconscious social utility of furthering the social pattern of male dominance, and that the perceptive acuity or psychological realism of such literature is in a sense wasted, devoted to a cause that is now lost, since its conception in injustice has now been discovered. "Now" is here an imprecise term; certainly the feminist movement made the discovery at its inception, more than one hundred years ago; it is as well seventy-five years since the suffragettes, thirty years since women in America took factory jobs alongside men, matched the accomplishment of men in the professions here and in Russia, England, Israel, and India. Yet the fictional representation has changed very little; it carries on its acuity and psychology in much the same terms, with a durability and persistence that give rise to the question whether it *can* be changed. It is not of much help, but notable, that we have long had novels of which it can be said that the sex of the writer is impossible to guess (a situation satirized by James in *The Death of the Lion*); it has been immemorially true that talented individuals of either sex can mimic or adopt attitudes and interests of the other, whether those be biologically dictated or assigned by social convention. At any time, as well, there are males of markedly "feminine" outlook, and females of a correspondingly "male" toughness of mind.

As always amid such discussions among males, there arises a need to "get down to" the physical differences between the sexes, and then (tacitly) come back up from them to support intellectual, emotional, and social differences, deriving surface structure from deep structure, as it were. The problem (for males) is that it has become increasingly more difficult to get far back up: Studies of emotionally deprived children amply support the thesis that lack of early and sustained loving care by adults is the cause of their trouble (a recent study has even indicated that the unloved child may grow up to be physically smaller), but they fail to show a distinction between the sex of the adults who might give the loving care. In the traditional male domain, we find that physical strength is increasingly irrelevant to a machine-oriented technology. In the matter of physical assault, the gun has been the "Great Equalizer" of unequal muscular strength since the advent of weatherproof percussion ignition of gunpowder in the nineteenth century. In the nineteenth century, any woman could learn to handle a pistol, but few women drove carriages; they were not strong enough to. The contemporary technology did nothing to reduce the steering input of a team of horses below the level of male strength because there was no need to, and because it lacked the means to do so within economically sound limits. Nowadays the reduction of steering input of vehicles, automobiles or airliners, can easily be carried down to a level approaching zero, and a woman who would be defeated by a single balky horse can drive three hundred horses in a four-thousand-pound car as well as a man. Few remaining machine controls are beyond women, or cannot be built to suit women as well as to suit men; no accumulation of biceps can stop a fission reaction; states of awareness and alertness, stimulated by chemical or social means, have demonstrably leveled out for the two sexes. Only the predisposed are more frightened by the specter of a menstruating pilot landing a jetliner than they are by that of a pilot simply tired or inattentive; menstruating automobile drivers, for instance, have for long maintained a markedly lower accident rate than their male counterparts. That the latter group is more given to drunkenness, excitement, and hostility in cars undoubtedly has something to do with this.

There is, also, a literature of *real* sexual difference. Erotic literature of the type that specifies the details of sexual acts and, for that matter most novels, even *Little Women* or *Men Without Women*, that make use of sex-specific roles have a component with a biological basis. But the question is rather whether the traditional novel is to be dismissed as hopelessly enmeshed in the male dominance pattern, or whether it may be retained as doing something more than historically testifying to a state of affairs between the sexes that the contemporary era is bringing to a long overdue end. There is no ready path to the wished-for elements in the novel of the past by sexual clues—most simply, there is no indication that women novelists saw any better through the social organization that imposed inferior status on them. Shelley's impassioned effort to celebrate the ideal and equal union of the sexes found little echo among English poetesses. Virginia Woolf's novels have the gleam of superior understanding that puts the great artist above his or her sex, and Virginia Woolf was a woman keenly resentful of the status of her sex; yet the heroines of her most telling novels—Mrs. Dalloway in *Mrs. Dalloway*, Mrs. Ramsey in *To the Lighthouse*—are maternal and "feminine" to a heightened degree, semimystical presences of a womanhood more usually so exaggerated and sentimentalized by a male writer, such as, to take one of equivalent period and stature, E. M. Forster, with his Mrs. Wilcox of *Howards End* and Mrs. Moore of *Passage to India*. In George Eliot and Jane Austen, the greatest authoresses in the traditional English novel, there are, respectively, an outlook quite indistinguishable from a masculine one, analogical to the assumption of masculine clothes and name by the writer, and a marvelously acute view of social *mores* and individual motivation, but nothing to indicate a consciousness that the world could or should be organized any other way.

This search for a Shelley of the novel is difficult to extend with any hope of success. Tolstoy deserves consideration if for no other reason than his preeminent mastery of the form. No one else has done all that he did, and from such a wide, serene, and generous point of view. That point of view grew increasingly aware of the absurdities and illogicalities in human social arrangements, but did it ever see in and around the lives of men and women in such a way that what unites them is as clear as what separates them? Tolstoy could present the idea that women have souls as deep, and a capacity for understanding as large, as men do, but only that, and in that form: "as ——— as a man," the compliment set to a male standard, and perilously close to a cliché. And in his growing certainty that a woman was best occupied bearing and nursing children, he was as enslaved in his thinking as a New Guinea chieftain.

What then of Proust, the greatest novelist of love? The answer lies in that phrase: Proust was far too deeply enmeshed in the beauty and despair of courtship, the lover's examination of the extension of his feeling into the world, to see beyond the lover's situation. He was not a thinker, or one to reason out of or beyond his own social arrangement, its prejudices concerning the states "being a Jew" and "being a homosexual" notwithstanding.

That is a crux to which we are forced to return. The thinking is most often done outside the novel, outside imaginative literature, even; and when it is done inside, the literature takes on a program character—the novels of Bellamy and Wells, the political poems of Shelley, the tracts of Mary Wollstonecraft. The contemporary hope, as I have indicated my belief, lies in science fiction, and the tragedy of science fiction is its wealth of imagination, its poverty of conceptualizing skill. What then of Henry James? To direct this inquiry to him is an act suspect of special pleading—Have I not set out to find notable precedents of several kinds in James? And indeed, James was no thinker, as we are reminded *ad nauseam* by those who have taken their cue from T. S. Eliot's memorable phrase. But it may be that by a process of elimination we are forced to consider him. He is the greatest rival to Proust in English, sharing nearly the full extent of Proust's keenness of observation and feeling, while demonstrating the control and sense of form that Proust lacked. The two men had something close to the same observational base, a lifelong aversion to the expected and conventional male roles of lover of women, father of children, *paterfamilias*. Add to that an acute sympathy for the female role and the possibility of a peculiar advantage to observation of this kind in the presence of a homosexual inclination (amply documented and "lived" in the case of Proust; sparsely documented and of uncertain extent in the case of James).

The idea of outlining the ideal novelist through listing qualities of mind, education, and experience is of course quite ludicrous (he should be well-read, travel a good deal, have worked in a bank, hospital, law court, have seen action in wartime. . . .); we may be thankful that art displays a complexity of genesis that insulates it from such behavorial-psychological gropings. But, given the taint of curiosity in the matter, what fascinating possibilities arise when you posit the brain of a Henry James, the equal of the brain of a Tolstoy, set in something like the reversed image of the life and times of a Tolstoy, a Proustian removal from the traditional theaters of male activity, *along with* a monkish abstention from lovemaking—there you have the ultimate observer, the ultimately disinterested judge of human affairs. If you do not have a fiend in human form, that is, the observer that Hawthorne and Goethe assumed could only be the devil. Yet James needs no defense in the area of human feeling; not even the most Antiterran of critics has doubted its presence in his work. It is a feeling, however, that makes no distinction, to the disadvantage of either, between men and women. In that, it seems to me, it is very nearly unique, and uniquely "postmodern." In other words, it shows us something that we have been unable, despite our busy casting down of the idols of the sexist past, to find or create for ourselves in this context, that of great fictional art.

The general three-part chronology I have used throughout this study may be applied here as well, in the matter of the treatment of sex and the consciousness of women in the novel: at one end the nineteenth century, Victorian and Edwardian prudery, of which James has been taken as a prime example; at the other end the contemporary situation, difficult to label so neatly but incorporating a public freedom of reference to sex and a public assertion of the equality of women; and, in between, the "modern" period, of self-conscious revolt from the world that was supposed to have ended in 1914. There are naturally overlaps and interlocks: The 1920s and 1960s shared shortened skirts and a quantum jump toward greater sexual freedom taken by youth in defiance of age; deliberately nonsensical art (Dada and the Happening, or Conceptual burlap sandwiches); a unisex assertion, with women assuming mannish dress,[141] deemphasizing their breasts, taking up sports and outdoor life along with men. "Modern" must also include together the reactionary 1940s and 1950s along with the truly revolutionary 1920s and 1930s, at least until a more satisfactory terminology is agreed upon. The 1920s show, in the literary sexual *Darstellung*, a contingency, a dependence upon that which is denied, that is matched today in the left wing of Women's Lib, with their manic and pathetic rejection of their own bodies, the childbearing role, sexual relations with men, so infected do they remain with the self-hatred inculcated by the old system. America's best-known and most revolutionary erotic writer, Henry Miller, is a clear example of this contingency, this need for the top hat of nineteenth-century public virtue and standards of taste at which to hurl the childish snowball. His *Tropic of Cancer* (1934), with its anachronistic fellow *Sexus* (1949), remains a monument to literary re-creation of male treatment of women as *objects*, in the sense Simone de Beauvoir applies, and that Kate Millett has sufficiently established by the method of *explication de texte* to make it unnecessary for me to quote samples here. In these works, women are vessels of wrath, recipients of "the primal male urge" to take vengeance on the yielding flesh, to humiliate, play the lord of the harem, reduce to submission with the great weapon of the phallus. And, of course, all the while, to put an end once and for all to prudishness, modesty, and other such effeminate virtues, to establish a we're-all-men-together atmosphere, and everything else is cunt pure and simple, cunt, cunt, cunt. This certainly blows Victorian pretensions to smithereens (all those fancy-dressed broads pretending they're not cunt), but it also sets the general tone light years *behind* the Victorians, or any other period in modern history, and as effectively closes off the avenues of the heart and mind between men and women as any hypothetical descent to savagery.[142] Miller's world is exactly that of schoolboys, derived, we might say, from the world of Edwardian schoolboys, for whom, as more than one English writer has testified, the shame of confessing to having a *sister*, and so being tainted with the proximity of female flesh, was only exceeded by the shame of being found out to have a *mother*, with all *that* entails vis-à-vis female flesh.

If the work of Henry Miller is what modern literature has to counter the omissions, what Roman Ingarden calls the *Unbestimmtheitstelle* ("Indeterminacy-spots"),[143] of the nineteenth-century novel, then it looks as though we were better off where we were before. D. H. Lawrence, although a writer far superior to Miller, has been as effectively exposed by Simone de Beauvoir and Kate Millett. With his phallic didacticism and his relentless reduction of women, he appears in perspective today in much the same place as Miller, as far as sex is concerned—that is, a writer "liberated" by Freud and the social changes attendant upon World War I to preach a garbled doctrine of ancient mystification and male supremacy.

Nabokov, like Miller and Lawrence, is chronologically a "modern" (born in 1899, his first novel published in 1926), with the difference that he is today a potent force in contemporary fiction, a Luis Buñuel of the novel. Yet the lovemaking in *Ada* (1969), excitedly announced as a "new erotic masterpiece," ranges from outright parody of Victorian pornography to a Sadean intellectual coldness. It is barren ground on which to search for signs of new growth in traditional male conceptions of women:

> He groped for and cupped her hot little slew from behind, then frantically scrambled into a boy's sandcastle-molding position; but she turned over, naively ready to embrace him the way Juliet is recommended to receive her Romeo. She was right. For the first time in their love story, the blessing, the genius of lyrical speech descended upon the rough lad, he murmured and moaned, kissing her face with voluble tenderness, crying out in three languages—the three greatest in the world—pet words upon which a dictionary of secret diminutives was to be based and go through many revisions till the definitive edition of 1967. (*Ada*, p. 121)

This is Ada and Van's first lovemaking, and initially rather smooth sailing—though some readers could certainly find object-overtones in "hot little slew"—until it takes a sudden turn into philology, which is a turn for the worse, and the puncturing of the representational surface, and thereby of the lives of all characters but Van. For he is the author of *Ada* ("Ada's" being, like Mrs. Sam Clemens, manuscript corrector, does not noticeably affect that relationship) as well as of imaginary trilingual dictionaries. Ada the girl, under the withering gaze of Nabokov's besetting nominalism (a nominalism with sadistic overtones), is finally a *word*, one of whose avatars is "hell" in Russian; in this context it is no surprise that Don Juan's road to hell, paved with the bodies of women, and Don Quixote *enchanted* by Dulcinea, figure in the narrative's embroidered layers, all of which are subordinated in one way or another to entomological metaphor, butterflies and insects whose mating habits are juxtaposed in the text with such scenes as that of first love quoted above. Here is the position of Romeo and Juliet put into the book's perspective:

> Some of the perils and ridicule which attend the missionary position adopted for mating purposes by our puritanical intelligentsia [reads Van to "entomologically-minded Ada"] . . . are pointed out by . . . the mating habits of the fly *Serromyia amorata* Poupart. Copulation takes place with both ventral surfaces pressed together and the mouths touching. When the last throb (frisson) of intercourse is terminated the female

sucks out the male's body content through the mouth of her impassioned partner. (*Ada*, p. 135)

To argue that Van falls under the same misanthropic pall, the bleakly disillusioned comparison of mankind to insects that strikes Ada—that if she is the *mante religieuse* of male folklore, then Van is nothing but poor worm—this is not quite possible. For as we have seen, in chapter 6, the preponderance of narrative in *Ada* is male adolescent wish-fulfillment, by the requirements of which women, no matter how desired, pursued, vowed to or hymned over, remain irrevocably objects of lust rather than equal partners. For all their beauties, Nabokov's other novels of importance—*Lolita, Pale Fire, Bend Sinister*—bear the same stamp. They may avoid the crudities of Miller, but they express the same basic psychological pattern.

While there is little justice in dismissing a generation of writers on the basis of such a short survey, there is no evidence I can find to fault feminist literary critics in their surveys of the modern writers. Ernest Hemingway and F. Scott Fitzgerald, for instance, shared Nabokov's background to the extent of education and youth before World War I, and their representation of women is as conventionally rooted. Greater writers, like Proust and Thomas Mann, did merely what all great writers do—penetrate so well into the general human consciousness that women as well as men are convinced by their "truth"—but that is a matter common to Shakespeare and Aeschylus, something of neither particular application to, nor derivation from, the modern world. Jean Genet receives and deserves high praise from Kate Millett for exposing the masculine charade, but this is a negative accomplishment, put as well at one remove from the area of the discussion by its homosexual framework. The novels of Colette serve Simone de Beauvoir in the same way that those of Genet serve Millett, as a rich mine of dramaticized embodiment of the injustices of male domination. Their underview, that of a woman, is more central than that of a man acting woman to other men, but there is little place granted to Colette in the modern pantheon, outside her own country. The work of the emerging black writers in English—Ralph Ellison, James Baldwin, Richard Wright, Leroi Jones—has even less to offer. The man-woman inequality can be read out of the white-black injustice portrayed, conservatism, *idées reçues,* and tradition being in both cases the motive force, along with fear, of a state of affairs demeaning to the human condition; but the reading-out process is forced and artificial, ironically undercut by the fact that black consciousness tends toward a more rigorous and traditional "separate and unequal" treatment of the sexes (Black Muslims being only an outstanding example) than does white.

Sophisticated and essentially conservative writers like Nabokov and James Purdy have escaped the influence of modern sexual positivism, which started with Freudian psychoanalysis and has come down to Kinsey and to Masters and Johnson in our own time, throwing off Esalen Institutes, organized touching, and articles on "How to Enjoy Sex" in popular magazines along the way. Its theme is literally a mindless one, one that displaces the mind by the body, holding (with Miller tacitly, and with Lawrence as a matter of doctrine) that truth lies in the body, that the body and its natural functions relieve one of all the harm the mind can do and will bring about, if given their way, a reign of love and truth. Thus, modern positivism approaches modern innocence, while clinging to ancient dualism. Masters and Johnson themselves, the most respected workers in the field of sexual therapy, have chosen to move away from mental (or psycho-) analysis in their treatment of "sexual dysfunction" or "sexual inadequacy,"[144] finding a direct behavioral approach to physical acts the most promising cure. Their standards of normal or "functional" sexual performance are high, at least in that they take a wide territory for the domain of their curative technique. They are quoted by their commentators, Fred Belliveau and Lin Richter, as stating, "A conservative estimate . . . would indicate half the marriages [in the United States] as either presently sexually dysfunctional or imminently so in the future."[145] But the causes of this widespread dysfunction are essentially superficial: "Sociocultural deprivation and ignorance of sexual physiology, rather than psychiatric or medical illness, constitute the etiologic background for most sexual dysfunction."[146] And the hope for cure is bright indeed: "It has been found more effective . . . to assign a total of three weeks to accomplish reversal of symptomatology" (p. 20). The symptoms being the heart of the matter, that means cure.

169 • The Erotic

While this may in fact be true, and does look true for the cases Masters and Johnson report with apparent candor and professional concern for accuracy, it has, to an American ear, unfortunate echoes of all those promises of compressed time and manufactured happiness that surround us—learn a foreign language over the weekend, increase your reading speed by a factor of ten, master the piano in twelve easy lessons, electronics in your basement, any skill or trade, and live happily ever after on the social and economic rewards derived therefrom. Presumably, given enough of the special three-week clinics, modeled on that of Masters and Johnson, that are now springing up in other American cities, as well as a general spread of the new knowledge of sexual physiology—both worldwide—the optimistic prophecy made by Masters and Johnson in the preface to their *Human Sexual Inadequacy* will be realized: "It is to be hoped that human sexual inadequacy . . . will be rendered obsolete in the next decade" (p. v). "Obsolete" is a term, interestingly enough, of strong associations to machine technology. If the American figure of 50 percent dysfunction is taken as even roughly indicative of the situation in all the other nations, the indicated process will have to have the speed and force of a tidal wave, unmatched in its career by that of any other American skill or product in its global career. Henry Miller's heroes would be proud of that spread of healthy copulation, that general clearing of cobwebs out of closets and cupboards!

With normal intercourse as their standard, Masters and Johnson have a simple and direct way with the often queer relationships people work out between themselves. Here is an example:

[A] clinical failure to reverse the symptoms of ejaculatory incompetence involved the man with no personal regard for, no interest in, and no feeling for his wife. . . . Once the depth of the husband's personal rejection of his wife was recognized, the unit [sic] was discharged from therapy. Divorce was recommended to the wife, but her immediate reaction was to hold on to her concept of a marriage. (p. 134)

The divorce counseled here seems a bit self-serving statistically, since a dysfunctional marriage that is dissolved, in the same way as one that is cured, counts as "one less dysfunctional unit." But further, it seems an irregular incursion into the mental domain, for who knows what kind of adjustment to each other this couple may have made, without psychoanalysis? Not a conventionally happy one, surely, but except for their coming together to the clinic there is no evidence that they had not made an arrangement whereby their sexual needs were met—with other partners, or by transposition into other areas of life. Certainly the wife had something in this marriage she was unwilling to give up. It could have been nothing but a life of leisure, but the question here is of the *assumptions* made. To take an initial one (one that, to give Masters and Johnson credit, it must be said that they seem here on the verge of questioning), can you assume that people who come to you for help actually want it? There are stranger things in heaven and earth than sexual positivism knows of; one suspects Masters and Johnson would cut the Gordian knot of James's *The Portrait of a Lady* by counseling Isabel Archer to get a divorce.

Masters and Johnson must be granted a victory nevertheless: Such benefits as there are to rationality and optimism they reap. Their campaign for mutual orgasm accompanied by ejaculation has the effect of raising woman's erotic satisfaction to the level of man's, and that is a great improvement, one trusts, on the traditional feminine masochism and passive acceptance of whatever crumbs fall from the table, as it were, of their male partner's sexual banquet. Without resorting to such fatuity as Kate Millett's assumption that female capacity for multiple orgasm proves the superiority of the female organism to the male, it seems safe to say that female orgasm has a natural role in sexual intercourse, more or less as male orgasm does, so normal intercourse may be presumed to feature orgasm for both partners. To decide otherwise would be to miss something about human physiology, to relegate the female orgasm to masturbation, the use of treadle sewing machines, Japanese *rin-no-tama*, and so forth. In that light, those of Miller's characters who assault women as if with a desire to humiliate them rather than to give them pleasure may be said to be missing something, one-half of what sexual *inter*course is about; while those of D. H. Lawrence who actively strive to prevent the woman from achieving orgasm in sexual intercourse may be said to be sadistically per-

171 • *The Erotic*

verted—no matter how many masochistic women may derive pleasure from reading such material, or being made love to in such a way.

The younger contemporary writers who have taken up the revolutionized treatment of love in the novel show little progress, on the whole, beyond the turbulence and natural confusion in the fiction of the 1920s, when the dam first broke. This is strange, considering the rate of change in twentieth-century society, and the rate of change in the novel. Norman Mailer, for instance (b. 1923), shows little progress beyond the stage Miller (b. 1891) marked out, of free-speaking male sexual violence, except that he has a greater grasp of feminine psychology. Burroughs has given us the most striking use of sexual fantasy in science fiction, but he pays little attention to women characters; Hubert Selby, Jr., in some ways a latter-day Céline, directs his obsessive narratives in primarily sadistic channels. Robbe-Grillet's haunting parables of illusion have a sadomasochistic character that is at least as far removed from the question at hand. There is little evidence here of any digestion of the knowledge the new science of sexual therapy has given us: Selby's *Last Exit to Brooklyn* and *The Room*, for instance, might be judged by an extraplanetary observer to have sprung from one of the most sexually benighted and repressed periods in Earth's history—seventeenth-century Spain, or Geneva at the same time, rather than America under the beneficent influence of birth control, sex education, clean laundry, and Masters and Johnson. More normal, or typical, passages of sexual description, like the two following, would show less than impressive development:

Billy was on top of Valencia, making love to her. One result of this act would be the birth of Robert Pilgrim, who would become a problem in high school, but who would then straighten out as a member of the famous Green Berets.

Valencia wasn't a time traveller, but she did have a lively imagination. While Billy was making love to her, she imagined that she was a famous woman in history. She was being Queen Elizabeth the First of England, and Billy was supposedly Christopher Columbus.

Billy made a noise like a small, rusty hinge. He had just emptied his seminal vesicles into Valencia. . . . Now he rolled off his huge wife, whose rapt expression did not change when he departed.[147]

I saw my father and the lieutenant standing in the doorway. I saw many men standing around, perhaps ten. And Maryann was there, lying on a bottom bunk. Her skin was wet, on a hot night, wet with sweat? No, worse. No one moved toward her at first. . . . My father came to her. They spoke. Nothing moved, none of the people there. . . . Then I remember Maryann's dark arms reaching up, my father bending, kissing her goodbye. Holding her hand one moment more. And then turning, leaving. The others standing motionless, strangers, thinking about how they will go again into, into her.[148]

The first of these is from Vonnegut's *Slaughterhouse-Five*, a book I have treated as important in its use of science and its embodiment of contemporary fictional developments. The scene here is its most direct description of lovemaking, a type of description that I take as critical, if present, to a novelist's representation of female consciousness. Here the tone is comic, gently so, as if from the point of view of a wise and experienced—given the plot, even extraterrestrial—observer. It is hard to see in Valencia a more ridiculous, alienated figure than Billy, especially if we include Billy's fatuous thoughts immediately following, over the bourgeois dream of success—an all-electric home and $30,000 a year—that his marriage to this fat girl no one else would marry has brought him. Yet Valencia is what a Miller hero would consider the most awful of repulsive fat cunts, hardly human. Where Vonnegut's sympathies lie is made clear by his 1970 play, *Happy Birthday, Wanda June*, which is, among other things, nearly a doctrinaire program for women's sexual rights and the puncturing of male sexual vanity, domination, and the violence it breeds (this last is made clear in *Slaughterhouse-Five*, whose subtitle, "The Children's Crusade," serves as ironic reflection of Eisenhower's phrase for the 1944 invasion of Europe). Vonnegut has not tried, beyond some short stories which he now violently disavows, to show the relations of the sexes on another basis than the comic-allegorical; we cannot look to him for more than a trace of what we seek. It is clear, though, that his heart is in the right place.

The second passage forms the climax of Thomas McMahon's

173 • The Erotic

Principles of American Nuclear Chemistry (1970), in which a young woman abandons her body to the soldiers in a Los Alamos barracks the night before the first atomic explosion. She, Maryann, has been the mistress of Harold McLaurin, one of the leading scientists at the atomic bomb project (otherwise only lightly fictionalized by McMahon, with "Ferrini" for Fermi, "Sandeman" for Oppenheimer, "Orr" for Bohr, and so forth), and in the absence of McLaurin's wife, who refused to accompany her husband to the project, has acted as a kind of mother—and sexual instructress—to Timmy, his son and the book's narrator. At the time of the episode in the barracks, Maryann is married to one of the other scientists on the project, but the bond between her and the father is felt by both of them, and by the boy, so that it is natural for them to go to her—even though the father in later years, rejoined to Timmy's mother, claims he barely remembers her. That the relationship was important to Maryann too is obvious. Even though she could only be mistress, not wife, domesticated by an odd chance of war and by another chance, that the war work was secret, combined with the father's scientific single-mindedness, which made it impossible for her to share in the driving force of his life—despite all this, her being with this man, who brought her to Los Alamos from her childhood home in Tennessee, was the central fact of her life. Her falling to pieces starts when she leaves the father and marries the other man—the same man who had callously told her that he had selected her to provide solace and comfort to Timmy's father so that his efficiency as a scientist would not be impaired, a revelation that, to borrow a phrase from Henry James's *Washington Square*, had broken the spring of her affection.

I take up this work because it is one of the few attempts to put into the novel the matter of Los Alamos, the invention of the atomic bomb, and the changes it brought to the world. It is not an altogether ineffective attempt to put science into contemporary literature on a factual-historical level, but its means, the way the girl Maryann is used to comment on science and the Bomb, reflect a feminine psychology more mystical than factual, strange to find in 1970. The book's cover, done by Alan Magee, showing Maryann's face merged with the mushroom cloud of the Bomb, represents the terms of the plot accurately; Maryann does provide the inspiration to keep the scientists working fruitfully, as psychologically or romantically naive as that may sound—Timmy's father, whose bed she shares, and Nachtigall, who marries her, and others, who come to the house and are guests at breakfast, served by her in a diaphanous nightgown. She is scientific Muse, and Venus *Victrix*, while at the same time her role as Venus *Verticordia*, turner of the heads of men, is a dangerously disturbing one, full of the darkness and disorder that threaten masculine clarity and direction. Men seriously at work are best left alone—or are they best left alone, when what they are working on is a superbomb, a small boy's dream of a firecracker big enough to blow up the world? (It is the vestal virgin of physics, the beautiful Selina Meisner, whose serene attention to her work and unconsciousness of the effect her beauty has on the men earns her the name of Cockteaser, who presents them with the possibility of just that happening, that the bomb "could light the air").

Sex and scientific accomplishment don't mix, when out of any other context than male scientists being given nocturnal solace by women who have no other part in their affairs. With a docile Maryann, and out of the grasp of a complaining and querulous wife, Timmy's father does his best work. But Sandeman nearly ruins himself going off to San Francisco on a fool's errand to rescue an ex-girl friend in trouble with her Communist lover (Oppenheimer's involvement with Jean Tatlock, which was used against him in the hearing, is distinctly recognizable here); Selina decides, with Maryann's advice, to take a lover, and "fucks away" her professional abilities—her physics becomes second-rate. Equally magical is the effect of Maryann, or the sexual mystery she represents, upon Timmy. Timmy is in a profound sense unmanned by his Los Alamos experience, being unable to progress into responsibility and maturity after the troubled adolescence he spent there. A day in which Maryann and another girl had taken him out into the countryside and there given him a partial sexual initiation returns to him in a dream sequence, in which he sees dead testicles—his own—in her hand.

Maryann's quotidian behavior is as saturated with the eternal feminine as her symbolic role suggests—she is as unsteady as water, nearly running off with a roustabout for whom she has conceived an instant infatuation on the way from Oak Ridge to Los Alamos with Timmy and his father, then at Los Alamos suffering from moods and vapors and fits of pointless, somewhat malicious gossip. She is basically childish, being delighted and amused, for instance, to discover that she can stain her fingers blue with the cheap dye in paper toweling. Her representation, in sum, is a compendium of male folklore of the female; she is the Eve Adam couldn't live with, and so returned to God in exasperation, but then found he couldn't live without, and so had to go and ask for back again. While the novel, like so many others of our day, advances from censorship to a larger and truer picture of sexual physicality itself, it still frames that picture with traditional bias. McMahon clearly and aptly shows that the truth of Maryann, the represented human being, is just that she needs recognition as a human being and cannot get it from the men, who have other interests, who are distracted by the adventure of their work, who are incapable, finally, of seeing her as more than a sexual object. But from his own, authorial, point of view he suffers from the same limitations they do; his mythological and transcendent frame has the same origin as their immanent and literal one. Both testify to the staying power of the male conception of the female as the Other—described so well by Simone de Beauvoir near the end of the modern period, now a quarter of a century ago.

That staying power, so little affected by mere increase of *knowledge* and so little challenged by imaginative literature, with all its freedoms, poses a question too absurdly large to be taken up here, but surely this clue of "the Other" is useful and opens up a connection to the consideration of the Other earlier in this volume. Maryann is symbolically tied to the atom bomb, made almost a Pandora in relation to the awe and terror in it, which is the possibility that it is a lid or door to the unknown, an unknown potentially filled with all the evils man has not hitherto managed to loose upon himself. She can be so tied because she is of her nature apart from man, an other that can thus serve as *mediatrix*, standing between man and the Other beyond all humankind. Woman's heights

(Muse, Angel, Mother of God) and depths (Whore, Angel of Death, pure animal carnality) are beyond man's. No man can imagine another man so much in the grip of the unspeakable as Maryann in the military barracks—her skin glistening with sweat? no, something worse . . . ; no man can imagine, with final satisfaction, once in the grip of the mythology, another man—an Einstein, even, or an Oppenheimer, made into the foolish Sandeman of the book—as embodying in his person the infinite mystery of the atomic explosion. The intrusion upon the secrets of the atom and space travel, the propelling of man beyond the planet Earth, are both the greatest accomplishments of man in his history, and the two facts that have transformed the contemporary world, putting a gulf between it and all previous history as boundless as the eternal deep. Is it not another example of the same predilection of the male imagination that Mailer, with his *Fire on the Moon* the first of our contemporaries to attempt an application of literary art to the landing on the moon, should propose the image of the astronauts as seeking sperm voyaging toward the great closed passive female egg of the Moon, the secrets of life locked within it?

The converse of this is to do what Simone de Beauvoir felt Stendhal had done, to recognize that woman is the same as man, a human being just like him, no more and no less; not *other* but *another*. To allow this fact, that woman is not above us and below, is to leave her just beside us, shorn of the magical powers we know we as men very well lack. By recognizing that she is not *other* we are left without our last defense or interposed entity between ourselves and the Great Other, and Other that the gods and angels and saints and heroes immortally conceived once kept in check on our behalf. To accept woman as one of us, to give up her mystification, alternately suppression and exaltation, is to recognize and accept that we are, in our own world, alone.

Henry James is one of those writers who got there ahead of us, for the eerie *absences* in his work, inside a dense and dramatic representation of society in England, America, France, and Italy, express what we can only now better see. It was not made much of, in James's lifetime, that there is no discernible or conventional transcendent entity in his *authorial* frame, partly because readers had not become accustomed (as they did after James's own practices and critical writing, developed into a critical school, had alerted them) to seeing the novel as technique, a matrix of embedded points of view. Novelists and readers, like M. Jourdain, had been doing it all along without thinking about it, since you cannot tell a story without a point of view, and you cannot create a character without giving him a point of view, which can by definition never be identical with your own. Secondly, and consequently, readers were accustomed—and still are, both in general and in the columns of learned journals, so natural is the response—to identifying in some vague way the thought of the author with that of the character or characters who seem sympathetic or right-minded. A good deal of modern criticism, whether or not in the direct line from James's *Prefaces* to Percy Lubbock and Joseph Warren Beach, to the New Criticism and Wayne Booth, has been a succession of nasty surprises for such readers as one after another of such "safe" characters has been blown up, whether in Swift or Dickens, Joyce or James.

The same has been true of the represented women in James's novels: They are there, in all appearance like women in other books. In the absence of authorial measuring points, we are free to *assume* that James saw them as we are used to seeing them, that is, as mothers, wives, inferior helpmates, objects; in the frustrations and ecstasies involved in courtship and mating, as angels, devils, and various intriguing mixtures of the two, the matter of the mixture being something to which females are especially given and which gives them their fascination. It is even today conventional in James scholarship to so take the portrait of Christina Light, the fatal woman of *Roderick Hudson* (1877), later made the title figure of another novel, *The Princess Casamassima* (1886). She is fickle, vain, untrustworthy, capable of leading a man to his ruin—as it can be said she does in both novels. In the manner so dear to Victorian fiction, she is the "dark" woman, with disreputable secrets in her past, a European or eastern background, capable of extremes of passion, adultery, incest, even murder (so Miriam in *The Marble Faun*, James's primary model for *Roderick Hudson*). She is set against the pure, sweet, hometown girl, who is western, American, blond, or blond in soul, the one the hero will, or should, marry, and who will be a good mother to his children, guardian of the hearth, companion in his declining years (Hilda the Dove in *The Marble Faun*, Mary Garland in *Roderick Hudson*).

In *Roderick Hudson*, written at a time when James was just learning his craft, we hardly expect to see him go far beyond his models, and indeed there is none of the subtlety of language and tone that we find in the novels of the "major phase." Yet James seemed to be able to start off in full flight as far as imaginative conception of womanhood was concerned. Christina Light, surrounded as she is with an aura of *femme fatale*, of object and "other" status, is a lucid portrait of, simply, a person, a human being with the misfortune (for a woman) of being born both intelligent and beautiful. She enjoys her own beauty and its effect on men—which means that she has a natural pride in her body—but she is disgusted by the show her mother makes of it in an effort to make a great match for her. A great match means money and social position to be gained, and Christina cannot bring herself to despise the idea—what else, after all, is she able to bring off as an accomplishment in life? To turn it down would be to condemn herself to a dreary stretch of further years in the company of her harpylike mother, listening to her reproaches. As Alessandro Manzoni's Gertrude is schooled and trained and *expected* to become a nun, Christina Light is to become a great match, and equivalently to serve the interests of her parents in doing so. That she would, in such a situation, be attracted to Roderick Hudson, the beautiful and talented but penniless young artist whose passion for her beauty is so loudly and sincerely proclaimed, but that she should try to put him off at the same time, is easy to understand. Yet to Rowland Mallett, the observer-narrator of the novel, this conduct is *prima facie* evidence of heartless flirtation, moral irresponsibility, childishness, willfulness, and vanity. When Christina breaks off her engagement to the wished-for *parti*, Prince Casamassima, with his great southern lands and his millions, Rowland is disgusted and curses her inwardly, for he can only see that such an act amounts to an invitation to Roderick to run off with her. Rowland feels himself responsible for Roderick's being held to the paths of righteousness, and Roderick is engaged to another girl, the virtuous Mary Garland. For Roderick to take up with Christina would be, in Rowland's mind, the culmination of his ruin. He is also alienated from sympathy with Christina by seeing her cruel treatment of the prince, a dull but honest fellow who has done nothing to deserve being jilted practically at the door of the church. That the girl might naturally let things go so far without actively meaning harm, that she could be so rude to a man merely because she does not love him and he, knowing that, could still want to marry her, and that she could use Hudson's infatuation as a weapon in this crisis, is outside the comprehension of Mallett. Since Mallett is the calm, reasonable, right-minded narrator, it is most natural to interpret these events through his eyes. What is outside his comprehension tends to be outside ours, too—but not outside James's. To Rowland, women are supposed to get married or resign themselves to spinsterhood; their function vis-à-vis men is marriage. He can sympathize when he sees the dire intensity of Mrs. Light's intention to force the daughter into marriage with Casamassima, but he is without response when Christina explains to him that she feels suffocated by this direction of her life into marriage, that what she wants is a different relation, a relation with an artist or free spirit, like Roderick, but as a brother, not a husband. To Rowland this is feminine theatrics; his displeasure is allied to that he feels over the figure of the unmarried lady artist in Rome, Augusta Blanchard, a woman taking on, and miserably failing at, the independence and creativity natural to a man. That Christina could also admire him, and wish to act so as to please him, is as lost upon him as is the admiration of Daisy Miller for Frederick Winterbourne. Thus, when Christina turns off Roderick in response to Rowland's appeal, Rowland only observes that the manner in which it was done was too abrupt and therefore harmful; when she tells him that what gave her the courage to turn off Casamassima with his millions was her realization that Miss Garland, the morally inner-directed New Englander, would not marry such a one for such a motive, Rowland can only reflect that Mary Garland is Roderick's fiancée, and therefore a natural enemy of Christina's, and that the abrogation of the engagement to Casamassima provides a cunning blow against the engagement of Mary to Roderick. That Roderick does not love Mary and proposed to her in a moment of twilit enthusiasm cuts no ice with Puritan Rowland; a contract is a contract.

When Christina, now married (by force) to Casamassima, meets Roderick in Switzerland and gives him a distinct romantic invitation, Rowland sees, and we might say that we see as well as he does, that such a woman is morally irretrievable, a closed chapter in the history of female wickedness. The parallel to *Daisy Miller* is again at least potentially striking: So thought Winterbourne when he saw Daisy in the Colisseum at night. There is no escaping the evil represented—to Casamassima, as richly deserved as it may be—by this adultery Christina proposes, and from which she is only saved by Roderick's tumbling off an Alpine cliff on his way to meet her; but there is in the novel a realization open to us, if not to Rowland Mallett, that such behavior is the revenge, feeble enough, but the only one open to her, taken by an aggrieved and desperate woman against the social structure that imprisons her. As "the most beautiful woman in Europe" she has been treated strictly as an object, and the one way the object can show it has teeth is by disrupting the system of possession, by giving the pleasure of the object-body to a man or men other than the one who bought and paid for it. Christina's chapter is therefore not closed for James.

An apothegmatic analogue for the whole occurs in a little scene toward the middle of this novel: Rowland, who is used to strolling about drinking in the wonders of Rome and who is willing, if properly appealed to within his own proclivities as regards the fair sex, to shepherd a female around to see the sights (giving her guidance, as he does to Mary Garland), meets Christina, who is out doing the same—without a man to accompany her. That means she cannot let her face be seen and is swathed in veils—barely able to see, in fact. Rowland has no comment; we presume he puts it down to the willful unconventionality of the girl. If a girl wants to improve her aesthetic education, let her arrange for a man to take it in charge, as he will take in charge her personal transportation.

James's other novels bear out the impression given by a second look at Christina Light; while there is no identification in them with the "cause" of womanhood, and no denunciation of male supremacy (indeed, the shrill emptiness of Lesbian feminism is dramatized in *The Bostonians*, and the domination, by default, of American society by the women is described with asperity in *The American Scene*), there is an effortless grasp of a woman's thoughts and actions within a framework that includes a man's natural knowledge of the tenor of the thoughts of a man. Jane Austen avoided scenes in which men are alone together, for fear she would misrepresent their speech; James had no such fear of representing women together. Indeed, his biographer, Leon Edel, has suggested that he cast himself as the heroine of several of his fictions, and E. S. Nadal, who knew James, noted that "he seemed to look at women rather as women looked at them. Women look at women as persons; men look at them as women."[149]

Kate Millett has written that Jean Genet "appears to be the only living male writer of first-class literary gifts to have transcended the sexual myths of our era,"[150] but at the outset of "our era" there was Henry James, there more fully too than the women writers tacitly assumed to have been able to show the truth. As we have seen, it is easy to find a woman writer who expresses the injustice, but hard to find one who can show the truth, who is not as limited in her perspective as Genet is in his. The truth is a difficult thing; men and women are closer together than they think, and the writer who shows that may be forced to write so that you can easily miss it.

CHAPTER EIGHT
Nothingness

A contemporary writer who treats the world in the same essentially melodramatic terms that Henry James did one hundred years ago, at the beginning of his career, is John Barth (b. 1930). His best book, to my mind, is his most direct description of contemporary society, *The End of the Road* (1958), an encapsulation of *nada* nearly as overwhelming to the reader as to its central character. And the *nada* is nowhere so clear as in the lovemaking described in the book. It starts with the central character, Jake Horner (a name apparently compounded ironically of "horn" in its sexual connotations and "Little Jack Horner" of the nursery rhyme), seducing the wife of a faculty colleague, Rennie Morgan, and ends with her pregnancy and death. The seduction, move by move, is inhumane even in comparison to the series of letters in *The Red and the Black*, or the stages of capture in the *Chin P'Ing Mei*, for all their nasty mechanicity; it is more like the Pavlovian orgasm-triggering used by the (robotlike) Russian spy on the American girl in Arthur Koestler's *Age of Longing*. The physical consummation is given this description by Jake:

> I could illustrate this phenomenon, in the case at hand, clear up to the point—well, up to the point where the cuckolding of Joe Morgan was pretty much an accomplished fact; but delicacy, to which I often incline, forbids. We spent a wordless, tumultuous night together, full of tumblings and flexings and shudders and such, exciting enough to experience but boring to describe; for the neighbors' sake I left before sunrise.[151]

Jake's attitude here seems partly the Victorian gentleman with a sense of humor ("delicacy ... forbids"), partly the Hemingwayesque modern hero, masculine and laconic (to talk about it spoils it). The "boring to describe" goes a little too far in that direction, however, and gives the "wordless" of the opening clause a sardonic cast. Jake goes on to add a summary dismissal—"the whole business was without significance to me"—a dismissal that would be only callous if it were not for the long campaign of devious seduction he has carried on, a campaign that has included an undermining of Rennie's faith in her husband, Joe. This latter process culminates with an unsubtle invitation to intrude upon his privacy in a way that replicates the most Dostoevskian intrusion upon the soul. It is a violation of the *person* through the body. Noticing that the living-room window, behind which Joe is working alone, is not completely shaded, Jake, bringing Rennie home from horseback riding, suggests that they spy on him. "Come on, be a sneak!" he whispers, "It's the most unfair thing you can do to a person" (p. 57). She resists, protesting that Joe, as a *real* person, is just the same when he is alone as he is with others; but she looks. What they see is Joe parading around and trying on different expressions—undignified and comical, disturbing only to an insecure woman who looks upon her husband as a sustaining pillar of strength. What follows is no less human, if unlikely, but of magnified consequence:

> He snapped out of it, jabbed his spectacles back on his nose. Had he heard some sound? No. He went back to the writing table and apparently resumed his reading, his back turned to us. The show, then, was over. Ah, but one moment. Yes. He turned slightly, and we could see: his tongue gripped purposefully between his lips at the side of his mouth, Joe was masturbating and picking his nose at the same time. I believe he also hummed a sprightly tune in rhythm with his work.
>
> Rennie was destroyed. She closed her eyes and pressed her forehead against the window sill. I stood beside her, out of the light from the brilliant living room, and stroked and stroked her hair, speaking softly in her ear the wordless, grammarless language she'd taught me to calm horses with. (p. 58)

The lovemaking between Rennie and Jake, coming after this scene, is built on the ruins of her world. It is, once again, wordless, a grappling in the dark, to which the consequent event, the death of Rennie at the hands of an abortionist in grotesque melodrama style, is a logically fitting pendant. Jake's heartlessness is matched by her hopelessness and helplessness, a condition of having no one and no thing on which to depend, and nothing within herself to sustain her. Jake himself is given to states of "weatherlessness," moral and physical catatonia that makes him incapable of any action at all; his uncertain grasp on sanity is partly maintained, and partly threatened, by the attention he receives from a black doctor running an illegal sanitarium. Though not suicidal, he is as dependent on outside direction as the woman he so thoughtlessly involves with him. For him, love leads to death, the death of the woman he shares with Joe Morgan. For him and the recklessly intellectual Joe, who would rather his wife commit suicide as an expression of her own will than stay in life with him and her children as an expression of his, this death leads to nothing—that is, *nothing*.

There may be a near-allegorical patterning in *The End of The Road*, in that Jake's doctor has a frighteningly keen intelligence, yet is very close to unhinged himself, and operates outside the (white) law, and that the asylum to which Jake repairs for therapeutic interviews with the doctor is "out in the country," unheard of by Joe Morgan or anyone else in the town; that the asylum is in the process of moving, having a peripatetic location; that the Morgans, the married couple of normal and productive work in the community, she with the children, he with his scout work, teaching, and Ph.D. thesis in preparation, are both beyond the pale. She is suicidal, living at the beck of a husband who is a pillar of straight, clean respectability and clear-eyed reasonableness, or rationality, a rationality carried to its logical and hellish end point, in which behavior so guided becomes indistinguishable from madness—sending his wife, for instance, after her confession of adultery and deep appeal for forgiveness, back to Jake, to make love again, and again, so that she may analyze her motives for having done it the first time and give him a rational explanation, on the basis of which they can make a decision about their further life together.

With such terms, the book reaches out to encompass, if not its represented modern world, at least its represented society, America of the 1950s, as an ill-fitting mask concealing the features of madness. As such it is the reverse of Ken Kesey's representation of America in *One Flew Over the Cuckoo's Nest* (1962), in which the central point of view is located in the madhouse, with the assumption that there is general sanity, the sane ones locked up being those who fail to make the adjustment to the roles of slave or petty master allowed in the industrialized and dehumanized outside world. Kesey's narrative allows the possibility that there is somewhere a power in charge that is benign, if neglectful—on the other side of the mountain, perhaps, like the God of the Old Testament covenant that another symbolically named hero, Jakov Bok of Bernard Malamud's *The Fixer* (1966), rejects on the basis of his punishing and forgetting about mankind by turns. But *The End of the Road* imposes a silence far more teasingly indicative of a bottomless, topless, infinitely extensible nothing. It holds our faces almost too unremittingly and didactically against the abrasive surface of this assertion, much in the spirit of the classroom in which Jake presses home the paradoxes of prescriptive grammar with grim nihilistic humor. We have Rennie asking Jake, "You think I'm a complete zero, don't you?" (p. 47) and describing herself in those terms. When she first met Joe and came under his influence, she says, "I realized then for the first time what a complete blank I was!" Her analysis extends to Jake himself: "You cancel yourself out. You're more like somebody in a dream. You're not strong and you're not weak. You're nothing" (p. 55). And Jake explains their relationship in equivalent terms: "I think Rennie's attraction for me lay in the fact that, alone of all the women I knew, if not all the people, she had peered deeply into herself and had found *nothing*" (p. 55).

Rennie's interest in Jake is therefore almost consciously suicidal: Once she has found the abyss, the next step is to drop into it. That drop is, however, something; the *end* of Rennie's life, though accident rather than suicide, is the major event, the *catastrophe*, of the book. For Jake there is, again, simply nothing, or nothingness, which will, finally, come to a natural end. The last word of the text is Jake's instruction to the driver of the cab he calls to take him away, "Terminal." Which is to say, The End of the Road.

In 1952 Paul Tillich summed up the state of modern man in words that we have since heard in a thousand forms, that we have taught in our college courses, that we have, in many cases, come to live by, either employing the outer envelope of faith that Tillich himself argued for, or abandoning it with Camus or Sartre:

Twentieth-century man has lost a meaningful world and a self which lives in meanings out of a spiritual center. The man-created world of objects has drawn into itself him who created it and who now loses his subjectivity in it. He has sacrificed himself to his own productions. But man is still aware of what he has lost or is continuously losing. He is still man enough to experience his dehumanization as despair. He does not know a way out but he tries to save his humanity by expressing the situation as without an "exit." He reacts with the courage of despair, the courage to take his despair upon himself and to resist the radical threat of nonbeing by the courage to be as oneself. Every analyst of presentday Existentialist philosophy, art, and literature can show their ambiguous structure: the meaninglessness which drives to despair, a passionate denunciation of this situation, and the successful or unsuccessful attempt to take the anxiety of meaninglessness into the courage to be as oneself.[152]

The specificity of "Existentialist" in this passage could even be removed; for every modern who calls himself or his art existentialist there are hundreds who have simply lost the spiritual center and have entered the area of awareness of *Angst*, the dread of meaninglessness. Vonnegut's *Cat's Cradle*, which is of no proclaimed philosophical school, makes the point as clearly as Sartre's *Nausea*; Barth's *End of the Road* as clearly as Camus's *Myth of Sisyphus*, if somewhat more indirectly. Irving Howe's *Decline of the New* (1970) can speak in general sociological terms of a "modernist outlook" suffering from an "emptying out of the self, a revulsion from the wearisomeness of both individuality and psychological gain." His immediate reference is to the work of Beckett, but his specification recapitulates the philosophical *Angst* practically word for word: "The modernist sensibility posits a blockage, if not an end, of history: an apocalyptic cul-de-sac in which both teleological ends and secular progress are called into question, perhaps become obsolete."[153] This is the "Loss of the self in modern literature and art" that Wylie Sypher made the title of his 1962 study; the "sovereignty of the void" taken as the theme of Ihab Hassan's *Dismemberment of Orpheus* (1971).

This situation predates World War II; in some respects it predates World War I. The general application of it to "Twentieth-Century Man" is useful, for while the general loss of religious faith was sufficiently marked in the nineteenth century to be noted and bewailed by Matthew Arnold and Sören Kierkegaard or celebrated by Nietzsche, the terrible slaughter of the two world wars and the social and economic upheaval between them formed the catalytic agent needed to bring about an accompanying loss of faith in science, and a focusing of the general collapse of those elements which had given security into despair.

In 1975, however, this whole philosophical stand can be seen as having no more basis in science and contemporary knowledge than it would have been considered to have in 1175. Modern man may well feel a loss of the self, that he is *ohne Eigenschaften,* what with the progress made by totalitarian and totalitarian-minded bureaucracies around the world, the pressure of conformity amid growing populations, and the loss of economic independence, but in respect to scientific knowledge he is once more at the center of the universe, though in a new way: not because God crowned his created universe with the setting of man on earth, but because man cannot help being at the center; he has no other way of seeing and interpreting. I have had occasion to mention the development of modern physics and Heisenberg's indeterminacy principle in my opening discussion of the loss of certain boundaries, along with the increasing apparency in the late 1950s and the early 1960s that neutrality or "laboratory conditions," "pure data," were unobtainable in psychology, perhaps culminating with the present imminent collapse of Freudian, or materialistic-deterministic, psychiatry; the experiments of Richard Gregory, Gunnar Johansson, and others in vision, showing the extent to which the supposed cameralike objectivity of seeing is a matter of structured selection and reworking of data; the linguistic revolution of Chomsky and the M.I.T. group, which has lent heavy support to the idea that language does not work in an open-ended relation to reality, but according to preexistent pathways and relations in the brain. All these have shown that there is no such thing as man the observer standing to one side and apart from the physical reality he observes, whether he thinks that observation is subjective (full of self) or objective (impersonal and selfless). Man is inescapably part of what he observes and *changes it by observing it;* he has no way of escaping the centrality in the universe his observation gives him. J. A. Wheeler has cited, from

Robert Dicker, the following rational parable, which we may see as being in line with Gödel's concern for the construction of a philosophy to catch up with contemporary physics in the matter of the relation between subject and object: Why does the universe have dimensions of several times 10^9 light-years?

To observe the universe requires a mind of a certain degree of intelligence. So far as we know, a brain of this complexity cannot be produced without carbon. Carbon in turn needs for its manufacture thermonuclear reactions in the stars. To carry through the manufacture requires several billion years of stellar evolution. In order to have several billion years of time available for this manufacture, the universe must be several billions of light-years across. Thus the circumstance that the universe has the size that it does is conditioned by the fact that we are here to observe it![154]

It might be said that we knew all along that we are part of nature; my point here is that we are only now prepared to see what the full consequences of that truth are. We knew all along, you might say, that the people we interact with alter their actions according to what they think we think of them—it did not take the famous passage in James's *What Maisie Knew* to show us that. But in the face of the new science, the determinist view of nature, if not to say the positivist, can hardly last intact. As for the loss of the self in the wider social arena, this means there is no place in which to lose it. But the consequences have not spread very far; the only thinkers who have had to alter their behavior directly are the physicists. The psychologists, the behaviorists, the psychiatrists, and those who feel the *Angst* inherent in the loss of self, all look much the same, we might say. Only a little peaked. They will change in the future, when the new basis for the self, replacing the already discredited form initiated by European romanticism, has penetrated both the entire scientific consciousness and greater parts of the public intellectual and lay consciousness.

Such future predictions do not immediately concern us; our subject is literature already written. What are the consequences for literature, or for our view of literature? Speaking of what we know, the situation as it exists, we can say there has been a wide abandonment of the normal man as we know and feel him as observer and as hero, for such a viewpoint entails the operability of the human will upon physical conditions. *Angst* and despair rule out such confidence: Given an uncontrollable universe, possibly directed by forces inimical to man, and man helpless in the grip of those forces, what point is there in celebrating what man can think and do? He is better seen for what he is, as foolishly trusting and pathetically underequipped in his reasoning as a dog (so Kafka's *Investigations of a Dog*), as loathsome to himself and others as an insect (so Kafka's *Metamorphosis*). He is insane to think he can set himself against the forces, so isn't he better shown as insane? Faulkner's *Sound and Fury* is a tale told by an idiot; Nabokov's series of novels, from *The Defense* and *Despair* to *Lolita* and *Pale Fire*, all have insane protagonists; so do, very possibly, Robbe-Grillet's *Last Year at Marienbad*, *Jealousy*, *The Erasers*, and *The Voyeur*. Sylvia Plath's *Bell Jar* has the power of a more-than-personal testament; Kesey's and Barth's use of the metaphor we have glanced at. Man the image of his Maker, apex of creation, becomes a bad joke: The form of his creator may be nothingness; the only ability with which he can show himself superior to the animal and plant forms surrounding him is that of self-destruction. Why not, then, a plant or animal for hero, or at least a goat-boy, or a deformed midget? What seems attractive for literary use is any form of consciousness that is not the normal consciousness of mankind and gives a point of view of strangeness suitable to the new strangeness of the world.

The developed antihero, a product of nineteenth-century naturalism, works in two main strands through this literature that might be called Monsieur Blot and Ubu Roi. The first is the passive, recording consciousness of the man incapable of real action or of staving off the fate carelessly prepared for him by he does not know whom or what, the *petit bourgeois* in a labyrinth peopled by mirror images of himself. He can only think "Why me?" when fate seeks him out; he faces it dramatically (Camus's *Stranger*), or pathetically (Arthur Miller's *Death of a Salesman*), or terribly (Kafka's *Trial*). The second strand, that of Ubu, represents the assertive, thrusting mind-pattern of the grotesque and absurd, the ironic comedy of disorienting the world to suit the disorientation in a consciousness deprived of the normal, traditional joys and sorrows of mankind. In contemporary American, that means if the world is a screwed-up place, Mailer's D. J. (*Why Are We in Vietnam?*) and Purdy's Cabot Wright (*Cabot Wright Begins*) are going to get out there and join in the screwing, carry it to any extreme necessary. Ubu and Giles Goat-Boy and Oskar Mazerath are grotesque jokes, put-ons concealing another truth that lends irony and deliberate concealment to their narratives.

Where is that higher truth? To what extent are we being toyed with by the author, and by whatever he is in contact with? How much can we believe? Such are the questions put to us by these modern Tales of Tubs, and even an answer from the writer himself is insufficient, for the terrible snarl he has created contains truths and fictions beyond his wit to recognize, remember, and identify. In a third-person omniscient author frame like that Theodore Dreiser used in *An American Tragedy* (1925), we may say that the information is given; with Dreiser as with Zola, there is a clear indication of social and environmental forces operating on the hero and guiding him on his fated way—the antihero is "explained." But Dreiser was behind his time with that novel, more in Zola's time, in a nineteenth-century world. Well before 1925, in English, Joyce and Woolf had begun to map out the world of indefinableness that was to dominate "modern" fiction, and Henry James had established its mold with *The Beast in the Jungle* (1903). Typically, these works lack authorial omniscience, so that there is no indicated "way out" of the represented events.

That Joyce, Woolf, and James belong on the Monsieur Blot side, and Grass, Robbe-Grillet, and Mailer on the Ubu, does not distinguish them in the matter of whether or not the reader should take the narrative at face value. Whether it is a cockroach talking or an *apparatchik*, a suicidal Harvard student or a Cambridge don, delusion and illusion are the stuff of their existence. To appeal to a character description I offered in the discussion of women's roles, none of these characters is "safe." As Wayne Booth has argued cogently in *The Rhetoric of Fiction* (1961), James allowed the characters of his narrators, originally selected for objective and impersonal "telling," to grow in importance and move over into the action itself, in stories like *The Liar, The Aspern Papers*, and *The Turn of the Screw*. The literary fault, according to Booth, is that James's love of complexity and ambiguity made him render the character of the narrator as a person "profoundly confused, basically self-deceived, or even wrongheaded or vicious,"[155] thus corrupting at the source the flow of narrative information. If we cannot trust the narrator, how can we possibly interpret the story?

As far as it goes, the argument is incontrovertible. When we step back, however, to view its surrounding metaphysics, we see that its tacit assumption involves an impossibility—that a situation as exactly complex and ambiguous as that in any of the three stories mentioned could be objectively observed and reliably narrated by anyone, fictional in being or not, close enough to the events to understand them and know them. The observer is part of his observing, and his observing changes what he observes. This is the generally overlooked point of *The Sacred Fount*, an extended treatment of the observer problem alone. We can thus say that in twentieth-century literature there are no reliable narrators, and that Henry James demonstrated this to us at the century's beginning.

Up to the century's beginning there was, in the Newtonian mechanics, a confidence in the immutability of physical laws that enabled a prediction of a future state from a present one—*any* present one. If you knew, for instance, the exact velocity and direction of the bowling ball you had just sent on its way, you could confidently and exactly predict the number of pins you would knock over, with their directions and velocities. The ultimate such knower would be some superperson (he exists in physical speculation as Laplace's Demon) who knew not only the direction and velocity of your bowling ball but of all other objects, all constituent parts of all things, including those making up you—in short, the position and motion of every atom in the universe. With that knowledge he could predict the future of the universe.[156] That is a nice analogue of nineteenth-century determinism, and it fits as well the role taken for themselves by many novelists of the past. In fact, most novelists before Henry James. When a critic concludes, with Wayne Booth, that "one must say that an author has an obligation to be as clear about his moral position as he possibly can be" (p. 389), he is asking that the reader, too, be allowed a share of the

Demon's role. The novel or the story is to have clear boundaries, a clear point of view, a posited position and motion. In going this far I am already being unfair to the complexities of Booth's skilled and wide-ranging argument, but the logical end to this is the practice of writers like Thackeray and Trollope, who openly treated their characters as puppets, dolls, mechanical tools of the effects they had planned for them. To a lesser degree, it is the practice of Stendhal and Balzac, who again always kept superior knowledge and kept the total control of the author-creator well in view, and who marshaled characters to illustrate the moral truths they had selected for illustration. It is this ordered world that the "antinovelists" like Robbe-Grillet, unconsciously following in James's steps, have set out to counteract and purge from the novel.

I think Henry James is the writer who showed us the *necessity* of the development away from what we now call "reliable narration" in the novel, that to continue with it suited neither our culture's growing command of the novel form, nor the discoverable facts of physical reality. That James set himself down notebook plans for stories of admirable clarity and brevity, and was as unaware of the importance of Einstein as he probably was of that of Newton, is immaterial, sufficiently described by W. K. Wimsatt's intentional fallacy. He belonged without knowing it to his culture, just as we belong without knowing it to ours; being a great artist he was working well beyond his own consciousness, toward the boundary between what was in his own time and what was to be beyond his own time. What he thought or saw is immaterial to what he did, and what he did was to put human consciousness, with all its imperfections and capacity for self-deception, into the center of the novel, and thereby impose a limit on that which could be known. There is, in *The Golden Bowl* as much as in *The Turn of the Screw*, only a partial knowledge of motive and event, and there never will be a full knowledge, for it is a requirement of these fictions that there be only partial knowledge. The roles of Laplace's Demon and of the "objective observer" were closed to the reader by Henry James, and, in the sense of artistic realization, they have been closed ever since. Thereby he opened, or reopened, to us a more fitting role, that of true human being rather than imitation god. It is the role that gives us back the "lost self" of modernism.

Thus, I prefer to see James not as the pioneer sower of confusion into the classic novel, but as Heisenberg saw Josiah Gibbs, as a pioneer of a new, if complex, truth:

> When we know the temperature of a particular system, it means that the system must be considered to be only one out of a whole set of systems. This set of systems can be described accurately by mathematics, but not the particular system with which we are concerned. With this Gibbs had half-unconsciously taken a step which later on was to have the most important consequences. Gibbs was the first to introduce a physical concept which can only be applied to an object when our knowledge of the object is incomplete.[157]

Gibbs, by being the first to use a concept only applicable to something when that something is incomplete, in the sense that our knowledge of it is incomplete, took a pioneer step in the direction of the new physics, in which incomplete knowledge is a prerequisite of any statement. James and Gibbs both pointed the way to the fact that the observer's incomplete knowledge is a condition of his observation. The true meaning of "Emma Bovary, c'est moi," that insubstantial and often misapplied utterance, is "We are all unreliable narrators," and by that admission we become one with the reality surrounding us. Such is the state of contemporary knowledge. The future may hold discoveries of a totally different order, but we have been laggard in catching up to the present.

In a work of genius it is always possible to press beyond the assumed boundaries, but there are differences in the assigned nature of the boundaries; and in a great deal of the fiction of the present period, as we have found, the assignment is of the nature of a nothingness, an absence that leads not in the direction of an "other," but nowhere, to nothing. Or to the "Terminal." Looking at the situation from the outside we can see that in a state of nothingness, whatever there is must be of our own supplying; whatever meaning is derived must be derived by ourselves in the knowledge that it can never be independent of ourselves. Our failure to escape our own observation, our own "unreliability," is therefore doubly pressed upon us. We are in *process*, a state of suspension until a pattern is found and a meaning derived. It is always open to the writer to make it impossible for us—if by no other means than writing gibberish. But it is also possible for him to make that very suspension his subject, to dramatize the process and the waiting suspense. It is not surprising that one such dramatization, Beckett's *Waiting for Godot (En Attendant Godot*, 1952), has been taken almost from the date of its appearance as a key work of our time. For that reason, it is hard to imagine it having been written much before 1952, and certainly not before World War II. Yet James's *Beast in the Jungle*, of 1903, is also such a dramatization, and it is with a comparison of it and Beckett's drama that I would like to conclude this chapter.

The "world" of Beckett is certainly not comparable to that of James. Beckett, spanning as he does both English and French literature, is the acknowledged master of nothingness in the contemporary scene. Linguistically, his equivalent is silence, a paradox that Ihab Hassan has dealt with imaginatively (*The Literature of Silence; The Dismemberment of Orpheus*). His characters die into silence, literally or figuratively; they fall into attitudes of static despair, careless immobility at the verge of extinction. There are vague hints of something beyond that may contain meaning, or will, or a destiny for man: Knott and Godot exist, offstage, mysteries that cannot be shown to contain more of the same nothing until they are plumbed; there is malignant power from without in the existence of the cylinder of *The Lost Ones*, the mechanical tortures of *Act Without Words*, and the shrill bells and advancing sand of *Happy Days*. But the distance between this exterior and the world of the characters is never bridged, and the characters themselves are always powerless to alter the conditions in which they find themselves. In James, on the other hand, it is rare indeed that any hint of an "exterior" is given, and it is commonly shown that the efforts of the individual are of the highest importance. *The Turn of the Screw* and *The Beast in the Jungle* are exceptional cases.

The situation in *Godot* is of two people waiting—for their destiny, we may say without too much overstatement, for there is no serious question of their not waiting, or ceasing to wait. They fear punishment; they can take no further action until their suspense is over, until they reach Godot, or Godot comes and tells them his decision—what he will do. But there is no marked hope of his ever coming; he has refused to come before, and during the action of the play refuses to come again. Even what it is they have asked of Godot, or what they expect of him, not to mention who he is, or what powers he has, is vague in their minds. This is, with a difference in particularities, the situation of James's Marcher, who waits to see what special condition destiny has prepared for him (he feels it is something big, but knows nothing, and has no way of knowing anything), and May Bartram, who agrees, in an unspecified way, to wait with him. He attempts to define it to her:

"It hasn't yet come. Only, you know, it isn't anything I'm to *do*, to achieve in the world, to be distinguished or admired for."
"It's to be something you're merely to suffer?"
"Well, say to wait for—to have to meet, to face, to see suddenly break out in my life; possibly destroying all further consciousness, possibly annihilating me; possibly, on the other hand, only altering everything, striking at the root of all my world and leaving me to the consequences, however they shape themselves."[158]

For Marcher there is no question of living normally, of going on to something else, until this question is settled; and May Bartram, by her sympathetic identification, also puts her life into a state of artificial suspension. That Marcher and May Bartram live in a "jungle" that is actually Victorian London, while Gogo and Didi are apparently marooned in the midst of a nearly featureless landscape, does not reduce the strain of the wait for them. Nor is there any final assertion, in Beckett or James, that the world inhabited by such characters is *the* world. The largest and busiest city in the world surrounds Marcher, but it might as well be on the moon for all it can do to break through the "detachment" that holds him and May. In the later Beckett narratives we have no certainty whatever about the locale. There is a suspension in space—but then, you never know who will come along. In *Happy Days*, for instance, an English couple appear, gape at Winnie "stuck up to her diddies in the bleeding ground," argue, and disappear, "gone—last human kind—to stray this way."[159] In *Godot*, Pozzo happens by with Lucky, and a boy reports from Godot's place of residence, and there may be unseen men, offstage, who nightly pummel Estragon—all of which lightens the hopelessness of the situation of Vladimir and Estragon no whit. Like Marcher and May, they will continue to wait for nothing until the end.

May Bartram, who follows Marcher's lead much as Estragon does that of Vladimir, does hold the key to his situation: She knows that he could join life while waiting for the momentous thing to arrive. He could join her, that is, by marrying her. It may even be that she knows that what he waits for is nothing. Estragon holds no such key; his questions (What exactly did we ask him to do for us? Why can't we go?) are only a whimpering in the dark; Vladimir and Marcher know, or are brought to know, that there is nothing but the nothing of their waiting. Of a momentary diversion Vladimir cries, "Let's get to work! In an instant all will vanish and we'll be alone again, in the midst of nothingness!";[160] Marcher sees, finally, that "he had been the man of his time, *the* man, to whom nothing on earth was to have happened" and "that all the while he had waited the wait was itself his portion" (p.401). There are not many other literary works before *Godot* that so neatly encapsulate this modern *suspension*. Kafka worked at it, with his usual ineffable skill, in *The Castle (Das Schloss)*, but, fittingly, never finished!

Putting it another way, we can say that this century, with its global war and growth of the nation-state into a cannibalistic monster, brought into literature the nightmare of "In the night they are coming for me," its most notable expressions being Kafka's *Trial*, Koestler's *Darkness at Noon*, Orwell's *1984*, and Alexander Solzhenitsyn's *First Circle*. In the present literary and philosophical situation that nightmare has become old-fashioned, despite its continued possibility of occurrence for us all in the nonliterary sphere of existence, for it assumes there is a "they," whatever its shape, that takes an interest in *me*, for no matter how dire a purpose. What we have now is a different nightmare, which has gathered shape in sources as diverse as the *lishniy chelovek* (superfluous man) of Russian romanticism and the dreams of sleep in H. P. Lovecraft, was concretized fleetingly in James, and attained full flower in Beckett and Ionesco. It is this: "In the night there is a hole over an abyss of nothingness, and I am going to fall through it."

Wallace Fowlie has written of *Godot* that there occurs between it and the viewers "a suspense that is exceptionally related to the lives of those watching the play. We are facing the void in our own lives, the nothing that happens in our lives."[161] Vladimir puts it as well:

What's certain is that the hours are long, under these conditions, and constrain us to beguile them with proceedings which, how shall I say, which may at first seem reasonable until they become a habit. You may say it is to prevent our reason from foundering. No doubt. But has it not long been straying in the night without end of the abyssal depths? (p. 80)

CHAPTER NINE
Postscript

In a sense, the topics taken up in the foregoing discussion are not assimilable; their connection to one another is simply that they occur in contemporary literature and are important to it. My effort in bringing them together here is to argue for their importance and to note their links to a nineteenth-century writer who in one way suffers from no lack of appreciation, and in another suffers from the wrong kind, an adulation based on the assumption of his withdrawal from and irrelevance to the work of science in the modern world. In bringing James and science into the same context, I have also tacitly argued for a criticism that accepts the natural kinship between science and literature, or between—as Scott Buchanan put it in 1929 in the title of his undeservedly neglected book—"poetry and mathematics." But the affinity of these two, with their complementary attitudes, does not result in their combining, as so many have predicted and as might seem the situation described in the previous chapter, to produce nothing. To that point a few more words may be directed.

In 1925 José Ortega y Gasset noted that twentieth-century culture was causing, through such artistic movements as abstractionism, a "dehumanization" of its art.[162] By that he meant to complete a circle of influence: Art comes out of life; it is a kind of dehumanization in life that leads to the same thing in art. And we have indeed lived through a period in which the development of abstractionism, along with the atomization of futurism and cubism, paralleled a break-up of man into presumed machinelike elements, inputs and outputs of a "behavioral" or "black box" model that had no need of his interior, or for aspects of him that could not be located objectively. Machine models for sociology, economics, the study of cash flow or passenger vehicle flow, city planning, and architecture came to rule a wide range of human activity, throwing off features such as mass calisthenics, Art Deco interiors, the celebration of speed in automobile and aircraft racing, and the pursuit of records, the resultant streamlining becoming an aesthetic end in itself, to be applied to toasters and the Chrysler Building as well as to the Chrysler Airflow sedan. Walter Gropius and the Bauhaus school acted to reduce the human element in architecture; Josef Albers started his series of paintings dedicated to geometric forms.

None of this is dead; most of it retains its fascination, along with some of its less presentable advantages. Despite abundant evidence that people take on the wasteful and deprived ways of insects, the Dostoevskian ant heap, when they live in featureless and labyrinthine tower blocks of apartments constructed along the lines of modern rational architecture, city planners continue to construct them. But since the 1950s there has grown up an active resistance to the machine model in art and life, something of a flowering of the principles of D. H. Lawrence, an exaltation of the human element, a new respect for nature and natural forces, a protective attitude toward the natural environment, a return of the human figure in painting, a new erotic freedom, a celebration of consciousness heightened first by drugs, then by ancient and preliterate methods of mystical concentration, a celebration of consciousness in electronic light and musical forms, in replacement of a direct handling of visual or "outside-world" sensory inputs. A good deal of this has been reaction, rather than pure action, in much the same way that Rousseauism, its most recent antecedent, was popularized in reaction to the rationality of the *philosophes* and the expanding authoritarian state, as well as to the encroachments of the machine, with its displacement of hand labor. Its narcissism and asocial tendencies, as in the eighteenth century, are accompanied by an enthusiasm for social reform that carries with it an equal element of fanaticism. Fanaticism, as always, derives its strength from abstract principles.

But popular culture rarely does more than parody the new, and often obscures it. The equation of life is different now that the unknown is in the hands of science. We have always been free to find our own interior abyss or our own interior salvation, but now there is the possibility that the extension of man's mind into machines will turn up the knowledge behind the superficial, but so disturbing, triumphs of science in the past, starting with tool-making power and ending with the reading of the book of the earth by nineteenth-century geology. The *danger* in the future has once more returned to what it was for Western man a thousand years ago, when the destruction of the world by an angry or impatient deity was, with some logic, predicted for the millennial *anno Domini*. The logic of our machines today is somewhat more pressing and poses the interesting problem of a race in time between the extension of knowledge, sufficient to bring wisdom, and the arrival of points at which lack of wisdom combined with the power of the machines can become critical and explode, returning the survivors of humanity to their starting point, the bottom of the hill of Sisyphus.

The contemporary reaction is in this sense irrelevant, for the machines are with and of us, and there is no going back from the knowledge they express and embody. Put on the simplest level, half of Western humanity would perish within months if all the machines were stopped, say by a devoted and widespread band of Laurentian true believers. On a more complex level, we could come back from space now, but we will not; the emotions stirred by this possibly infinite New-found-land are too intense. But we *could* come back, in the sense that only a few curious men and machines have gone out so far. Once our economy goes out, once we incorporate the wild adventure into the machinery that enables us to live, there will be no more a possibility of coming back than there is today of sending the population of the planetary New World back into the Old. The self will never be wrested from the grasp the machine has gotten on it; the choices open to us are rather concerning uses of the self, and its engrafted machines.

In 1939 Henry Miller wrote that "the loss of sex polarity is part and parcel of the larger disintegration, the reflex of the soul's death, and coincident with the disappearance of great men, great deeds, great causes, great wars."[163] Whether a sardonic irony is implicit in the last two items we need not inquire, for Miller was in an important sense right: The glorification of masculinity implicit in sex polarity has a lot to do with the appearance of Hitler and Napoleon, the Crusades, and Making the World Safe for Democracy, and little to do with love, learning, and peace. And it is science, along with its handmaiden technology, that has made it possible for man to make the highly artificial move away from sex polarity. "Artificial" in the sense that living in a house rather than a cave is artificial, or cooking prepared food rather than taking wild animals by a chase on foot. To move beyond sex polarity is to move beyond Miller and Lawrence and all the other apostles of freedom from civilization, and to move in the direction of that which makes men human, and which men share with women—their minds. Toward what Henry James called consciousness. In that direction lie the stars.

Notes

Index

Notes

For the reader's convenience, the notes have been numbered consecutively throughout the book, rather than chapter by chapter.

Chapter 1. Introduction

1. See, for example, the typical (over)statement, in parallel literary application of Pierre de Boisdeffre: "At the beginning of the twentieth century the new physics had just set out, in effect, the boundary markers of a universe of discontinuity. It had dismantled the reassuring edifice that nineteenth-century science had raised over our heads. . . . Everything changed in 1940. Our 'Christian and humanist' civilization suddenly slid into the abyss" *(Où va le roman* [Paris: del Duca, 1962], pp. 64, 86). The translation here, and those elsewhere when not otherwise noted, are my own.

2. For a literary expression of this medical *hubris*, an easy mastery of the secrets of life, see Henrik Ibsen's *A Doll's House* (1879, Dr. Rank) and G. B. Shaw's *Doctor's Dilemma* (1906, Dr. Ridgeon). Shaw's *Doctors' Delusions* may also be cited; its epigraph is apt: "Invited to contribute a series of articles in a Manchester paper in reply to the question 'Have We Lost Faith?' Mr. George Bernard Shaw gives his answer in this single sentence: 'Certainly not; but we have transferred it from God to the General Medical Council' " *(Doctors' Delusions, Crude Criminology and Sham Education* [London: Constable, 1932], p. 1).

3. "As far as the laws of mathematics refer to reality they are not certain, and as far as they are certain they do not refer to reality," quoted in James R. Newman, ed., *The World of Mathematics* (New York: Simon and Schuster, 1956), p. 1646.

4. D. Hilbert, "Mathematical Problems," *Bulletin of the American Mathematical Society*, 8 (1902), 445. Hilbert remained a child of the nineteenth century in his outlook, maintaining as late as 1930, the year of Gödel's theorem, that "the true reason . . . why Comte could not find an unsolvable problem lies in the fact that there is no such thing as an unsolvable problem" (quoted in Constance Reid, *Hilbert* [Berlin: Springer Verlag, 1970], p. 196).

5. Howard DeLong, *A Profile of Mathematical Logic* (Reading, Mass.: Addison Wesley, 1970), p. 226.

6. There are even disconcertingly parallel evidences in experimental psychology and education: The level of performance of students or laboratory animals can be varied by telling the teacher or researcher what to expect from them; or, as the irrepressible *Journal of Irreproducible Results* puts it, "The behavior of rats in a laboratory studying the psychology of rats generally fits the theory of the head of the laboratory" (December 1970, p. 43). For the good reasons, in science, for resisting such truths (the value of paradigm), see T. S. Kuhn, *The Structure of Scientific Revolutions*, 2d ed. (Chicago: University of Chicago Press, 1970), p. 24 and passim. On the higher animals,

see Robert Rosenthal and Lenore Jacobson, *Pygmalion in the Classroom: Teacher Expectation and Pupils' Intellectual Development* (New York: Holt, Rinehart, 1968); and Robert Rosenthal and Donald Rubin, "*Pygmalion* Reaffirmed," in *Pygmalion Reconsidered. A Case Study in Statistical Inference: Reconsideration of the Rosenthal-Jacobson Data on Teacher Expectancy*, ed. Janet Elashoff and Richard Snow (Belmont, Calif.: Wadsworth, 1971), pp. 139–55.

7. The phrase "Newtonian model" here and elsewhere is meant in the sense of accepted thinking, as opposed to "Newton's model," which lacked, in several respects, the mechanicity and simplicity attributed to it by later generations, often (as here) for purposes of contrast to twentieth-century physics. Ralph M. Blake, Curt Ducasse et al. point out, for instance, that Newton "emancipated himself from the current notion that our understanding of nature can ever reach embodiment in an absolutely certain and definitive science" (*Theories of Scientific Method: The Renaissance Through the Nineteenth Century* [Seattle: University of Washington Press, 1966], p. 120). Both Newton's force of gravity and the infinitesimal of his calculus are imaginative creations, as paradoxical and insubstantial as the puzzling concepts of the twentieth-century science we discuss.

8. In a 1945 essay, S. W. Hayter claimed this effect for the painting of Wassily Kandinsky: "After 1915 a different order of space makes its appearance. The basal plane is eliminated and the space figured appears not only to be continuous in all directions, but its coordinates are no longer referred to a solid plane. Like inter-stellar space it is to be referred only to remote points in terms of motion" ("The Language of Kandinsky," in Wassily Kandinsky, *Concerning the Spiritual in Art* [*Über das Geistige in der Kunst*], ed. and trans. Nina Kandinsky, The Documents of Modern Art, vol. 5 [New York: George Wittenborn, 1966], p. 16). See also Marshall McLuhan and Harley Parker, *Through the Vanishing Point* (New York: Harper and Row, 1968), p. 25: "Beyond the environment of this planet there is no space in our planetary or 'container' sense. The gravitational point once transcended, the astronaut must have his own environment with him, as it were . . . outer space is not a frame any more than it is visualizable."

9. For contemporary accounts, see R. D. Pretty and D. H. R. Archer, eds., *Jane's Weapon Systems*, 6th ed., 1974–1975 (London: Macdonald, 1974); K. Tsipis, "Physics and Calculus of Countercity and Counterforce Nuclear Attacks," *Science*, 187 (1975), 393–97; and Herbert F. York, "The Nuclear 'Balance of Terror' in Europe," *Bulletin of the Atomic Scientists*, 32, no. 5 (1976), 9–16.

10. Roland Puccetti's remarkable book, *Persons: A Study of Possible Moral Agents in the Universe* (New York: Herder and Herder, 1969), is one of the very few efforts made to reconsider Christianity in the context of contemporary science, and to draw logical conclusions.

11. For the *troika*—Copernicus-Shapley-Baade—see D. W. Sciama, *The Unity of the Universe* (Garden City, N.Y.: Doubleday, 1959), p. 73. The point has evolved into a social cliché as regards Einstein's theories; as Jeremy Bernstein puts it in his *Einstein* (New York: Viking, 1973): "The irony of this is that Einstein's work is understood by such a small percentage of the people whose lives and intellectual outlook have been, often unwittingly, influenced by it" (p. ix).

12. "Man must at last wake out of his millenary dream; and in doing so, wake to his total solitude, his fundamental isolation. Now does he at last realize that, like a gypsy, he lives on the boundary of an alien world" (*Chance and Necessity: An Essay on the Natural Philosophy of Modern Biology* [*Le Hasard et la nécessité / essai sur la philosophie naturelle de la biologie moderne*], trans. Austryn Wainhouse [New York: Knopf, 1971], pp. 172–73).

13. The existence of a multiform critical case to the contrary should not be ignored, no matter how unconvincing one finds it. For the numerous reflections of contemporary science, mainly superficial, in Joyce's *Finnegans Wake*, see *James Joyce Quarterly* and *A Wake Newslitter*, passim. Rudi Prusok has argued that Mann's magnificently old-fashioned novel, *Der Zauberberg*, "entails a reconsideration of the nature of man in the light of Einstein's Relativity Theory and modern medicine" (*PMLA*, 88 [January 1973], 52–61). Stephen Ullmann has related Proust and Einstein in *Language and Style* (Oxford: Blackwell, 1964) and *The Image in the Modern French Novel* (Cambridge: Cambridge University Press, 1960). Sartre, in his "Qu'est-ce que la littérature?" in *Situations II* (Paris: Gallimard, 1948), decreed changes in the novel to fit the world of Einsteinian relativity, but his concept of *littérature engagée* and his Marxist politics seem to outweigh whatever might be called "Einsteinian" in his writing. Among literary prophets and patrons who proclaimed the influence of the new science on literature during the modern period, Eugene Jolas, with his Paris journal *transition* (1927–1938), certainly deserves notice, but the innovations he cherished were for the most part trifling or short-lived, those of the rather unscientific James Joyce being the single exception. Other critical gleanings are equally spare; the individual exceptions are not impressive. It is, after all, in *Parsifal* (1882) that Wagner gave Gurnemanz the highly Einsteinian line, "Du siehst, mein Sohn, zum Raum wird hier die Zeit" ("You see, my son, time here turns into space"), (I, i).

14. (New York: Oxford University Press, 1965), p. 13.

15. Examples of impingement or prefiguration are, of course, not hard to find. In Kipling's *Letters of Marque* (1887) there is, in the description of the horror felt by the traveler at the Gau-Mukh of Chitor, a substantial likeness to what E. M. Forster was to feel, as another Englishman in India, at the Ellora caves in 1912 ("Indian Entries," *Encounter*, 18, no. 1 [1962], 20–27). The material in Kipling's hands went no further, being essentially unassimilable to a *Zeitgeist* that stressed moral choice and the power of the human will; in Forster's "twentieth-century" hands it became the central core of *A Passage to India* (1924) and one of the most powerful expressions of mortality and metaphysical emptiness in modern fiction. Kipling's passage might be compared to Balzac's *Sarrasine* as seen by Roland Barthes, "one of those limit-texts which, in the work of a great writer, represent strange temptations that cause him sometimes to foresee modernity" (*Les lettres françaises*, March 5, 1970, p. 11; quoted in Stephen Heath, "Towards Textual Semiotics," in *Signs of the Times: Introductory Readings in Textual Semiotics*, ed. S. Heath, C. MacCabe, and C. Prendergast [Cambridge: Granta, 1971], p. 30).

16. Nor do I attempt to join my own arguments to that general one I may seem to be paralleling, that of "relevance." Every past writer is "relevant" to our existence in the

widest sense of the term; no past writer is "relevant" in the narrow sense of speaking directly to our present social condition, from the simple fact that his social conditions cannot, as part of the past, be ours. If a past novelist devoted himself to specific social problems of his day we must admit that those problems are not ours, and if he avoided involvement with such problems we must admit that his moral outlook was clearly a moral outlook, to be analyzed in the terms of his own society and then in terms of ours. This we do when we read anyone whose world is not that of our own present day and present geographical location. If the only relevant novels are those about my own city today, then certainly there is no reason to recognize the novel at all, to allow it to put a fictional layer of artifice between the mind of the observer and the reality that cries out for social action.

Chapter 2. The Henry James Murder Mystery

17. The asteroid belt beyond Mars could be the remains of an exploded planet (for arguments advancing and rejecting the idea, see M. W. Ovenden in *Nature*, 239 [1972], 508; W. Napier and R. J. Dodd in *Nature*, 242 [1973], 250–51). Martin Gardner speculates, in *The Ambidextrous Universe* (New York: New American Library, 1969), that the planet might have been one where sentient beings had carried their investigations of matter, some billions of years ago, one critical step too far!

18. Perhaps its best-known ancient form is that of Epimenides the Cretan, "All Cretans are liars"; one of its modern (logical) forms is that of Ludwig Wittgenstein, "Alle Sätze der Logik sagen aber dasselbe. Nämlick nichts" ("But in fact all the propositions of logic say the same thing, to wit, nothing"), Proposition 5.43, *Tractatus Logico-Philosophicus* (London: Routledge and Kegan Paul, 1961).

19. Kurt Vonnegut, *Cat's Cradle* (New York: Dell, 1970), p. 182. Further page references are in parentheses in the text.

20. See Quentin Anderson, *The American Henry James* (New Brunswick, N.J.: Rutgers University Press, 1957), especially chap. 9, "Manifest Providence: II," for a sustained attempt to associate *The Wings of the Dove* with Christian allegory and metaphysics. A broader treatment may be noted in Randall Stewart's 1958 study, *American Literature and Christian Doctrine* (Baton Rouge: Louisiana State University Press), which tends to make James Christian by default: "I call Hawthorne, Melville, and James 'counter-romantics' because they recognize Original Sin, because they show man's struggle toward redemption, because they dramatize the necessary role of suffering in the purification of the self. They do not apotheosize the self, as romantics like Emerson and Whitman do, but warn against its perversities, its obsessions, its insidious deceptions. They side with the orthodox, traditional Christian view of man and the world" (p. 106). Both Graham Greene, in his "Henry James: The Religious Aspect" (in *The Lost Childhood and Other Essays* [London: Eyre and Spottiswoode, 1951], pp. 31–39), and Robert M. Slabey, in "Henry James and 'The Most Impressive Convention in All History' " (*American Literature*, 30 [1958], 89–102), try to associate James with the Catholic faith by the flimsiest of indirect evidence, leaving the reader only with the very correct impression that James was often taken by the tone and

majesty of cathedrals, was awed by Rome, and took an interest in the dead. It is left for F. O. Matthiessen, first in the field and in so many ways its master, to summarize the situation economically and accurately, in a passage I offer as well for its bearing on the argument of this chapter:

> HJ was scarcely concerned with man's relation to God; he fixed his attention exclusively on the fact of human consciousness. . . . It was remarked, shortly after HJ's death, that he 'was in love with the next world, or the next state of consciousness; he was always exploring the borderland between the conscious and the super-conscious.' That is one way of describing the final refinement of his method no less than of his content, and how he took the drama of intelligence as far from the confining body as it could be made to go. One thinks in particular of what he tried to symbolize by the eerie presences in his ghost stories, or how he carried to its extreme, in the unfinished *The Sense of the Past*, his way of suggesting what lurks just behind the words of conversation to beckon us into the realm of the unspoken. It is none the less clear that HJ is not a religious novelist as Hawthorne and Dostoevsky are. (*The James Family* [New York: Knopf, 1947], pp. 587, 592)

21. For a review of the literature of the great *Turn of the Screw* argument, see Dorothea Krook, *The Ordeal of Consciousness in Henry James* (Cambridge: Cambridge University Press, 1962), and T. M. Cranfill and R. L. Clark, *An Anatomy of The Turn of the Screw* (Austin: University of Texas Press, 1965). There are other such surveys, and the river of ink has flowed on since then, of course, branching into areas where the question of possession, or madness, seems more applicable to the scholarship than to the story. In 1967, for instance, a psychiatrist, Dr. C. Knight Aldrich, published in *Modern Fiction Studies* (13, pp. 167-78) a study, "Another Twist to *The Turn of the Screw*," that undertakes to prove that neither supernatural agents nor a hallucinated governess is the cause of little Miles's death, but the housekeeper, Mrs. Grose! My treatment of James's story as a murder mystery has been paralleled in John Griffith, "James's *The Pupil* as Whodunit: The Question of Moral Responsibility," *Studies in Short Fiction*, 9 (1972), 257-68.

22. *The Complete Tales of Henry James*, ed. Leon Edel (Philadelphia: Lippincott, 1964), vol. 10, p. 133. Further references to this edition are given in the text.

23. She did speak to Miss Jessell on "the incongruity" of "Quint and the boy . . . perpetually together" (p. 64), but only on the basis of social class boundaries ("*she* liked to see young gentlemen not forget their station"). That she values the children's welfare very highly seems clear—she felt powerless precisely because there was nothing, besides this superficial matter of class taboo, that she could put her finger on.

24. James himself, with his usual elaborate self-depreciation, referred to it as a "bogey-tale" (letter to Louis Waldstein, October 21, 1898); a "pot-boiler" about "spooks" (letter to H. G. Wells, December 9, 1898); as well as "a very mechanical matter" (letter to F. W. H. Myers, December 19, 1898); all in *The Letters of Henry James*, ed. Percy Lubbock (New York: Scribners, 1920), vol. 1.

25. The governess does use the words "demon" and "work of demons," telling Mrs. Grose that Quint and Jessel as *revenants* are doing the work of demons; with none but the vaguest of contexts it is difficult to apply any denotation to the word, and the distinction between the governess as neutral recording consciousness and as interpreting brain must as well be kept in mind by the reader.

Chapter 3. Murder as a Literary Art

26. For an articulate statement of the traditional critical distinction between a murder mystery and "a work of art which deals with murder," I refer the reader to W. H. Auden, "The Guilty Vicarage," reprinted in *Detective Fiction: Crime and Compromise*, ed. Dick Allen and David Chacho (New York: Harcourt Brace, 1974), p. 409.

27. R. M. Albérès used much the same language to describe the traditional, or nineteenth-century, novel in France: "Dans le style traditionnel de la narration, une longue description établissait d'abord *un décor familier et normal dans lequel un événement devait se produire;* elle rassurait le lecteur sans le heurter, lui montrant que l'aventure est un accident exceptionnel, seulement destiné d'ailleurs à lui donner un frisson de plaisir et d'anxiété, dans un univers ordonné et bien classé" (*Bilan littéraire du xxe siècle*, 3d ed. [Paris: Lib. A-G Nizet, 1971], p. 17). On the modern development of the murder mystery away from rational intelligence and faith in justice to hero-as-tough-guy, violence, sadism, and other more visceral effects, see George Orwell, "Raffles and Miss Blandish" (1944), in *Collected Essays, Journalism and Letters of George Orwell*, vol. 3, *As I Please: 1943–45*, ed. Sonia Orwell and Ian Angus (New York: Harcourt Brace, 1968), pp. 212–24; and Stuart Hall and Paddy Whannel, *The Popular Arts* (New York: Pantheon, 1965), chap. 6, "The Avenging Angels."

28. Typical of the extreme theoretical position on this is Wylie Sypher, *Loss of the Self in Modern Literature and Art* (New York: Vintage, 1962), p. 70: 'The destruction was so total during and after the second World War that art went down with everything else; and as Czeslaw Milosz remarks, we have almost no literature of modern frightfulness because the artist was overborne by the scale of the calamity."

29. See Theodore Ziolkowski, *Dimensions of the Modern Novel* (Princeton: Princeton University Press, 1969), chap. 9, "The Artist as Criminal," for a good English-French-German survey of the form.

30. Alain Robbe-Grillet, *La Maison de Rendez-Vous*, trans. Richard Howard (New York: Grove, 1966), p. 112. Further page references in the text are to this edition.

31. Eugène Ionesco, "Selections from the Journals," *Yale French Studies*, 29 (1962), 8.

32. In 1949 Mann found it possible to agree with Georg Lukasz that the earlier story showed "the danger of a barbarous underworld existing within modern German civilization," and this element underlies the link to *Dr. Faustus:* "What this does is to lay bare prophetically the relationship between the Venetian novella and *Faustus*" (*The Story of a Novel: The Genesis of Doctor Faustus*, trans. Richard and Clara Winston [New York: Knopf, 1961], p. 142).

33. This applies to *Death in Venice* and to Mann's fiction in general; *Dr. Faustus*, less

from religious conviction than from the author's desire to dredge up the whole German past and find therein a suitable, if absurdly elevated, Hitler metaphor, features the devil prominently, "as the secret hero of the book" (*Story of a Novel*, p. 71).

34. Heinz Politzer, "Heimito von Doderer's *Demons* and the Modern Kahanian Novel," in *The Contemporary Novel in German*, ed. Robert Heitner (Austin: University of Texas Press, 1967), p. 57.

35. *Das Versprechen* (Zurich: Verlag der Arche, 1962). Page references are to this edition and to the English translation, *The Pledge*, by Richard and Clara Winston (London: Jonathan Cape, 1959).

36. "Denn jedes Publikum and jeder Steuerzahler hat ein Anrecht auf seine Helden und sein Happy-End, und dies zu liefern, sind wir von der Polizei and ihr von der Schriftstellerei gleicherweise verpflichet" (*Das Versprechen*, p. 18).

37. "Hier wird der Schwindel zu toll und zu unverschämt. Ihr baut eure Handlungen logisch auf; wie bei einem Schachspiel geht es zu, hier der Verbrecher, hier das Opfer hier der Mitwisser, hier der Nutzniesser; es genügt, dass der Detektiv die Regeln kennt und die Partie wiederholt, und schon hat er den Verbrecher gestellt, der Gerechtigkeit zum Siege verholfen. Diese Fiktion macht mich wütend. Der Wirklichkeit ist mit Logik nur zum Teil beizukommen" (*Das Versprechen*, pp. 18–19). The last sentence is very close to one in Werner Heisenberg's *Physics and Philosophy*: "Therefore, it will never be possible by pure reason to arrive at some absolute truth" (New York: Harper and Brothers, 1958), p. 72.

38. Not only that, but the senseless crime is easier to commit. Dr.H.'s reflections cover both aspects: "With other crimes our task is simpler. We have only to consider the motives—money or jealousy, say,—and we can light on the suspects. But this method is no use in a sex-murder. A man on a business trip catches sight of a girl or a boy; he gets out of his car—no witnesses, no one notices a thing—and in the evening he is back home in Lausanne or Basle or where you will, and there we are without a single clue" (p. 54). ["Bei jedem anderen Verbrechen haben wir es leichter. Wir brauchen nur die Motive zu überlegen, Geldmangel, Eifersucht, und schon lässt sich der Kreis der Verdächtigen enger ziehen. Doch bei einem Lustmord ist diese Methode sinnlos. Da kann einer auf der Geschäftsreise ein Mädchen sehen oder einen Knaben, er steigt aus seinem Wagen—keine Zeugen, keine Beobachtungen, und am Abend sitzt er wieder zu Hause, vielleicht in Lausanne, vielleicht in Basel, irgendwo, und wir stehen da, ohne Anhaltspunkte" (p. 66).]

39. Dwight MacDonald, *On Movies* (Englewood Cliffs, N.J.: Prentice-Hall, 1969), p. 50: "The objection to introducing a mentally disturbed person into a drama, whether as criminal or as victim, is that he or she is by definition a 'wild' card in the deck, unfair artistically, since anything can happen, also severely limiting the meaning, since madness is eccentric, in the literal sense of being outside the central human experience as well as being impenetrable to all but psychiatric specialists. Also, contrary to popular belief, the madder, the duller."

40. R. B. Heilman, "The Lure of the Demonic: James and Dürrenmatt," *Comparative Literature*, 13 (1961), 346–57.

Chapter 4. Terror in Henry James

41. F. O. Matthiessen and K. B. Murdock, eds., *The Notebooks of Henry James* (New York: Oxford University Press, 1961), p. 361.

42. The work of J. W. Dunne (1875–1949), embodied in *An Experiment with Time* (1927), *The Serial Universe* (1934), *The New Immortality* (1938), and *Nothing Dies* (1940), will be discussed further in chapter 6.

43. *Notebooks*, p. 364.

44. Ibid.

45. New York: Bantam Books. References in the text are to this edition.

46. For Gardner's discussion, see *Ambidextrous Universe*, pp. 119–20. In Blish's case, it is the "cat" who is reversed, not the milk; this is much more dangerous. J. B. S. Haldane also noted, in *Possible Worlds and Other Essays* (London: Chatto and Windus, 1927): "On going through the looking-glass, Alice would have found her digestive enzymes of no more use on the looking-glass sugars than her Yale key on the looking-glass locks" (p. 27). In fact, a large number of Yale keys are symmetrically reversed duplicates of others, so Alice would do better opening locks than eating cake.

47. *The Complete Tales*, vol. 12, p. 201. Further page references are given in the text.

Chapter 5. Science Fiction

48. T. S. Shklovski and Carl Sagan, *Intelligent Life in the Universe* (New York: Delta, 1966), p. 363. For Milton and astronomy see, among others, A. J. Meadows, *The High Firmament: A Survey of Astronomy in English Literature* (Leicester: Leicester University Press, 1969).

49. Despite the perfectly reasonable attempts to view *The Tempest* or *Gulliver's Travels* as science fiction (see Kingsley Amis, *New Maps of Hell* [London: Gollancz, 1961], p. 30). For Donne's science see Marjorie H. Nicolson, *The Breaking of the Circle: Studies in the Effect of the "New Science" Upon Seventeenth-Century Poetry* (Evanston, Ill.: Northwestern University Press, 1950).

50. For the connection of science fiction to the future and Utopian fantasy, see H. B. Franklin, *Future Perfect: American Science Fiction of the Nineteenth Century* (New York: Oxford University Press, 1966); and Mark R. Hillega, *The Future as Nightmare: H. G. Wells and the Anti-Utopians* (New York: Oxford University Press, 1967); as well as Amis, *New Maps*, the best general coverage of the subject, rivaled only by Brian Aldiss's more factitious *Billion Year Spree* (New York: Doubleday, 1973).

51. Ames, *New Maps*, p. 18.

52. *Best SF: Science Fiction Stories*, ed. with intro. by Edmund Crispin (London: Faber and Faber, 1955), p. 9.

53. The distinction of "space fiction" from science fiction proposed by Montgomery (introduction to *SF Five*) seems unnecessary, for space exploration fictionally conceived belongs to science fiction as long as we maintain that genre classification. On the other hand, the prose description of the *actual* doings of astronauts in space

exploration, a budding department of literature, belongs to journalism and to history and may earn a special title, given such imaginative efforts as Norman Mailer's *Fire on the Moon*. But it is not fiction.

54. Teilhard de Chardin, *Building the Earth* (Wilkes Barre, Pa.: Dimension Books, 1965), pp. 34, 119.

55. Kurt Vonnegut, *Slaughterhouse-Five* (New York: Dell, 1969), p. 87.

56. One contemporary writer at the center of this rearrangement of genre is Michel Butor, whose work bridges the *roman policer–science-fiction–nouveau roman* in France. See Xavier Delcourt, "Pour Michel Butor les frontières entre science-fiction et littérature tendent à s'effacer," *La Quinzaine Littéraire*, January 13–17, 1976, pp. 5–7.

57. These were the work of "the Little Green Men that Cambridge originally thought caused pulsars" (T. Gold, "Rotating Neutron Stars and the Nature of Pulsars," in *The Physics of Pulsars*, ed. A. M. Lenchek [New York: Gordon and Breach, 1972], pp. 101–09).

Chapter 6. Time and the Visible World

58. Modern literature has, therefore, many passages of contrast between the invading time consciousness and the older patterns. D. H. Lawrence's *Mornings in Mexico* (1927) puts it in his inimitable way:

> Now the white man is a sort of extraordinary white monkey that, by cunning, has learnt lots of semi-magical secrets of the universe, and made himself boss of the show. . . . [He] has curious tricks. He knows, for example, the time. Now to a Mexican, and an Indian, time is a vague, foggy reality. There are only three times: *en la mañana, en la tarde, en la noche*: in the morning, in the afternoon, in the night. There is even no midday, and no evening.
> But to the white monkey, horrible to relate, there are exact spots of time, such as five o'clock, half past nine. The day is a horrible puzzle of exact spots of time. ([Harmondsworth, Eng.: Penguin Books, 1960], pp. 33–34)

59. If there is an invariant interval in nature, it is a very small one—we now use an interval of $\frac{1}{9,192,631,770}$ of a second to keep time (that is, the present international time unit, the atomic second, is defined as equivalent to 9,192,631,770 cycles of the hyperfine resonance frequency of the ground state of the Cesium 133 atom).

60. W. F. Twaddell, *The English Verb Auxiliaries*, 2d ed. (Providence, R.I.: Brown University Press, 1963).

61. R. A. Jacobs and P. S. Rosenbaum, *Transformations, Style, and Meaning* (Waltham: Xerox College Publications, 1971), p. 66.

62. The one on which I mainly draw here is in Ziolkowski, *Dimensions of the Modern Novel*, "The Discordant Clocks," pp. 183 ff.

63. Mircea Eliade, *Cosmos and History: The Myth of the Eternal Return*, trans. Willard Trask (New York: Harper, 1959), pp. 44–46.

64. "Längst verstorbene Kaiser werden in unseren Dörfen auf den Thron gesetzt, und der nur noch im Liede lebt, hat vor kurzem eine Bekanntmachung erlassen, die

der Priester vor dem Altare verliest. Schlachten unserer ältesten Geschichte werden jetzt erst geschlagen und mit glühendem Gesicht fällt der Nachbar mit der Nachricht dir ins Haus. Die kaiserlichen Frauen, überfüttert in den seidenen Kissen, von schlauen Höflingen der edlen Sitte entfremdet, anschwellend in Herrschsucht, auffahrend in Gier, ausgebreitet in Wollust, verüben ihre Untaten immer wieder von neuen. Je mehr Zeit schon vergangen ist, desto schrecklicher leuchten alle Farben, und mit lautem Wehgeschrei erfährt einmal das Dorf, wie eine Kaiserin vor Jahrtausenden in langen Zügen ihres Mannes Blut trank" (Franz Kafka, "Beim Bau der chinesischen Mauer," in his *Beschreibung eines Kampfes* [New York: Schocken, 1946], pp. 79–80). For an English edition, see *The Great Wall of China and Other Pieces*, trans. Willa and Edwin Muir (London: Martin Secker, 1933), p. 154.

65. Both accounts are from P. V. Glob, *The Bog People: Iron-Age Man Preserved*, trans. R. Breuer-Mitford (London: Paladin Books, 1969), pp. 46, 54.

66. From Hajime Nakamura, "Time in Indian and Japanese Thought," in *The Voices of Time*, ed. J. T. Fraser (New York: Braziller, 1966), p. 89.

67. For a survey of time psychology, see Paul Fraisse, "Perception et estimation du temps," in *La Perception*, vol. 6 of *Traité de psychologie expérimentale*, ed. Paul Fraisse and Jean Piaget (Paris: Presses Universitaires de France, 1963), pp. 59–95; or Paul Fraisse, *The Psychology of Time*, trans. Jennifer Leith (New York: Harper and Row, 1963).

68. See H. Woodrow, "Time Perception," in *Handbook of Experimental Psychology*, ed. S. S. Stevens (New York: Wiley, 1951), p. 1231.

69. H. Helson and S. M. King, "The tau effect: An Example of Psychological Relativity," *Journal of Experimental Psychology*, 14 (1931), 202–18. Helson proposed the name first in *Science*, 71 (1930), 536–37.

70. J. Cohen, C. Hansel, and J. Sylvester, "A New Phenomenon in Time Judgment," *Nature*, 172 (1953), 901.

71. Lester Grinspoon, "Marihuana," *Scientific American*, 221, no. 6 (1969), 19. The same expansion and dilation were noted by William James in his *Principles of Psychology* (New York: Holt, 1890), vol. 1, pp. 639–40: "In hashish-intoxication there is a curious increase in the apparent time perspective. We utter a sentence, and ere the end is reached the beginning seems already to date from indefinitely long ago. We enter a short street, and it is as if we should never get to the end of it."

72. See, for example, A. J. Weil et al., "Clinical and Psychological Effects of Marihuana in Man," *Science*, 162 (1968), 1240.

73. "Henceforth space by itself, and time by itself, are doomed to fade away into mere shadows, and only a kind of union of the two will preserve an independent reality" (H. Minkowski, in A. Einstein, H. A. Lorentz, H. Minkowski, and H. Weyl, *The Principle of Relativity* [New York: Dover, n.d. (1923)], p. 75).

74. M. M. Agrest, in Shklovskii and Sagan, *Intelligent Life in the Universe*, p. 454. It was left for Erich von Däniken to flesh out Agrest's idea with such journalistic fervor and slapdash disregard for causality as to establish it firmly in the area of popular Flying Saucerdom (*Erinnerungen an die Zukunft*, 1968; English translation by Michael Heron, *Chariots of the Gods?* [New York: Putnam, 1970]).

75. See Albert Einstein, *Relativity: The Special and General Theory*, trans. R. W. Lawson (New York: Holt, 1921), pp. 65–66.

76. I take this account from Milič Čapek, "Time in Relativity Theory: Arguments for a Philosophy of Becoming," in *Voices of Time*, ed. J. T. Fraser, pp. 434–54. Einstein's own most accessible description of the inadmissibility of the universal instant is in *Out of My Later Years* (New York: Philosophical Library, 1950), chap. 10, sec. A, "Special theory of relativity," pp. 42–45.

77. Quoted in Walter Sullivan, "Physicists Muse on Question of Time Running Backward," *New York Times*, January 30, 1966, sec. 4, p. 10, col. 1.

78. This problem, of whether a precognition can be real if acted upon, is treated interestingly by J. B. Priestley as "The Problem of the Dead Baby," in his *Man and Time* (London: Aldus Books, 1964). Transport faster than the speed of light — hypothetical tachyon travel—involves the same crux: If you returned before you left, what if, subsequent to your return, something happened to prevent you from leaving? Worse, what if nothing prevented you from leaving—again and again?

79. See P. T. Landsberg, "Time in Statistical Physics and Special Relativity," *Studium Generale*, 23 (1970), 1125. That entropy establishes the arrow of time (Eddington's position) is not accepted by all physicists. A universal isotropy of time is advanced by H. Mehlberg, "Physical Laws and Time's Arrow," in *Current Issues in the Philosophy of Science*, ed. H. Feigl and G. Maxwell (New York: Holt, 1961), pp. 105–38, and others; the anisotropic position, for one-way time, is expressed in several essays in J. T. Fraser, F. C. Haber, and G. H. Müller, eds., *The Study of Time* (New York: Springer Verlag, 1972), esp. O. Costa de Beauregard, "No Paradox in the Theory of Time Anisotropy" (pp. 131–39), and K. G. Denbigh, "In Defence of the Direction of Time" (which rebuts Mehlberg, pp. 148–58).

80. *Things to Come* (London: Cresset Press, 1935), p. 139.

81. "The Man Who Could Work Miracles," in *Tales of Space and Time* (1900), reprinted in *Works*, Atlantic ed. (New York: Scribner's, 1935), vol. 10, pp. 351–75.

82. Translation from George Steindorff and Keith Seele, *When Egypt Ruled the East* (Chicago: University of Chicago Press, 1963), p. 71.

83. Heinrich von Kleist, "Über das Marionettentheater," in *Prosa Stücke* (Stuttgart: Philipp Reclam, 1964). The link between puppets and extended time I take from Arthur Sewell's brilliant *Character and Society in Shakespeare* (Oxford: Oxford University Press, 1951), p. 144.

84. For a survey of the philosophical and political aspects of *The Time Machine*, along with an effort to attribute Swiftian literary complexity to it, see Robert Philmus, "*The Time Machine*; or, the Fourth Dimension as Prophecy," *PMLA*, 84 (1969), 530–35.

85. Chandrasekhar, "Geodesics in Gödel's Universe," in *The Nature of Time*, ed. T. Gold (Ithaca, N.Y.: Cornell University Press, 1967), pp. 68–74; Gödel's diagram is on p. 69. See also Čapek in *Voices of Time*, ed. J. T. Fraser, pp. 434–54; and Richard Swinburne, *Space and Time* (London: Macmillan, 1968), p. 169 n. In a letter of March 21, 1955 (a month before his death), Einstein wrote, "The separation between past, present and future has only the meaning of an illusion, albeit a tenacious one."

86. *The Time Machine* (New York: Random House, 1931), p. 5.

87. *The Sense of the Past* (London: Collins, 1917), p. 71. Further references to this edition are in parentheses in the text.

88. *The Art of the Novel* (New York: Scribner's, 1950), p. 164.

89. Reprinted in Geoff Conklin, ed., *Great Science Fiction by Scientists* (New York: Collier, 1962), pp. 61–82.

90. Matthiessen and Murdock, eds. *Notebooks*, p. 364.

91. *Ada or Ardor: A Family Chronicle* (New York: McGraw-Hill, 1969), p. 81. Further references to this edition are in parentheses in the text. In the matter of a technology arrested by law at something like a late Victorian level, Nabokov's Antiterra bears a resemblance, and *Ada* a possible source relationship, to Samuel Butler's *Erewhon* (1872).

92. Shklovskii and Sagan, *Intelligent Life in the Universe*, p. 361.

93. Perhaps the worst case is the matter of Van's sadistic punishment of Kim the Kitchen Boy (pp. 441–46) for snooping with a camera and attempting blackmail: He blinds him, or has him blinded, but in respect for his love of photography, supplies him with brailled works on the subject.

94. "Mathematical Games," *Scientific American*, 224 (April 1970), 108.

95. Harlow Shapley, in *Beyond the Observatory* (New York: Scribner's, 1967), estimates "at least one hundred thousand million billion stars in our universe, the number of attached planets must be similarly great, and probably there are many more planets in the detached category" (p. 64). This gives comparable figures: 10^{21} stars, plus 10^{21} attached planets (at one to a star, far more conservative than my hypothetical ten to a star), plus (x) times 10^{21} detached planets = a minimum of 3 x 10^{21} planets total. See also L. A. DuBridge, *Introduction to Space* (New York: Columbia University Press, 1960), p. 77. If there are other universes "nesting" within the space we observe, then all counts mentioned would be too conservative. See T. Gold, "Multiple Universes," *Nature*, 242 (1973), 24–25.

96. The figures in the last two sentences are taken from Shklovskii and Sagan, *Intelligent Life in the Universe*, pp. 345, 130.

97. V. A. Firsoff, *Life, Mind, and Galaxies* (Edinburgh: Oliver and Boyd, 1967), p. 95. Similarly Shapley, *Beyond the Observatory*: "If only one star in a trillion has a planet that harbors life, there would be, nevertheless, a hundred million of them" (p. 123); and, on the development of man and his brain: "This rising dominance of mind has probably been long ago attained in other inhabited worlds" (p. 126); or G. Eglinton, J. R. Maxwell, and C. Pillinger, "The Carbon Chemistry of the Moon": "It seems increasingly likely that we are not alone in the universe. There may be millions of inhabited planets like our own" *(Scientific American*, 227, no. 4 [October 1972], 81).

98. *Paradise Lost*, IX, 914–15.

99. The earthly location of hell (*iz ada*) has echoic resemblance to Butler's Erewhon, in which Dr. Gurgoyle's philosophy posits, through vicarious existence, "a true heaven and a true hell" (Samuel Butler, *Works* [New York: AMS Press, 1968], vol. 16, p. 105). Both Terra and Erewhon are "nowhere" because they are *here*, us, ourselves as distorted by mirror-image reversal.

100. *Ada* here resembles one of the most remarkably imaginative science-fiction novels of the postmodern era, Arthur Clarke's *Childhood's End* (1954), in which Earth is connected to another world of winged manlike creatures, already in Terran consciousness, by a process of "remembering the future," as the horned and winged devils of medieval Christian lore.

101. That does not prevent him, as author of *Ada*, from supplying us with clues plentiful enough to indicate that they are the twelve apostles adumbrated—they are "mysterious pastors" (p. 276), twelve in number, with "sad apostolic hands" (p. 268); their gestures as they spread a meal are "ritually limited"; they wear "old Sunday suits"; they draw back into the forest pulling their picnic cloth "like a fishing boat" (p. 269); they present "a most melancholy and meaningful picture—but meaning what?" and leave on their departure a collar and tie hanging on a bush, as if "they might have dispatched and buried one of their comrades" (p. 276)—in all, a rather Joycean-Beckettian picture.

102. Cited by Henry Margenau, *The Nature of Physical Reality* (New York: McGraw-Hill, 1950), p. 164. See Einstein, *Relativity: The Special and General Theory*, chap. 31, pp. 128–34, "The possibility of a 'finite' and yet 'unbounded' universe" (this being the sphere to 2-D inhabitants of its surface; our universe of curved space to us).

103. The fact that a 2-D figure has no thickness, and therefore cannot be visible from within its own plane, or on its edge, is necessarily fudged in the interest of dramatic illusion.

104. Dionys Burger, *Sphereland* (New York: Crowell, 1965), p. 87.

105. Martin Gardner notes this progression among Terran idealists: "The Kaluza-Klein suggestion of a fifth dimension, perpendicular to the four coordinate axes of space-time, understandably appeals to any Platonist who thinks of this world as a shadow projection of a higher space. . . . [likewise] the concept of a *fourth* dimension was taken over by early Spiritualists. Since relativity theory, the 'other' world of many occultists has been the *fifth* dimension of Kaluza-Klein" (*Ambidextrous Universe*, p. 236).

106. In this description of antimatter I have drawn from Hannes Alfvén, *Worlds-Antiworlds: Antimatter in Cosmology* (San Francisco: W. H. Freeman, 1966), chap. 3 and passim.

107. *The Nature of Time*, p. 229.

108. Alfvén, *Worlds-Antiworlds*, p. 61.

109. Gardner, *Ambidextrous Universe*, pp. 232, 230.

110. *Pale Fire* (New York: Lancer, 1966), pp. 108 (emphasis added), 98.

111. Ernest Jones, "The Problem of Paul Morphy," reprinted in *The Chess Reader*, ed. Jerome Salzmann (New York: Greenberg, 1949), pp. 237–70.

112. Charles Davy, *Words in the Mind* (London: Chatto and Windus, 1965), pp. 91–99. There is a physical analogue to this in both dreaming and sleep paralysis, where a sense can exist that "giving in" to the power of the vision on the mental screen would entail no way of return, and a loss of the waking physical self. It is also of interest that this contemplation of pure pattern goes one critical step further than that of Nabokov's grand master in *The Defense*. He closets himself with the bare

board, dispensing with the pieces; Davy's prodigy dispenses with the pieces and the board as well.

113. *The Sense of the Past* is nearly as open to the physical analogy of reversed time as is *Ada*: It, too, has two time levels between which little or no communication is possible, the earlier London being as locked into our past as another planet with reversed time, and getting farther from us every minute, almost as if it were proceeding in a different direction. In a real sense it is both what we were—our ancestors—and coexisting, in that by crossing a threshold one can walk into it, and find it going on, but in its progression immutably removed from our time (this opens up the alarming prospect of every moment of time, once "passed," moving on in its own reality). But again, the characters of the former time and those of the present have a strong interconnection. James's hero and one of them are even twins, and fatal traps for each other.

114. Coleridge's own association of the boy with imaginary time can be derived from his remarks in the preface to *Sibylline Leaves*, in which the poem first appeared. There he gives a possibly disingenuous account of the poem as merely a description of the state of a schoolboy's mind on his return from vacation. An earlier passage in *Anima Poetae*, far more complex (and obscure) in its terms, gives a plan for a poem that most probably took the form of "Time, Real and Imaginary." For an indication of modern critical puzzlement over interpretation, see *Explicator*, 3, no. 1 (October 1944), item 4 (F. H. Heidbrink); 3, no. 4 (February 1945), item 33 (A. A. Raven); and 19, no. 7 (April 1961), item 46 (J. R. Byers).

115. In John Barth, *Lost in the Funhouse* (Garden City, N.Y.: Doubleday, 1968).

116. Einstein, *Relativity: The Special and General Theory*, p. 66.

117. John Cohen, "Psychological Time," *Scientific American*, 211, no. 5 (1964), 124.

118. Lewis Carroll, from the prefatory verses to *Alice's Adventures in Wonderland*.

119. *The Elementary Structures of Kinship*, trans. James H. Bell, John R. von Sturmer, and Rodney Needham (London: Eyre and Spottiswoode, 1969), p. 457.

Chapter 7. The Erotic

120. That of Sir Edward Tylor (1832–1917), and long dominant in anthropological thinking. See, for example, Tylor's *Primitive Culture*, 1871.

121. Vladimir Nabokov, *The Annotated Lolita*, ed. Alfred Appel (New York: McGraw-Hill, 1970), p. 62. Subsequent references are given in the text.

122. G. Legman, *Rationale of the Dirty Joke: An Analysis of Sexual Humor* (London: Granada, 1972), vol. 1, p. 94.

123. Edmund Wilson, "The Ambiguity of Henry James," *Hound & Horn*, 7 (1934), 385–406, reprinted in his *Triple Thinkers* (New York: Oxford University Press, 1948).

124. Reprinted in Roger Gard, ed., *Henry James: The Critical Heritage* (London: Routledge and Kegan Paul, 1968), p. 282. It is interesting that Maxwell Geismar, in his *Henry James and the Jacobites* (New York: Hill and Wang, 1965), calls the novel a "dialogue of incest" (p. 175).

125. His likeness to Henry James as a *man* has been noted. He, like James, is aged

219 • Notes to Pages 139–149

fifty-five plus, has a house in the country which serves him as a refuge, is an outsider to London society, and a habitual observer (see Leon Edel, *Henry James: The Treacherous Years* [Philadelphia: Lippincott, 1969], pp. 250 ff.).

126. Henry James, *The Awkward Age* (New York: Doubleday, 1958), p. x. Further quotes from this edition are put in parentheses in the text.

127. Choosing between them takes us into another area of Jamesian projected sexuality that is better explored in another context. This is the matter of male inversion: Vanderbank, whose central characterization of the "sacred terror" must contain a sexual component, is frozen in inaction, only dubiously balanced by an excess of (illicit) action in the direction of being the mother's lover (the position Humbert Humbert found himself in at the most frustrated stage of his machinations). Mitchy, on the other hand, is full of passion, which he freely declares, but it takes the issue of masochistically marrying the girl in whom Nanda takes an interest and whom she commands him to marry as a test of his devotion to herself. While James often favored this type of romantic self-abnegation in his plots (cf. *The American*), he shows here its destructive consequences.

128. This is a matter of dialect, not easily substantiated in the speech of eighty years ago, but compare James's *What Maisie Knew:* Maisie, a girl of social origins similar to Nanda's but ten years younger, speaks with greater maturity.

129. The plan is given in the New York edition preface to the novel. James was consistently somewhat inaccurate in his comments on his work, particularly in the matter of his claims to have removed authorial presence and directing consciousness. This was missed by his early critics and followers, like Percy Lubbock, who took the prefaces at their word, but in recent years more and more noted. In the case of *The Awkward Age*, see F. Gillen, "The Dramatist and His Drama: Theory and Effect in *The Awkward Age*," *TSLL*, 12 (1971), 662–75.

130. It might be noted that it is *Mr. Longdon's* offer of money that plays a role in this stance, for Vanderbank feels (or takes as an excuse) that once the offer has been made he will open himself to the charge of having been bought if he proposes to Nanda.

131. The point is used in Claud Cockburn's comic novel, *Beat the Devil* (1951). Gwendolyn Chelm, a middle-class English girl, and her husband converse as follows:

'I always wonder,' he said, 'that your parents left you in the charge of a dirty, ignorant old woman like she seems to have been.'
'They cared for nothing except to have me off their hands. . . . They'd have sold me to the White Slave market if they hadn't been afraid of scandal. Besides, my father was incompetent. I don't suppose he knew just how to contact the White Slave people.' (Harmondsworth, Eng.: Penguin Books, 1971, p. 12)

132. *The Art of the Novel* (New York: Scribner's, 1950), p. 117.

133. That is, she is a boy, and thus held safely inside private thoughts of capture and possession or degradation. The boy in the rocket in Thomas Pynchon's *Gravity's Rainbow* (1973) is a more direct variation, but also more fantastic.

134. "Wagner puzza di sesso," in Richard Ellmann, *James Joyce* (New York: Oxford University Press, 1965), p. 393.

135. For instance, in his "English as a VSO Language" (*Language*, 46 [1970], 286–99), James McCawley cites the fact that "God is loved by Spiro" is funny in a way that "Spiro loves God" is not. Most English speakers perceive this immediately, but neither they nor grammarians have an accepted explanation for it.

136. *The Art of the Novel*, p. 49.

137. Letter to Morton Fullerton, July 14, 1893, in *The Selected Letters of Henry James*, ed. Leon Edel (Garden City, N.Y.: Doubleday, 1960), p. 181. The bordello subject was probably mistakenly remembered by James as Goncourt's; presumably the writer was Maupassant, planning *La Maison Tellier* (see Leon Edel, *Henry James: The Conquest of London* [Philadelphia: Lippincott, 1962], p. 266).

138. *The Art of the Novel*, p. 173.

139. Ibid., pp. 176–77.

140. John Bayley, *The Characters of Love* (London: Constable, 1960), p. 30.

141. The woman's share of the greater reciprocity of dress change in the 1960s (men with purses, women with trouser flies) has been wryly commented on by Molly Haskell: "Men were entitled to grow long hair and wear beads and indulge in a kind of polymorphous passivity, and what did women gain in exchange? Pants" (*From Reverence to Rape: The Treatment of Women in the Movies* [New York: Holt, Rinehart and Winston, 1974], p. 356).

142. One such period, that of National Socialism in Germany (1933–1945), posited just such a descent for youth, along with its attendant suppression of women. In Hitler's words: "In meinen Ordensburgen wird eine Jugend heranwachsen, vor der sich die Welt erschrecken wird. Eine gewalttätige, herrische, unerschrockene, grausame Jugend will ich. . . . Das freie, herrliche Raubtier muss erst wieder aus ihren Augen blitzen. . . . So merze ich die Tausende von Jahren der menschlichen Domestikation aus. So habe ich das reine, edle Material der Natur vor mir" (quoted in Hannah Vogt, *Schuld oder Verhängnis? Zwölf Fragen an Deutschlands jüngste Vergangenheit* [Frankfurt: Diesterweg, 1961], p. 137).

143. Roman Ingarden, *Vom Erkennen des Literarischen Kunstwerks* (Tubingen: Niemeyer, 1968), pp. 10, 49.

144. Neither term is explicitly defined in their *Human Sexual Inadequacy* (Boston: Little, Brown, 1970), but both may be taken as equivalent to "inability to copulate."

145. Fred Belliveau and Lin Richter, *Understanding Human Sexual Inadequacy* (Boston: Little, Brown, 1970), p. 3.

146. *Human Sexual Inadequacy*, p. 21. Further quotes are in parentheses in the text.

147. Vonnegut, *Slaughterhouse-Five*, p. 102.

148. Thomas McMahon, *Principles of American Nuclear Chemistry* (New York: Ballantine, 1970), p. 204.

149. See Edel, for example, *The Conquest of London*, p. 399; *The Treacherous Years*, p. 321. Nadal's remark was first published in *Scribner's Magazine*, July 1920; is reprinted in Simon Nowell-Smith, *The Legend of the Master* (New York: Scribner's, 1948); and is quoted in Edel, *Conquest*, p. 359.

150. Kate Millett, *Sexual Politics* (New York: Avon Books, 1971), p. 22.

Chapter 8. Nothingness

151. John Barth, *The End of the Road* (New York: Avon Books, 1958), p. 81. Subsequent references are in parentheses in the text.
152. Paul Tillich, *The Courage to Be* (New Haven: Yale University Press, 1952), pp. 139–40.
153. Irving Howe, *Decline of the New* (New York: Harcourt Brace, 1970), pp. 5–6.
154. J. A. Wheeler, "Three-Dimensional Geometry as a Carrier of Information About Time," in *Nature of Time*, ed. T. Gold, p. 91. The only literary work of my acquaintance that uses an analogue to this idealistic paradox is A. C. Clarke's *2001* (with its allied work, "The Sentinel"), in which the opening up of the universe to man is contingent upon man's undertaking the effort of discovery, his capacity to discover being established by his finding the "sentinel" on the moon put there for him to find.
155. Wayne Booth, *The Rhetoric of Fiction* (Chicago: University of Chicago Press, 1961), p. 340.
156. Laplace calls him "une intelligence" in his *Essai philosophique sur les probabilités* (Paris: Courcier, 1814), p. 2: "Nous devons donc envisager l'état présent de l'univers, comme l'effet de son état antérieur, et comme la cause de celui qui va suivre. Une intelligence qui pour un instant donné, connaîtrait toutes les forces dont la nature est animée, et la situation respective des êtres qui la composent, si d'ailleurs elle était assez vaste pour soumettre ces données à l'analyse, embrasserait dans la même formule, les mouvements des plus grands corps de l'univers et ceux du plus léger atome: rien ne serait incertain pour elle, et l'avenir comme le passé, serait présent à ses yeux." (For an English edition, see *A Philosophical Essay on Probabilities*, trans. F. W. Truscott and F. L. Emory, [New York: John Wiley, 1920], p. 4.)
157. Werner Heisenberg, *The Physicists' Conception of Nature (Das Naturbild der heutigen Physik)*, trans. Arnold Pomerans (Westport, Conn.: Greenwood Press), pp. 37–38.
158. *The Complete Tales*, vol. 11, p. 360. Further references are in parentheses in the text.
159. Samuel Beckett, *Happy Days* (London: Faber and Faber, 1962), pp. 32–33.
160. Samuel Beckett, *Waiting for Godot* (London: Faber and Faber, 1956), p. 81. Further references are in parentheses in the text.
161. Wallace Fowlie, "A Stocktaking: French Literature in the 1960s," *Contemporary Literature*, 11, no. 2 (Spring 1970), 148.

Chapter 9. Postscript

162. José Ortega y Gasset, *La Deshumanización del arte* (Madrid: Revista de Occidente, 1925). A recent edition, with a translation by Helene Weyl, is *The Dehumanization of Art, and Other Essays on Art, Culture, and Literature* (Princeton: Princeton University Press, 1968).
163. Henry Miller, *The Cosmological Eye* (Norfolk, Conn.: New Directions, 1939), p. 120.

Index

Abbott, Edwin, 109, 113, 126
Aeschylus, 167
Agrest, M. M., 75
Albers, Josef, 199
Alcott, Louisa May, 137, 161
Aldiss, Brian, 212n50
Alfvén, Hannes, 114
al-Hakīm, Tawfīq, 29
Amis, Kingsley, 57
Antimatter: defined, 113–15; in Nabokov, 120; and time, 120
Asimov, Isaac, 63
Astronomy: and "demotion" of Earth, 9; Newtonian, 62; and planets, hypothetical number of, 100; and time, 77, 78
Atom bomb: in McMahon, 173; as threat, 3–4; in Vonnegut, 18
Austen, Jane, 152, 162, 181

Baldwin, James, 167
Balzac, 12, 158, 192
Barth, John: *End of the Road*, 182–85, 193; *Giles Goat-Boy*, 190; "Menelaiad," 125; mentioned, 12, 17, 63, 182, 189
Bayley, John, 158
Beach, Joseph, 177
Beauty and the Beast, 153
Beauvoir, Simone de, 164, 165, 167, 175, 176
Beckett, Samuel: *Waiting for Godot*, 14, 17, 194–95, 196–97; mentioned, 12, 14, 186, 197
Bellamy, Edward, 57, 83, 162
Bergson, Henri, 71, 75
Bildungsroman, 73
Blish, James: *Spock Must Die!*, 50–52, 55; mentioned, 93
Blot, M., 189, 190
Bond, James, 36
Booth, Wayne, 177, 190, 191, 192
Borges, Jorge Luis: *Garden of Forking Paths*, 123; mentioned, 12, 17, 63, 119

Breuer, Miles, 86, 87
Brontës, 152, 153
Broome, Richard, 56
Buñuel, Luis, 158, 165
Burger, Dionys, 109, 113
Burgess, Anthony, 36
Burroughs, William, 14, 136, 171
Butler, Samuel, 70
Butor, Michel, 213n56

Camus, Albert, 185, 186, 189
Cannabis sativa, 73
Čapek, Milič, 85
Capote, Truman, 36, 45
Carroll, Lewis: *Alice in Wonderland*, 128; chess in, 118; *Sylvie and Bruno*, 71; *Through the Looking-glass*, 50, 114, 118; mentioned, 86, 124, 145
Chandrasekhar, S., 85
Chateaubriand, 106
Chess: as life-analogue, 117; in literature, 116, 117–18; in Nabokov, 117, 119; solipsism in, 134–35
Childhood: as key to *Ada*, 128; as sexual goal, 145
Chomsky, Noam, 128, 187
Christianity: in Dunne, 123; in Grass, 40; as inner mystery of *Ada*, 217n100–01; in Ionesco, 34; in James, 21; renewed crisis in, 4
Christie, Agatha, 29–30
Church, Alonzo, 5
Clarke, Arthur: *Childhood's End* and *Ada*, 217n100; "The Sentinel," 221n154; "Third Law" of, 76; *2001*, 58, 221n154; mentioned, 12, 17, 63, 83, 93
Cockburn, Claud, 219n131
Cohen, J., 72, 128
Coleridge, Samuel Taylor, 120
Colette, 167
Conrad, Joseph, 136
Cosmology: Copernican, 9, 80; Newto-

nian, 127; Ptolemaic, 80. *See also* Astronomy
Crab Nebula, 77
Crispin, Edmund, 58

Dada, 164
Däniken, Erich von, 214*n*74
Davy, Charles, 118
Demons: *Die Dämonen*, 37; Demon Veen, 96; Laplace's, 191, 192; as observers, 163; mentioned, 23, 107, 210*n*25
Dickens, Charles: *Bleak House*, 140, 153; and marriage, 13; mentioned, 10, 12, 92, 177
Dicker, Robert, 188
Dickey, James, 132
Doderer, Heimito von, 37
Don Juan, 166
Don Quixote, 166
Donne, John, 56
Dos Passos, John, 10
Dostoevski, Feodor: *Crime and Punishment*, 48; *The Double*, 115; use of murder mystery, 30; mentioned, 158, 183, 199
Double: in Blish, 50–51; of Earth, 101, 108; in film, 104; in Hawthorne, 51, 115; in James, 50–55, 116; in literature, 49, 115; in Nabokov, 101–02, 115
Doyle, Conan, 28, 43
Dreams, in literature, 124–25
Dreiser, Theodore, 14, 190
Dunne, J. W., 47, 48, 73, 78; 93, 123, 124, 131
Durrell, Lawrence, 29
Dürrenmatt, Friedrich, 42–46

Edel, Leon, 181
Einstein, Albert: clock paradox of, 15, 74, 112; fable of dimensions of, 109, 113; and fourth dimension, 76, 87, 127; on mathematics, 5; theory of relativity of, 6, 63; and time travel, 74, 75, 83, 85; mentioned, 3, 61, 93, 192
Eliade, Mircea, 70
Eliot, George, 13, 87, 152, 162
Eliot, T. S., 9, 10, 142, 163

Ellison, Ralph, 133, 167
Entropy, 6, 71
Erotic, the: in chess, 119; as beyond physicality, 13; and sadism, 36; and sexology, 13; of "twin" lovers, 115. *See also* Sex
—in literature, 132–81 *passim*; James Bond and, 36; incest and, 132–33; D. H. Lawrence and, 13; masturbation and, 135; *My Secret Life*, 97; Nabokov and, 165–67; Mickey Spillane and, 36. *See also* James, Henry: *Awkward Age*, *Roderick Hudson*, *Turn of the Screw*; Women characters in literature
Existentialism, 186
Extraterrestrial life, 15, 101

Faulkner, William, 10, 189
Fiedler, Leslie, 64
Film: in *Ada*, 104–05; as illusion, 104–05, 106; *Last Laugh*, 144; in *Lolita*, 144; mentioned, 36
Firsoff, V. A., 101
Fitzgerald, F. Scott, 167
Flaubert, Gustave, 10, 152, 193
Forster, E. M., 162
Fowlie, Wallace, 197
Freud, and Freudianism, 13, 21–22, 73, 150, 165

Gance, Abel, 105
Gardner, Martin: in *Ada*, 95, 99; mentioned, 50, 114, 131
Genet, Jean, 167, 181
Gibbs, Josiah, 193
Gide, André, 11, 130, 136
Gödel, Kurt, 5, 83–84, 85, 86, 188
Goethe, 70, 163
Gold, Thomas, 114
Goncourts, 154
Grass, Günter: *Tin Drum*, 38–41, 43, 190; mentioned, 12, 14, 17, 136, 190
Gropius, Walter, 199

Hardy, Thomas, 136
Harris, Frank, 13
Hassan, Ihab, 186, 194
Hawthorne, Nathaniel: *Marble Faun*,

177, 178; and marriage, 13; *M. de Miroir*, 51, 115; mentioned, 88, 163
Heilman, R. B., 46
Heisenberg, Werner, 6, 187, 193
Helson, H., 72
Hemingway, Ernest, 161, 167
Herodotus, 81–82
Herschel, William, 3
Hilbert, David, 5
Hinton, C. H., 114
Hitchcock, Alfred, 43
Hitler, Adolph, 41, 200, 220n142
Howe, Irving, 186
Hoyle, Fred, 59, 93
Huxley, Aldous, 57, 130, 136

Ibsen, Henrik, 205n2
Incest: in *Ada*, 134; of imagination, 148; and society, 132–33
Indeterminacy principle, 6, 187
Ingarden, Roman, 165
Ionesco, Eugène: *The Killer*, 12, 33–34, 66; mentioned, 12, 14, 197
Irving, Washington, 92, 138

James, Henry: *American*, 156; *American Scene*, 181; *Aspern Papers*, 190; *Awkward Age*, 12, 47, 132, 137–49; 150; *Beast in the Jungle*, 14, 47, 48, 190, 194, 195–96; *Bostonians*, 156, 181; *Daisy Miller*, 151, 180; *Death of the Lion*, 160; *Golden Bowl*, 11, 82, 87, 138, 147, 150, 157, 158, 192; *Jolly Corner*, 47, 49–55, 116, 117, 123; *Liar*, 190; *Portrait of a Lady*, 82, 87, 138, 156, 170; and repressed sex, 13; *Roderick Hudson*, 87–88, 177, 178–81; *Sacred Fount*, 191; *Sense of the Past*, 12, 47, 80, 82–83, 86, 87, 88–93, 94, 129, 130; social vocabulary of, 151; *Turn of the Screw*, 12, 18, 21–27, 28, 37, 46, 48, 92, 149–59, 190–91, 192, 194; *Washington Square*, 173; *What Maisie Knew*, 150, 188; *Wings of the Dove*, 88; and women, 14, 176–81; mentioned, 3, 10, 16, 17, 123, 130, 136, 141, 151, 158, 163, 177, 181, 190, 198, 201
James, William, 21

Johannson, Gunnar, 187
Jones, Ernest, 117
Jones, Leroi, 167
Joyce, James: *Finnegans Wake*, 72; *Ulysses*, 10; mentioned, 9, 71, 136, 150, 158, 177, 190

Kafka, Franz: *Castle*, 196; *Great Wall of China*, 70; *Investigations of a Dog*, 189; *Metamorphosis*, 189; *Trial*, 10, 189, 196; mentioned, 9, 10, 12, 14
Kalidasa, 139
Kandinsky, Wassily, 206n8
Kenner, Hugh, 156
Kesey, Ken, 184, 189
Kinsey, Alfred, 13, 15, 168
Kipling, Rudyard, 207n15
Kleist, Heinrich von, 82
Koestler, Arthur, 182, 196
Kubrick, Stanley, 36

Landsberg, P. T., 78
Lang, Fritz, 37
Language: deep-surface structure, 128–29; metalanguage, 131
Laplace, 191
Lawrence, D. H.: as sexist, 165; on time, 213n58; mentioned, 158, 168, 170, 199, 201
Lesbianism, 156, 181
Lévi-Strauss, Claude, 128–29
Lewis, C. S. 60
Little Green Men, 213n57
Lovecraft, H. P., 197
Lubbock, Percy, 177

Macdonald, Dwight, 43
Mailer, Norman, 171, 176, 190
Malamud, Bernard, 185
Malraux, André, 10
Man of Feeling, 140
Mann ohne Eigenschaften, 187, 197
Mann, Thomas: *Blood of the Walsungs*, 134; *Death in Venice*, 37; *Doktor Faustus*, 36–37; *Herr und Hund*, 39; *Magic Mountain*, 10; time in, 71; mentioned, 9, 14, 87
Manzoni, Alessandro, 178
Masters and Johnson, 13, 168, 169, 170, 171

Masturbation: and artist, 135–36; in Burroughs, 136; and chess, 134–35; in *Lolita*, 135; as preferred activity, 135
Maupassant, Guy de, 220n137
McMahon, Thomas, 172–75
Miller, Arthur, 189, 190
Miller, Henry: *Sexus*, 164; *Tropic of Cancer*, 164; *Tropic of Capricorn*, 13; mentioned, 164, 165, 168, 169, 170, 200, 201
Millett, Kate, 164, 165, 167, 170, 181
Milton, John, 56, 77–78, 157
Minkowski space, 122
Mirror: *abhijnaña*-nymphet and, 149; in antimatter analogy, 99, 114, 115; in Lewis Carroll, 118; existence in, as ideal, 130; reflection and reversal in, 103
Mirror effect: in space, 50; in time, 128
Mirror literature, 130
Modernism, 10
Monod, Jacques, 9
Montgomery, Bruce, 58
Morphy, Paul, 117
Movies. *See* Film
Murder mystery: and Dürrenmatt, 42–46; and Grass, 28–41; history of, 28; in Ionesco, 35; link to science fiction and "other," 66; metaphysical conservatism of, 29–30; in Robbe-Grillet, 35
My Secret Life, 97, 128

Nabokov, Vladimir: *Ada*, 12, 18, 61, 63, 87, 93–131, 133, 136, 150, 165; *Bend Sinister*, 167; *Defense*, 189; *Despair*, 72, 115, 189; *Lolita*, 12, 115, 128, 132, 135, 136–49 *passim*, 167, 189; *Pale Fire*, 95, 105, 115, 116, 129, 167, 189; *Speak, Memory*, 97, 127; mentioned, 12, 123, 124, 130, 141, 167, 168
Nadal, E. S., 181
Narrator, unreliable, 190, 192–93
Nazism: allegorized by Grass, 38–41, by Lang, 37, by Mann, 36–37; problem of, in German literature, 38; and violence, 36
New Criticism, literary, 177

Newton, Isaac, 6, 73, 76, 127, 191, 192
Nietzsche, Friedrich, 37
Nothing: in Barth, 182–85; in Beckett, 195, 197; as contemporary subject, 14; in Ionesco, 197; in James, 195–96; overthrown, 188; mentioned, 20, 26

Observer: as demon, 163; in Dunne, 47, 48, 73, 78, 93, 124, 131; in fiction, 87; imprisoned, by linear time, 89; in James, 47, 93, 163
Oppenheimer, J. Robert, 3, 173, 174, 176
Ortega y Gasset, José, 198
Orwell, George, 196
Other, the: in contemporary literature, 14; in James, 21; and science fiction, 59–60; in *Sense of the Past*, 89; mentioned, 12, 66. *See also* Double
Other side: on chess board, 117, 120; in time travel, 120

Parity: "fall" of, 79; in mirrors, 103; reversed in alternate world, 103, 112; among Terrans, 99–100
Peckinpah, Sam, 36
Plath, Sylvia, 189
Plato, 99
Poe, E. A.: *Annabel Leigh*, 144, 148; and murder mystery, 21, 66; and science fiction, 66; *William Wilson*, 49, 115
Positivism, logical, 13, 73
Pound, Ezra, 9, 10
Proust, Marcel, 9, 12, 71, 75, 149, 162, 163
Psycho, 43
Puccetti, Roland, 206n10
Purdy, James, 168, 190
Pushkin, Alexander, 46
Putnam, Hilary, 77
Pynchon, Thomas, 220n133

Radcliffe, Mrs., 152
Ramses II, 82
Robbe-Grillet, Alain: and Dürrenmatt, 42; *Erasers*, 12, 43, 84–85, 189; *Jealousy*, 189; *Last Year at Marienbad*, 21, 31–32, 34, 126, 189; *Maison de Rendez-Vous*, 12, 21, 32–33, 71, 126;

227 • Index

and murdery mystery, 21; *Voyeur*, 189; mentioned, 12, 17, 85, 136, 190, 192
Romains, Jules, 73, 87
Roman experimental, 73
Roman fleuve, 73
Rousseauism, 199

Sagan, Carl, 96
Sartre, Jean-Paul: *Huis Clos*, 10; *Nausea*, 10, 35, 186; mentioned, 10, 185
Science fiction: and *Ada*, 93–94; defined, 57–60, 66; history of, 18, 56–57, 64; and James, 83; quality of, 15, 63, 163; mentioned, 54, 55, 61, 163. *See also* Blish, James; Clarke, Arthur; Time travel; Vonnegut, Kurt; and Wells, H. G.
Selby, Hubert, 171
Serialism, 78. *See also* Dunne, J. W.
Sewell, Arthur, 215n83
Sex: differentiation of, 159–61; dysfunction in, 168; in James, 149, 150, 155–56, 157, 163; as literary subject, 158, 171–72; and nothingness, 182–86; and the nymphet, 143; revolution in, 133. *See also* Erotic
Shakespeare, 16, 56, 167
Shaw, G. B., 205n2
Shelley, Percy Bysshe, 133, 161, 162
Skinner, B. F., 62
Snow, C. P., 62
Solipsism: in chess, 134; literary, 130, 136; sexual, 134
Solzhenitsyn, Alexander, 196
Space: divorce of, from time, in *Ada*, 126–27; extraplanetary, 206n8; and fourth dimension, 127, 131. *See also* Cosmology; Einstein, Albert; Minkowski space; Newton, Isaac
Space travel: social resistance to, 64; and tie to murder mystery, 65; and time, 75; mentioned, 7, 61–62
Spillane, Mickey, 36
Star Trek, 50, 57
Stendhal, 158, 176, 182, 192
Story of O, 149
Superfluous man, 197

Swift, Jonathan, 56, 177
Swinburne, 136, 137
Sypher, Wylie, 186

Teilhard de Chardin, Pierre, 62, 65
Thermodynamics, second law of, 6
Thutmoses I, 82
Thutmoses IV, 81
Tillich, Paul, 185
Time: arrow of, 71, 79, 121; and clock paradox, 74; and clocks, 8, 67–70, 126; Dunne's theory of, 47, 48, 78; forks in, 12, 49, 123–24; as fourth dimension, 85–86, 87; and historical dislocation, 70–71; in language, 68–69; linear, 76, 89; in literature, 70, 71–80 *passim*, 83, 120, 122–23, 126, 127; not independent reality, 6; and physiology of perception, 72–73; psychological, 93, 128; and relativity, 74, 75, 76, 78, 131; reversed, 15, 78, 120; ruins of, 88; and serialism, 78; mentioned, 77, 81–82
Time travel, 49, 83–84, 119–20
Tolstoy, Leo, 16, 59, 124, 158, 162, 163

Ubu Roi, 189, 190
Unreliable narrator, 127, 192
Utopian fiction, 57

Vadim, Roger, 105
Velasquez, 131
Verne, Jules, 57, 60
Vonnegut, Kurt: *Cat's Cradle*, 12, 18–20, 27, 37; *Happy Birthday, Wanda June*, 172; *Sirens of Titan*, 130; *Slaughterhouse-Five*, 12, 61, 63, 79, 93, 171–72; mentioned, 12, 14, 17, 63

Wells, H. G.: and fourth dimension, 85–86; *Invisible Man*, 83; *Men Like Gods*, 57; *Shape of Things to Come*, 37, 80; *Time Machine*, 57, 80, 83, 85, 93, 129; mentioned, 60, 162
Wilde, Oscar, 86, 136, 137
Williams, Charles, 28, 31
Wilson, Edmund, 137
Wittgenstein, Ludwig, 131
Women characters in literature, 171–81;

as *Another*, 176; and atom bomb, 175; in Genet, 167, 181; in James, 176–81; in McMahon, 174–75; in Miller, 164–65; as *Other*, 175. *See also* Sex

Woolf, Virginia: *Mrs. Dalloway*, 161; *To the Lighthouse*, 161; mentioned, 9, 10, 71, 161, 190

Wordsworth, William, 71
Wright, Richard, 167
Wu-men Hui'k'ai, 71

Yang and Lee, 61, 79
Yellow Book, the, 136

Zola, Emile, 154, 190